Youth Identities, Localities, and Visual
Material Culture

# EXPLORATIONS OF EDUCATIONAL PURPOSE

## Volume 25

---

*Series Scope*

---

In today's dominant modes of pedagogy, questions about issues of race, class, gender, sexuality, colonialism, religion, and other social dynamics are rarely asked. Questions about the social spaces where pedagogy takes place – in schools, media, and corporate think tanks – are not raised. And they need to be.

The *Explorations of Educational Purpose* book series can help establish a renewed interest in such questions and their centrality in the larger study of education and the preparation of teachers and other educational professionals. The editors of this series feel that education matters and that the world is in need of a rethinking of education and educational purpose.

Coming from a critical pedagogical orientation, *Explorations of Educational Purpose* aims to have the study of education transcend the trivialization that often degrades it. Rather than be content with the frivolous, scholarly lax forms of teacher education and weak teaching prevailing in the world today, we should work towards education that truly takes the unattained potential of human beings as its starting point. The series will present studies of all dimensions of education and offer alternatives. The ultimate aim of the series is to create new possibilities for people around the world who suffer under the current design of socio-political and educational institutions.

For further volumes:
http://www.springer.com/series/7472

Kristen Ali Eglinton

# Youth Identities, Localities, and Visual Material Culture

## Making Selves, Making Worlds

 Springer

Kristen Ali Eglinton
Department of Sociology
Digital World Research Centre
University of Surrey
Guildford, Surrey, UK

Faculty of Education
University of Cambridge
Cambridge

ISSN 1875-4449    ISSN 1875-4457 (electronic)
ISBN 978-94-007-4856-9  ISBN 978-94-007-4857-6 (eBook)
DOI 10.1007/978-94-007-4857-6
Springer Dordrecht Heidelberg New York London

Library of Congress Control Number: 2012949325

Printed on acid-free paper

Springer is part of Springer Science+Business Media (www.springer.com)

# Preface

Globalisation and media proliferation, socio-politics and identity politics, the future of youth and the relevance of education – now more than ever the space where youth lives, 'visual material culture', and geography collide in the contexts of education demands critical examination. While popular visual material culture is a key pedagogical site – an 'unofficial curriculum' where youth learn about and construct their identities and worlds – in youth studies in education, there is limited focus on just how youth are actually using these forms to produce aspects of themselves and worlds with/in fast changing sociocultural contexts (Kennelly, Poyntz, & Ugor, 2009). It could be argued that, theoretically and methodologically, it is difficult to grasp youth identity-making from these forms as it is a process that is at once historic/dynamic, local/global, public/private, and individual/collective.

In this book, I engage with some of these challenges and provide an ethnographic account of the ways in which a small group of economically (and otherwise) marginalised black and/or Latino/a youth in a New York City after-school club, and white and Indigenous youth in a small sub-Arctic town in Yukon, Canada (aged anywhere between 8 and 15), used visual material culture (from rap icons to the built environment) to construct their racial, place-based, and gendered identities. Using a 'multi-sited' (Marcus, 1998) visual ethnographic approach, drawing on a wide interdisciplinary framework which includes human geography, anthropology, sociocultural theories, and cultural psychology, I aim to provide a relational account of young people's engagement with visual material culture – an account which places focus upon the intersection of youth lives, visual material culture, and aspects of local place (including the physical and social geographies).

Ethnographic fieldwork for this book was carried out between 2005 and 2006. Though the fieldwork was done for my doctoral studies, rereading some of the text years later, it is obvious that the ideas and research presented are a culmination of a rather idiosyncratic and unequivocally interdisciplinary path. In fact, while the focus of this research I summarised in the first two paragraphs of this Preface might sound sharp, it took years to develop: including years training as a visual artist – sculpture and multimedia to be more precise; time spent in New Mexico working with a local Navajo silversmith, and later travelling to Pueblos, and talking to

Indigenous youth about their lives and the ways they expressed themselves through traditional and contemporary media; and time training as a teacher followed by years working as a visual art, design, and media pedagogue in some of the most impoverished areas of New York including the South Bronx and Harlem. It was over the course of these years that I realised how the use of traditional and digital media, as well as expression through, for example, fashion and music, is paramount to youth identities – how it is a means for youth to build strong identities, comment on, understand, and change their worlds and in some instances a means of breaking the cycle of poverty which impacts the lives of so many young people I have worked with.

After my time teaching in New York City, the focus of this inquiry and my identity as a youth researcher and visual ethnographer was crystallised through doctoral studies at Cambridge. My work in the Faculty of Education there stretched across educational research, sociology, psychology, human geography, and, most profoundly, applied visual anthropology. Over time, my interests and passions were solidified: I found a home in youth studies in education; learned about the possibilities of ethnographic and qualitative research; experimented with the borders of visual media, arts, education, and social research; and during fieldwork, experienced how visual ethnographic participatory projects support access into identity processes and push into relief the ways in which geography, including local values, histories, and physical spaces, is intertwined with who we are and who we might become.

I feel my trajectory or maybe, more aptly, my movements to, from, and between visual arts, visual arts in education, educational research, youth studies in educa- tion, and the rest – movements always underpinned by perspectives from various disciplines – comes through in this book as I move from chapter to chapter touching on my early days as an art educator to issues in art education to issues in education broadly conceived. Though the dissertation on which this book is based was located in visual art education, given the opportunity to publish this project, I have worked hard to open the ideas to those concerned with the lives of young people in and out of educational contexts: with youth as they are learning every day – forming and reforming themselves and their worlds through the visual material culture which surrounds them. My hope is that the empirical data I present and narrative I weave will not only lend support to the multitude of perspectives, practices, and people eager to hear how youth are using the visual material culture around them, but will spark ways of thinking about how we might better support young people in this process.

As I mentioned above, fieldwork was carried out in two sites, one in New York City and the other in Yukon Territory, Canada. With respect to the Yukon site, which I have called 'Barlow', it was early 2005 when I met a visiting research fellow at my college who asked about my work. Though my dissertation was in its infancy, I had a general focus inspired by my work as a visual art, design, and media educator (see Chap. 1): I wanted to better understand the ways in which youth were using visual material culture in their everyday lives. Drawing on my background as an artist and growing interest in visual anthropology, I knew I would do so by using various visual methodologies including, say, film-making and photography. I was also certain of who I was going to work with: urban youth in New York City, and, to understand the role of geography, I would supplement this with fieldwork in a rural North American community populated by both Indigenous and non-Indigenous youth. Not only did I have a personal connection to Indigenous youth, I believed that the more different this supplemental site was from New York City, the more I might learn.

I told him about my interests, he told me about Barlow, a community that he worked closely with in Northern Canada. As he spoke, I was convinced I should go; I sought access, and a year later, I was off to the Yukon. While there, I learned about the unique problems facing northern youth (including educational issues, and health disparities among Indigenous populations) and about reciprocity, and, in the spirit of reciprocity, I left with the full intention of returning for further research. Something I am still working on.

As far as the New York City site, what I have called the 'Hope' after-school club, I note in the book, how it was through my sister that I found out about and contacted the Hope. With regard to my selection of an urban after-school club more broadly, in light of various factors (including insights from a pilot study I conducted in England and my teaching experiences in New York City), I speculated that research in a large urban environment would yield a great diversity of data. I was also aware that (at the time) few studies in art education examining youth cultural practices had been carried out in a New York City after-school club; connected to this, I also drew on Dimitriadis (2001) who cites the benefits of working in an after-school club during his own ethnography where the unofficial curriculum of popular culture could be more probed more deeply. I also knew from my experiences as an art educator both in and out of schools that youth cultural practices – for better or for worse – come alive outside the classroom.

More personally, in my selection of sites, with Heron and Reason (1997), I have always believed that when possible social research should seek out the voices of those often unheard. My experience is that all youth and, in particular, urban black and/or Latina/Latino youth and rural Indigenous youth face various forms of exclusions from mainstream contexts. Further, my experiences have long centred on working with youth and adults to support expression through cultural production (i.e. media- and art-making) – over the years I have learned forms of cultural production are potentially transformative in the sense that they enable the exploration of self and world. When starting this research, I wanted to support the use of these powerful tools in communities with youth that I believed not only faced various exclusions but who might not otherwise have opportunities to work with particular expressive media. Bringing threads together, I believed a free after-school programme in the Greenwich area of New York City with a majority of black and/or Latina/Latino youth might benefit from this project. Similarly, the rural town of Barlow which, despite having more advantages than most small communities, has a remote setting and high population of Indigenous youth and, therefore, might also benefit from taking part in this project.

While this research was underpinned by participatory, feminist, and 'new' ethnographic perspectives (e.g.. in Lather, 2001) which beckon researchers to continuously reflect on issues of power, authority, subjectivity, and ethics embedded in social research, I do feel some of the self-reflexive and participatory processes which characterised this study during fieldwork and the writing-up stage might have been smoothed over in the narrative I am able to present in this book. In Chap. 1, I talk more about some of these perspectives which guided the research, and in Chap. 8 I spend some time highlighting several of the ethical issues which continued to crop up throughout the research process – issues which I have continued to think about long after this study ended.

In fact, much has happened since I submitted the dissertation on which this book is based. In particular, I have been working on various youth projects including a visual participatory ethnography with youth who would be classified as homeless or marginally housed, and who have been excluded from a variety of educational institutions. I have also been working in South Africa with communities in an effort to understand the ways in which youth, adults, and Elders use, share, and depend on mobile multimedia (think camera phones) for their education, social, and cultural practices. As these new ethnographic experiences begin to clutter my brain, coming back to the study I present here has been difficult: representing the young people who took part in this research feels just as hard today as it did the day I finished fieldwork – then, as now, I struggle to make sense of the voices, sounds, smells, and my own changes as a researcher. I also struggle to put some of their words on paper, essentially freezing these young people in time, as I know some of their comments, be they racist or sexist, are not who these young people are – not then and not now. I would argue some of these difficulties and issues are ethical ones, and though they are not specific to me and to this research, they continue to occupy my thoughts.

Life has not only changed for me; it has, perhaps even more so, changed for many of the young people who so generously gave me a glimpse into their social worlds – those notorious spaces researchers are continuously trying to understand, recreate, and represent. Globalisation, in particular, has continued to shift and challenge the social landscape of these young people's lives and their communities. Moreover, the young people, whose words and practices I describe in this book, have moved on; and, while I still communicate with several of them, it is obvious that they have grown up, they are thinking differently, they are engaging with new forms of visual material culture, and forming new identities.

Change not only characterises my life and the lives of the young people you will read about but I believe also characterises educational scholarship where theoretically and methodologically the landscape looks different now than it did several years ago when I set out to do fieldwork. Theoretically, perspectives in educational research have inched forward. Geography, for example, is slowly seeping into the research agenda. We are learning that social phenomena is 'placed' – and as Moles (2010), for example, adds it is temporal too. In practice: books and papers, though not many, have started to come out which focus on youth movement and mobility and on the spatial in educational youth culture research (e.g. Dolby & Rizvi, 2008a, 2008b; McLeod, 2009). Of note is Dillabough and

Kennelly's (2010) work in Canada and educational echoes of Anoop Nayak and others who put space and place at the centre of their analysis – and who are developing accompanying philosophical ideas to understand processes of culture. Indeed, in educational research, we are catching up to ideas in anthropology where culture is not static but a process and where ethnography is not just method. As Youdell (2006, p. 59) writes and as I would vehemently argue: 'Understanding ethnography as a method. . . overlooks the theoretical and methodological debates over the meanings it uncovers or creates, the claims it can make, and the promises made on its behalf' (see also Willis, 2000).

Staying with methodology, ethnographers and qualitative researchers across the social sciences, and increasingly in education, have been playing with new tools to capture mobilities and the flows and processes of culture that I so tried to get at with visual methods when I carried out the fieldwork in 2005–2006. In fact, I started writing this Preface within hours of a National Research Methods Autumn School in the UK where just over 30 of us gathered for three days to talk about mobilities, place methods, GPS, 'walking tours' (Moles, 2010), and what it means to do research when geography counts. And, yet while there have been many changes – in context, in thought, in practice – since finishing this study, my own views on social research and some of the questions I seek remain fundamentally the same. A central question I have continued to intensely explore, one which occupies most of my scholarly time and one which is threaded through this book, is how to theoretically and methodologically access that space where youth lives, visual material culture, and the local places they live in and through meet in cultural practice. Moreover, my passion for empirical research that makes contributions across deeply interconnected areas including methodology, theory, and pedagogy in education continues to drive my work forward. As such, this book has distinguishable theoretical, methodological, and pedagogical contributions that I hope continue to move the field of educational research forward on the path it seems to be traversing.

Theoretically, in this interdisciplinary study, I have taken an original approach: reaching across disciplines, I have drawn on perspectives to rethink youth engagement with visual material culture as a highly active, spatial, imaginative, and relational process. Before Petchauer's (2009) call for educational research in the arena of popular culture which draws on sociocultural perspectives, I developed a novel theoretical framework drawn from sociocultural theories which demonstrates how the creative use of theory opens up the complexity of youth lives and penetrates those areas – such as the space between lives, VMC, and local places – that are often overlooked or under-conceptualised.

Methodologically, this book is timely: it is aligned with contemporary issues in youth studies which postulate the significance of spatiality (Kennelly et al., 2009); I draw on anthropological perspectives which speak to the potential of multi-sited work, and, in light of both the 'visual' and 'participatory' turn in the social sciences (see, e.g. Brownlie, 2009, for participation), this book begins to demonstrate how visual and participatory approaches might offer youth a space to explore their own meanings. Moving on to pedagogy, I conclude by suggesting an 'ethnographic pedagogy' as a means of bringing young people's complex experiences with visual material culture into the classroom; this approach asks researchers and pedagogues to put youth at the centre of their analysis and practice, to pedagogically and theoretically reposition youth as active agents who (re)construct both themselves and the world around them, to rethink youth engagement with visual material culture as transformative democratic practice, and to imagine places as both local and global, continuously produced, in part, by youth themselves as live with/in and through a visual material culture.

London, England                                                                        Kristen Ali Eglinton

# References

Brownlie, J. (2009). Researching not playing in the public sphere. *Sociology, 43*(40), 699–716.

Dillabough, J., & Kennelly, J. (2010). *Lost youth in the global city*. London: Routledge.

Dimitriadis, G. (2001). *Performing identity/performing culture: Hip hop as text, pedagogy, and lived practice*. New York: Peter Lang Publishing.

Dolby, N., & Rizvi, F. (2008a). Introduction: Youth, mobility, and identity. In N. Dolby & F. Rizvi (Eds.), *Youth moves: Identities and education in global perspective* (pp. 1–14). London: Routledge.

Dolby, N., & Rizvi, F. (Eds.) (2008b). *Youth moves: Identities and education in global perspective*. London: Routledge.

Heron, J., & Reason, P. (1997). A participatory inquiry paradigm. *Qualitative Inquiry, 3*(3), 274–294.

Kennelly, J., Poyntz, S., & Ugor, P. (2009). Special issue introduction: Youth cultural politics, and new social spaces in an era of globalization. *Review of Education, Pedagogy, and Cultural Studies, 31*(4), 255–269.

Lather, P. A. (2001). Postmodernism, post-structuralism and post (critical) ethnography: Of ruins, aporias and angels. In P. Atkinson, A. Coffey, S. Delamont, J. Lofland, & L. Lofland (Eds.), *Handbook of ethnography* (pp. 477–492). London: Sage.

Marcus, G. E. (1998). *Ethnography through thick and thin*. Princeton, NJ: Princeton University Press.

McLeod, J. (2009). Youth studies, comparative inquiry, and the local/global problematic. *Review of Education, Pedagogy, and Cultural Studies, 31*(4), 270–292.

Moles, K. (2010). *Time, place and understanding*. In National Centre for Research Methods Autumn School 2010, 3–5 Nov 2010, Southampton, UK. (Unpublished)

Petchauer, E. (2009). Framing and reviewing hip-hop educational research. *Review of Educational Research, 79*(2), 946–978.

Willis, P. E. (2000). *The ethnographic imagination*. Cambridge, UK: Polity Press.

Youdell, D. (2006). *Impossible bodies, impossible selves: Exclusions and student subjectivities*. Dordrecht, The Netherlands: Springer.

# Acknowledgements

Countless people have left their imprints on this research as our paths crossed over the course of this journey. And, wow, what an incredible journey it has been – from the early days at Cambridge in the UK, to fieldwork in New York City and Yukon Territory, to writing the PhD dissertation, and now, two years later, to reworking the dissertation into this book. Today, I have the sweet pleasure of reworking the dissertation acknowledgements; as I read them over, not only do they still hold true, they seem even more profound. Today, I see how my PhD colleagues and mentors have become dear friends, and how my oldest friends who have stuck with me for years have become part of me; I also can't help but think about all those people I have met since the PhD who have supported the reworking of the dissertation into this book and made it possible to get it done.

Foremost, I want to give a big mouthy shout-out to the young people I worked with at the Hope after-school in New York City and in Barlow, Canada – you *are* this project. Thanks all for teaching me, for your honesty and your zest for life. You have inspired me beyond measure, opened my thinking, and reshuffled my brain. Rock on with your brilliance! While confidentiality keeps me from citing the names of those amazing souls who supported the fieldwork for this book, I am grateful to the director and assistant director of the Hope programme in New York City for allowing me in and treating me like one of your own. Thanks to all the staff at the Hope who made a difficult job look effortless and impressed me day after day. In Barlow, to the outstanding school principal, First Nation education coordinator and education director, the spirited art educator whose class I hung around in for months, the generous people in the art centre, the awesome coordinator of the local college, and to the people of Barlow – thank you for teaching me through your actions the meanings of community, generosity, and reciprocity.

As this book is based on PhD research carried out at the University of Cambridge, Faculty of Education, several individuals across the university have in various and unforgettable ways helped bring this project to fruition. I'm indebted to my PhD supervisor Dr. Richard Hickman whose unique blend of scholarship, vision, empathy, and humour kept me believing in this project and who, since finishing the PhD, has continued to be my trusted and ever insightful advisor.

My gratitude to the examiners of this research, Professor Nick Stanley and Mr. John Finney, for engaging with this work in such a soulful way. Thanks also to Dr. Michael Evans, Dr. Rob Moore, Dr. Phil Gardner, and Dr. Jo-Anne Dillabough. At Clare Hall, my beloved college, much appreciation to the Senior Tutor Dr. Bobbie Wells, and to the people there, especially Irene Hills, Lynne Richards, and Liz Taylor.

My heartfelt thanks to Dr. Antonina Tereshchenko, Dr. Angeliki Triantafyllaki, Dr. Valeska Grau, and Dr. Muna Amr for all your love, empathy, brilliance, and affection; for your depth of understanding (personally and professionally); for reading, editing, and commenting on this manuscript; for discussing this project with me for the last seven years – through thick and thin my dear friends – you have been there. *Waqit jaied*! A special mention here to Antonina for tirelessly checking references on this manuscript – you're a super co-pilot. To Dr. Sharlene Swartz for her inspiring youth research and for advice on this manuscript, to Dr. Mark Dickens for late nights at the Ashby, and to the MRes class at Cambridge – you know who you are – in so many ways you have contributed to this book.

Appreciation to my field supervisor at New York University, New York City, Dr. Dipti Desai, to Professor Liora Bresler who impacted this journey in ways most likely unknown to her, to Dr. Joan Webster-Price who remains artist/professor extraordinaire, and to David Neufeld who listened to me, believed in this work, and supported me throughout this endeavour.

While friends (too many to name) beyond the Ivory Tower across the globe have undoubtedly supported this project through phone calls, love, and (tons of) empathy, my deepest thanks to Jerry Jennings for his work, compassion, and much-needed emotional support; to Veronica Salas for always sorting me out and checking references for this manuscript; to Ali Richards for being there through this research and making comments on parts of this manuscript; to Diana MacLean for her work on the manuscript and unconditional support; to Paul Scobel for keeping me in the family food budget; to Amanda Barragry for images and the NY job club Wednesday mornings; to Katrine Kaarsemaker for the images and amazing montages she made for this book; to Daniela Jadue, Paula Guardia, and Brooke Procida for help with referencing, editing, and formatting; to George Johnson for reading and providing help with Chap. 1; and to Andy Crowther, Liz Scofield, Carolyn MacDonald, Kelly Malloy, Eric Salas, Peggy Maher, Nuala Roberts, Simon Robinson, Elina Vartiainen, and so many others for excellent suggestions, late night talks, and support in various ways; to Dr. John Overell for his wisdom and for his immeasurable achievements. To Marion and Jimmy Eastwood (and Cameron, Nathan, and Margaret) for so generously taking me in, feeding me, and being there for me. Thanks are also due to Chris and Reg Eglinton for believing in this work – appreciation all – always.

The last months of drafting this book would not have been possible without the support of the Digital World Research Centre at the University of Surrey, Department of Sociology. Massive appreciation to Professor David Frohlich who has wholeheartedly supported this work through his caring, humour, and guidance; special thanks are also due to Kristina Langhein for her kindness and humanity, to Dr. Chris Lim for listening, to Connie Golsteijn who generously checked the quotations for this manuscript, to Dr. Alicia Blum-Ross for her always insightful comments on the manuscript, and to Jocelyn Spence for her meticulous help with revisions and for editing the manuscript.

My gratitude to Bernadette Ohmer and Harmen van Paradijs at Springer for seeing the value in this work and to Bernadette for her continued professionalism, kindness, and understanding over the last year of writing. Thanks to the external reviewer who made excellent comments and suggestions that have strengthened this work. To Professor Shirley Steinberg and Professor Kenneth Tobin for bringing this research monograph into this book series and helping me get the research out there. Special thanks to Shirley for being that speaker at conferences I would knock people over to listen to.

Various funding bodies have also supported this project. In particular, financial support was provided by the Northern Research Endowment Grant from the Northern Research Institute, Yukon College. Further support for fieldwork and travel expenses was provided by the Foundation for Canadian Studies in the United Kingdom in association with the Canadian High Commission and by Clare Hall and the Faculty of Education at the University of Cambridge.

Finally, to my treasured family – what can I say?! From start to now to forever, thank you for believing in my dreams. You all have travelled every inch of this road with me (and for that I apologise!). To my sisters Kim and Heather – for the phone calls, for listening to me talk incessantly about this project, and for all your love, and also for your time on this manuscript; to my brothers, grandma (and grandpa always), and my dearest Jackson and Quinny! To my phenomenal parents, Nancy and Fred – your belief in me and the work I am trying to do, your love, advice, unyielding support, incredible wisdom, and time have without question made this research possible – I am forever grateful and indebted. And, to Mark – a true creative maverick – thank you. Your own intense passions inspire me to do better and, as always, dream bigger.

# Contents

# List of Boxes

# List of Figures

# List of Tables

# Permissions

**Fig. 3.1** Brooklyn Bridge image courtesy Christopher Palmer
**Fig. 3.2** Images courtesy Amanda Barragry
**Fig. 3.3** Images courtesy Katrine Kaarsemaker

**Fig. 4.1** Images used with permission from youth in this study

**Figs. A2.1, A2.2, A2.3** All artwork used with permission from youth in this study

**Figs. 3.1, 3.2, 3.3, 4.2, A2.1, A2.2, A2.3** Graphics by Katrine Kaarsemaker

# Chapter 1
# Telling Stories, Forging Links, and Researching Lives

## Telling Stories

November 2010: I am sitting in the library of my old university, a place I used to know well, now a refuge to which I have returned. As I scroll through pages of fieldnotes, interview transcripts, thousands of images, hours of footage – searching for new meanings, old meanings, even reassurance – my loud sighs seep through the layered quiet of the Reading Room. The basic aim of underlining visual material culture (VMC) – think rap music, fashion, even the buildings surrounding us – as a central epistemological space where young people construct their identities and worlds, and arguing that youth identity-making from VMC is a relational process involving youth experiences, aspects of the social and physical places they live with/in and through, and VMC itself, is a task that appears daunting. Not only am I representing thoughts and perspectives written up 2 years before, about data generated over 3 years earlier, the importance of examining youth engagement with VMC is growing, and the task is becoming ever more complex.

While narratives can do many things – convey overarching themes, stretch the imagination, communicate moral (and immoral) accounts – I use it here more prosaically to talk about one of my first days as an art educator: in 1996, after graduate school, I took a job as an art teacher in what administrators considered the longest running 'failing school' in the South Bronx area of New York City.[1] Picture in your mind's eye a large inner-city school, identified by a number, not a name, a place where metal detectors and armed guards greet you at the door of a building covered in purposeless scaffolding, a structure easily mistaken for a long abandoned factory. This junior high school served 5,000 young people in grades seven, eight, and nine (generally between the ages of 11–16, depending on various individual and institutional circumstances).[2] My classroom on the third floor had

---

[1] A portion of this chapter has been previously published in Eglinton (2008).

[2] Junior high schools in the United States serve students between elementary and high school. Grades included vary between 6th and 9th grade.

K.A. Eglinton, *Youth Identities, Localities, and Visual Material Culture: Making Selves, Making Worlds*, Explorations of Educational Purpose 25, DOI 10.1007/978-94-007-4857-6_1, © Springer Science+Business Media Dordrecht 2013

three chairs and a big table. There were three windows; I took comfort in the fact that the main window, which had a hole shot through it (yes, from a bullet), was padlocked shut. I was told in the job interview that the art teacher who preceded me was dangled out of the window by a group of angry students. Even when the rain blew through the bullet hole, I felt comfortable knowing it was padlocked shut. To start the school year, I was given a big roll of white paper, a few boxes of used stubby crayons, and some dried-up glue sticks. Clearly well prepared to teach 1,980 or so youths that would ultimately make their way through my door, my aim was to somehow make art class meaningful.[3] In keeping with cutting-edge art education scholarship with its notion of opening up the canon to all VMC (most profoundly popular culture), I sketched out a plan that would include everything from paintings in museums to popular television programmes. The first project would examine graffiti. My clichéd equation here, I am ashamed to publicise: New York City youth equals graffiti.

As the first class pushed through the door, I felt relaxed. Graffiti was something 'I got'. After all, I had seen the Jean-Michel Basquiat show at the Museum of Modern Art, and, years earlier, I permanently inked an area of my torso with a trademark character by Keith Haring. I was ready to roll.

After a brief introduction, I explained the project: we would produce our own graffiti 'tags' (letters/images representing ourselves) and then, in conjunction with the other 1,947 or so young people I was to teach throughout the year, create a mural of tags on the roll of white paper now covering the back wall of the classroom. The goals set, I launched into a discussion about graffiti art – well, about my under-standing of graffiti art: Keith Haring, the meaning of his images, and so forth.

The memory still haunts me: there I was, a 25-year-old white woman from downtown Manhattan telling 33 black and/or Latina/Latino 13- and 14-year-olds from the South Bronx *the* meaning of Keith Haring's figures; treating these examples as decontextualised objects, something we could study and decode; using my own understandings and perspectives to teach youth about aspects of a VMC they were already using, or were living in and through; 'enlightening' them to Haring and Basquiat; and positioning myself as an authority. In fact, if pedagogy can be characterised as 'interactive productivity' – a dialectic involving teacher, learner, and knowledge (Lather, 1991, p. 15) – this was not pedagogy.[4] Without an understanding of the ways in which youth were engaging with their visual material world; without seeing VMC – in this case graffiti – as an epistemological space, a tool they were

---

[3] Though this number might seem high, I was only one of three art teachers in a school with 5,000 students. One art educator worked with 1,000 or so special needs students, and two of us worked with 4,000 remaining pupils. I taught 6 classes per day with approximately 33 young people in a class. I saw each class once a week for a term (approximately, 990 young people in a term). There were two terms in the school year, bringing the number of young people who walked through my door to around 1,980.

[4] Lather (1991) is discussing the work of Lusted (1986).

already using to understand themselves and shape the world around them; without any real ethnographic or 'thick' (Geertz, 1973) understanding of *how* or *what* young people might 'say, think or feel' (Hall, 1997b, p. 3) about their visual material world – I could not expect to meaningfully engage with youth. Five to ten minutes into the lesson, I heard the snap of the tenuous thread that connected us. In the end, the project fell to pieces. And the back wall of the classroom? Not exactly a collaborative Basquiat, though there was some artfully executed, and, in some cases, phenomenally obscene text and imagery.

## Forging Links

I begin with my own story not because it is singular but because it starts to hint at pedagogical, theoretical, and empirical issues and lacunae in education warranting attention if we are to take seriously the ways in which youth, in an increasingly globalised world, are engaging with VMC in their everyday lives.

To clarify, I start with pedagogy, the primacy I placed on my own experiences with graffiti, my reading of Haring's figures, and the production of my voice as 'the' authority was based on the common assumption that educators and/or researchers know the right answers and that youth 'are not already speaking' or not already '[intervening] in their own history' (Grossberg, 1989, p. 92). My practice that day in the Bronx reflects a typical construction of youth as passive non-agents and was based, in part, on an 'ideology of immaturity' (in Finney, Hickman, Morrison, Nicholl, & Rudduck, 2005, p. 87), where youth are not yet in a position to act and where the role of the teacher is to instil action and agency, to transform youth.

Trying to 'enlighten' youth to the meanings of graffiti also faintly echoes a pedagogical tactic that questions taken-for-granted or common-sense meanings and representations; here, the task of the educator is to use various theories to reveal meanings rather than to elicit them from the youth themselves (Dimitriadis, 2001). Arguably, this practice deepens chasms between theories examining VMC in the classroom and the ways in which youth *actually are* engaging with these forms. In media education, for example, Buckingham (2003, p. 315) cites Funge's (1998) recognition of 'the gap between her students' perceptions of gender in the media and the feminist theories on which much media education is based'. He describes Funge's acknowledgement of the difference between feminist theories focusing on the ideological analysis of popular culture and the conversely empowering experiences young girls are having with these forms. Though slightly different, my emphasis on Haring's figures and life clearly reflected my own interests at the time – as well as my age, where I lived, my past experiences, who my friends were, and a particular kind of visual analysis. What I failed to take into account was that youth were already drawing on graffiti in their own lives – and, as I found out years later, using graffiti to construct their understanding of New York City and of themselves as New Yorkers (see Chap. 4).

From a more theoretical standpoint, my focus on the text – the graffiti – alone rather than on the text and, say, the context of New York City and the lives of those particular students was based on a pervasive knot of assumptions that conceptually separates youth lives, from VMC and from contexts (i.e. social and physical landscapes). This *non-relational* understanding harbours and encourages further dichotomies separating culture from context, body from mind, and individual from society (see Gablik, 1991) and fosters a problematic 'aspatial' understanding that fails to recognise the idea that youth engagement with VMC is active, temporal, and contextual – intersecting time and place.

Since that first day in the Bronx, I have worked as an art pedagogue and visual ethnographer with thousands of young people across the globe and, along the way, have come to learn first-hand that young people are not only living with/in and through a VMC but that young people, like all people, 'live culturally' (Ingold, 1994, p. 300) and that their engagement with VMC is part of *relational* activity which at once shapes and is shaped by the sociocultural context. As I will try to make clear in Chap. 2, there is a mutual constitution of person and place where VMC serves as a kind of 'mediating artefact' (Cole, 1996). As I demonstrate in this book, the experiences youth have with VMC, the meanings they make, and the ways in which they engage with these forms are lived in and through those social interactions which constitute local places as well as through their own experiences as raced, classed, and, for instance, gendered subjects in a particular time and place.

Deepening chasms between theoretical perspectives, youth lived experiences and pedagogical practices are two interconnected empirical issues: first, there remains a need in educational research for a more sustained focus on young people's engagement with VMC from a more relational perspective: one which takes into account VMC, youth, and social and physical contexts. Second, inquiry into the ways youth use VMC to produce their identities and understand their worlds, in light of continuously changing social, cultural, and material processes – in this book grouped under globalisation – raises a host of theoretical and methodological issues that educational research is only just starting to address (see Dimitriadis & Weis, 2007; Dolby & Rizvi, 2008a, 2008b; Eisenhart, 2001).

To clarify, I am not arguing that youth engagement with VMC has been overlooked in education scholarship; on the contrary, it is a particularly rich area across many perspectives including critical pedagogy and, for instance, media education. But rather that what is needed is a more sustained empirical agenda that explores what young people are actually doing with VMC in their daily lives: research which could inform pedagogy as it gets at young people's meanings and posits youth as active cultural producers living with/in and (re) making their worlds.

Connected to this, Dimitriadis and Weis (2007) and others argue that to conceive of an inclusive and relevant education for all youth and to meaningfully enter into their lives, not only must we consider the complexity of youth experiences and learning, including those spaces both inside and outside formal schooling – most significantly VMC – that youth draw on to make sense of their lives, we also need to reconceive or 'reimagine our object of study' (p. 339). That is, I argue, we need to rethink the study of youth engagement with VMC in ways that more closely align themselves with the lives of contemporary youth by taking into consideration the constraints and affordances of geography and by seeing engagement with these forms as a productive process involving localities, young people's lives, and visual material culture itself.

With these ideas churning in my mind, in 2005, I set out on a year of ethnographic fieldwork in two different communities in North America to explore how young people were using VMC and the ways place or localities might be implicated in the process. In the first weeks of fieldwork, data strongly suggested that of the countless ways youth used VMC, the most salient was understanding self and world. I soon focused on the ways in which youth were using these forms to make sense of, construct, and negotiate aspects of their identities and the world around them. The concepts of self/selves and identity/identities are used interchangeably,[5] and place is implicit in my focus where I appropriate the notion of 'world' from Holland, Lachicotte, Skinner, and Cain's (1998) 'figured worlds', which for now can be defined as those spaces we at once produce and live through, for example, the overlapping figured worlds of school, race, gender, or politics, as well as, say, the figured worlds of youth in a particular area of New York City.

With this narrower focus, between 2005 and 2006, I examined the ways a small group of economically and otherwise marginalised black and Latina/Latino youth in a New York City after-school club I have called the 'Hope' and white and/or First Nations (Canadian Aboriginal) youth in a small sub-Arctic town in Yukon, Canada, I've called 'Barlow' engaged VMC in the construction of place-based, racial, and gender identities. The story I tell in this book and the findings and relationships I describe are based on this fieldwork.

I chose to focus on all forms of VMC rather than on only popular culture for number of reasons. First, my interest is in what youth are actually using in their daily lives – from fashion to the built environment to rap artists – not in what I assume they are engaging with. By narrowing the scope of the ethnography to popular culture, before fieldwork commenced, I might have closed off inquiry. Therefore, I left this study open to the exploration of VMC which includes all human-made objects, images, and events to which people attribute meaning: for instance, fine art, popular media representations, 'iconic forms' (Grossberg, 1989) or what I later refer to as 'embodied VMC' (such as actors, pop stars), films, websites, clothing, and the like (see discussions in Duncum, 2001, 2002; Freedman, 2003; Keifer-Boyd, Amburgy, & Knight, 2007, p. 19).

As it is difficult to delineate what is and what is not VMC (indeed, all aspects of the visual material world could be included in the broad category of VMC), during fieldwork I decided to focus only on those aspects of VMC that young people described in interviews and/or that I observed them engaging with when we were

---

[5] For clarity and brevity, I use the terms self/selves and identity/identities interchangeably. I do not, however, do this unreflectively and recognise there are literature and debates focusing on the relationship between self and identity (e.g. Fraser, 1999).

together (either at the Hope or in Barlow). Two significant implications come out of this decision: first, the findings and claims I make cannot be generalised to VMC as a broad category, but can apply only to the particular VMC that these specific youth spoke about and/or used during my time with them and that is mentioned in this book. Second, it could be argued that there are issues with respect to the role of advertising – without question a highly relevant form of VMC. While I believe that looking at the contexts of advertising in youth identity-making is important, the specific research problem, questions, and, as I illustrate throughout this book, methodology are underpinned by a quest for youth voice and meanings with a specific focus on the VMC youth themselves were engaging with and talking about. Over the course of this study, young people did not speak about advertising per se (not even when we spent time looking through magazines or exploring the Internet together). In addition, in Chap. 6, when focusing on gender, an area where there are rich connections to advertising, it was rap artists and other icons, and not advertising (though connected), that youth spoke about as embodying ideals of masculinity and femininity. This does not mean that advertising is not a ubiquitous form impacting all of our lives, meanings, and identities, but that my focus was on the specific VMC these youth spoke to me about, and, further, that in order to do the area of advertising justice would require further fieldwork and analysis.

My use of the term VMC is inspired by a contemporary shift in visual art education (my early pedagogical home and where this research finds its roots) to study the inclusive domain of visual culture. Using the term VMC engages this complex area of pedagogy located in the space between visual art education, aspects of media education in North America, and, in part, critical pedagogies. It is an area of education well positioned to provide the tools to better understand youth everyday experiences with VMC, through an area ripe with theoretical and pedagogical issues such as the ones I confronted in the Bronx. Also, while many authors separate visual culture from material culture, I bring them together to signify that material culture is visual and that engagement with 'visual culture is never wholly visual' but experienced through many modes (Duncum, 2005, p. 154; also Mirzoeff, 1998, 1999).

Furthermore, VMC is an expansive and inclusive term – an important point when exploring, as I did, youth engagement with visual material artefacts in communities with intensely different social and physical landscapes. As Mitchell (1995) writes of visual culture, it is 'connate with the human species, and flourishes in nonmodern, non-Western, and nontechnological societies' (p. 543). It includes the Aboriginal beadwork that was part of the visual material landscape of Barlow, as well as the blinking banners of Times Square in New York City. What is more, the study of visual material culture supports debates around localisation and globalisation in youth culture research. In visual culture studies, Mirzoeff (1999), drawing on the work of Appadurai (1990), underlines how the study of visual culture pushes analysts past a common focus on local resistance; examining VMC invites us to investigate the globalisation and localisation of cultural forms. VMC, in the tradition of visual culture studies, steers researchers, pedagogues, and scholars away from 'reading' images much in the tradition of media studies, and towards a focus on cultural practices, on people's everyday experiences with our world – it is concerned with the sensuousness of images and other cultural forms (see Mitchell, 1995). Finally, echoing the nature of this study which draws on various disciplines and perspectives, primarily anthropology, VMC is a wholly interdisciplinary enterprise, or as Mitchell (p. 542) writes of visual culture studies, it is '"indiscipline"': a 'moment of turbulence at the inner and outer borders of established disciplines'.

## Locality and the Global Postmodern

In 'reimagining' (Dimitriadis & Weis, 2007) youth experiences with VMC and trying to conceive a more relational understanding of youth engagement with these forms, geography plays a key role: not only is it a central player in youth identity production from VMC, but its entanglement with globalisation complicates how we might empirically conceive this engagement (Kennelly, Poyntz, & Ugor, 2009).

Though it started off as a hunch sparked by the literature and my own experiences, 'locality' or what I will more often refer to as 'place' quickly became a central concept during fieldwork. For example, in Chaps. 4 and 7, I illustrate how the discourses and relations constituting localities were implicated in youth identity construction from VMC – in the stories that they could 'tell themselves about themselves' (Geertz, 1973, p. 448). In Chap. 4, I highlight how youth in New York took the opportunity to represent life 'in place', to perform their place-based identities. These findings, I suggest, speak to a long-time relationship between youth identities, VMC, and localities across disciplines involved in youth studies (see Bennett, 2000; Holloway & Valentine, 2000; Hörschelmann & Schäfer, 2005; Massey, 1998; Pilkington & Johnson, 2003; Skelton & Valentine, 1998a, 1998b).

In particular, some youth scholars including Dillabough and Kennelly (2010), Nayak (2003), and others (e.g. Bennett, 1999; Dolby, 2001; Maira, 2002; Pilkington, 2004) have carried out and ignited an interest in ethnographically examining the ways in which global shifts and local places, including local histories and politics, are implicated in youth cultures and identities, including those forged, in part, through engagement with VMC. The work of these researchers underlines the importance of spatiality as a key conceptual tool and begins to push into relief an important connection between spatiality and globalisation (Kennelly et al., 2009; see also McLeod's, 2009 review).

Globalisation can be thought of as a historical and ongoing epoch characterised by uneven webs of economic, cultural, technological, and political flows leading to increased connectivity.[6] In the study of youth identities, place, and VMC, I suggest that Hall's (1997a) 'global imperial' and 'global postmodern' provide a useful distinction: while the global imperial is characterised by a kind of 'unity' of cultural form, power of the nation state, and cultural identity strapped to nationality, the

---

[6] See, for instance, in Appadurai (1990), Burawoy (2000a, 2000b), Hall (1997a), Jess and Massey (1995), Kenway, Kraack, and Hickey-Moody (2006), and Savage, Bagnall, and Longhurst (2005 p. 3), for definitions and debates within the field of globalisation.

global postmodern adjusts itself to migration, transnational movements, and mass media; it is a profoundly visual culture (Mirzoeff, 1999) that crosses national and sociocultural borders (see also in Burawoy, 2000a, 2000b).

The global postmodern arguably unsettles concepts such as place, culture, and identities – concepts which have long been the staple diet of social and cultural theories and have long anchored and framed ethnographic youth studies research and ethnography broadly (see Kenway et al., 2006). To clarify, in light of changing social and material relations, mass media, and heightened mobility, scholars across disciplines have highlighted problematic epistemological and ontological assumptions underpinning a notion of culture as a unified essential bounded form, something tied to a particular place.[7] Culture in the global postmodern is more like a medium, a process, and a product; in the study presented in this book, I draw on theories positing culture as patterns of artefacts which include VMC as well as language, beliefs, values, and the like (Cole, 1996; Cole & Engestrom, 1993; Hall, 1997b).

As culture moves across real and imagined borders, identities too move from seemingly stable, unified, and fairly fixed forms which draw their meaning from family, community, and the nation state (Buckingham, 2003, p. 311) to fragmented cultural forms which pull on a host of local, regional, national, and global discourses, as well as VMC in their formation (see in Dolby & Rizvi, 2008a). 'Everyday cultural flows and the mobility of objects', as Nayak and Kehily (2008, p. 32) put it, are 'transforming young people's identities in complex ways as they come to interact with and reconfigure process of globali[s]ation'.

Place and space are especially unsettled in the global postmodern, which is itself a spatial-temporal concept (Kenway et al., 2006). Space is no longer 'a container' (Nayak & Kehily, 2008, p. 31), but something socially constructed in and through human action, signs, symbols, and movements (Falzon, 2009). Space, as Massey (1993, 1998) and others argue, consists of flows of social, cultural, political, and economic relations. Drawing on Appadurai (1990, 1991), these flows or 'scapes', including ethnoscapes (flows of people) and mediascapes (flows of electronic media), become sources of youth identity-making. Place is interrelated with space as both material space (i.e. geographic and physical space) and a nexus of intersecting social relations, influences, and movements (i.e. sociocultural space) (Massey, 1993, pp. 65–66) (see also Chap. 2).

I suggest that localities – local places, with local actions, meanings, and values – are not erased in the global postmodern, but, as many have argued (e.g. in Nayak, 2003), take on an increasingly significant role in young people's lives. In fact, turning to methodology, globalisation, and its entanglement with spatiality – the 'spatial turn' in the social sciences – is profoundly impacting the ways in which we might empirically conceive the geographies of youth identity production from VMC.[8] The global postmodern not only beckons researchers to rethink their

---

[7] For example, in anthropology, see Hastrup and Olwig (1997), Faubion (2001), Fontana (1994, p. 44–5), Macdonald (2001).

[8] See, for example, discussions in Dimitriadis and Weis (2007), Falzon (2009), Kennelly et al. (2009), and Nayak and Kehily (2008).

theoretical frames, it unsettles the methodological tools often used to understand complex sociocultural processes (Marcus, 2009). As a basic example, a shift from culture as bounded to culture as de-essentialised and de-territorialised means the space of (educational) ethnography (i.e. a bounded 'site') is decentred and the object of study itself (i.e. bounded culture) now fragmented, dispersed, and hybridised (see Dimitriadis & Weis, 2007; Falzon, 2009).

## Researching Lives

I have pointed to the need for a more relational understanding of youth engagement with VMC – one that conceives of youth, VMC, and locality in the same frame and positions youth as active cultural producers constrained and supported by social and physical landscapes. I have drawn on Hall's (1997a) global postmodern to think about theoretical shifts and alluded to methodological complications involved in the study of contemporary youth identity-making from VMC. I now focus on the methodology, in particular on the multi-sited, participatory, visual-based ethnography used in this study. While my focus will be slightly more theoretical, I refer readers to Appendix 1 for a discussion of practical details including methods used, sample interview questions, phases of the research, data analysis procedures, and the like.

I worked as a researcher, and more loosely as an artist, in the Hope after-school club in New York City, United States, for just over 6 months and supplemented this fieldwork with 13 weeks of fieldwork in Barlow, a small sub-Arctic community in Yukon Territory, Canada.[9] In an attempt to attract youth with a genuine interest in the research, participation was voluntary: they were not required to participate because they were in a particular group or grade, but instead signed up to work on the project or sought me out after hearing about what I was doing through friends (see Chaps. 4 and 7 for accessing and meeting youth at the Hope and in Barlow respectively). Many young people between the ages of 8 and 15 came in and out of the study. Throughout my time at the Hope, approximately 28 young people participated in one or more of the visual-based projects and/or interviews. Of the 28 young people, 11 were boys, 17 were girls, and all except one identified as black and/or Latina/Latino. Approximately 34 young people in Barlow took part in projects and/or participated in an interview. Of this group in Barlow, 19 were girls, 15 were boys, and 17 of the youth identified as First Nations or 'Native', one as 'half-Native and half-white', one as 'part First Nations', and 15 as French Canadian and/or white. Not included in this breakdown are the dozens of other youth I spoke with who inevitably shaped the accounts I provide. Within each site,

---

[9] Names of all participants, community members, staff, and sites (except New York City and Yukon Territory more generally) have been changed.

I also focused more pointedly on 12–14 young people at the Hope and 5–10 in Barlow; these participants helped provide a deeper examination of individual biographies and the ways in which personal and collective experiences intersected with their use and meanings of cultural forms.

## A 'New' Multi-sited Ethnography

Hoping to align the ethnographic approach employed in this study with my desire to take seriously youth perspectives and everyday experiences with VMC and with changing conceptual understandings of culture, identities, and place, I drew on 'postmodern' (e.g. in Fontana, 1994) or 'new' (e.g. in Lather, 2001) ethnographic perspectives. Where traditional or modernist ethnographies might be characterised by the use of tools to observe, describe, and interpret the 'way of life' of a 'bounded culture' or group of people, postmodern ethnographies question the authority of the ethnographer as objective observer and, within the contexts of globalisation, modify themselves to consider culture as a destabilised object of ethnographic inquiry (Clifford, 1986; Faubion, 2001, pp. 4–8).[10]

New ethnographies start from a critical perspective: they recognise the situated, historical, and political basis of all research and expose the subject-object dualism underpinning traditional forms that postulate the researcher as either a decontextualised being or someone who can somehow shed their subjectivity. New ethnographic projects accept that *all* interpretations are historically and culturally situated. Recognising some of the pedagogical issues described earlier in this chapter with respect to positioning myself as an authority, new ethnographies challenge traditional researcher/researched relationships and illuminate issues involving voice, positioning, and ethics connected to power and hierarchy that are inevitably embedded in research (see Faubion, 2001; Kirsch, 1999; Macdonald, 2001, p. 69; Ramazanoglu & Holland, 2002; Youdell, 2006).

Though new ethnographies continue to use ideas and methods from traditional ethnography (e.g. participant observation), innovative tools and strategies are often employed to respond to shifting understandings of culture and place. For this research, I joined the growing discourse in educational scholarship, particularly among those interested in youth identities, VMC, and spatiality (e.g. Dimitriadis & Weis, 2007; Dolby & Rizvi, 2008b; Petchauer, 2009) and other scholars across disciplines by

---

[10] See also Hastrup and Olwig (1997) and Pink (2001). I contrast modernist and postmodern perspectives not because a sharp divide exists between them, nor to demonstrate a temporal picture, but rather to highlight differences in the kinds of ethnography. Fontana (1994, p. 220) writes: 'What makes... ethnographies postmodern is often a matter of degree and interpretation'. Though this research finds its home in interdisciplinarity, the approach used in this study focuses heavily, though not exclusively, on social and cultural anthropology. This does not mean that ethnography is exclusive to anthropology; Lather (2001, p. 477), for instance, describes ethnography as 'transdisciplinary'.

drawing on 'multi-sited ethnography' and/or 'global ethnography' (see Falzon, 2009; Marcus, 1995, 1998, 2009; as well as studies by Burawoy et al., 2000; Dillabough & Kennelly, 2010; Kehily & Nayak, 2008; Kenway et al., 2006; Nayak & Kehily, 2008; global ethnographies include multi-sited ethnographies). Multi-sited ethnography includes the ethnographic examination of the various sites (e.g. theoretical or physical) and scales (e.g. community, regional, national, global) intervening in a given process or phenomenon (Marcus, 1995, 1998). Using two vastly different sites (New York City and a small sub-Arctic community) helped push locality into relief, 'acknowledging the fundamental differences in local epistemologies that inform everyday practice, experience, and emotion' (Pink, 2006, p. 134). Arguably, the multi-sited approach I used aligns itself with the contemporary experiences of youth living in and through ever-changing and increasingly interconnected sociocultural contexts.

I have come to see ethnography as more than a method or set of methods: I imagine it as a porous, though hardly passive, form where particular theoretical and methodological perspectives move in and through, and are brought together, in infinite combinations. With my primary interest in youth meanings, perspectives, and practices, I locate this study among interpretive approaches, noting that these approaches overarch diverse perspectives, theoretical frameworks, and researchers' epistemological and ontological assumptions (Guba & Lincoln, 1994, p. 108; see also Kincheloe & Tobin, 2006). The research presented here is underpinned by a variety of theoretical assumptions that guide my relationship with youth, inform about power, and speak about the production of ethnographic knowledge.

Specifically, my understanding of researcher subjectivity and my validation of knowledge claims draw on a moderate social constructionist framework (Schwandt, 2000) and concepts from sociocultural theories (I have written about this in Hickman & Eglinton, 2010). These perspectives support the idea of knowledge and reality as continuously produced and shaped by available cultural resources or artefacts including values and beliefs, language, scripts, recipes, and, say, signs (Bruner, 1990; Cole, 1996). They also hold that while knowledge is in constant transformation, some constructions such as dominant discourses around race or gender are so historically rooted that they now appear reified. Effecting change or shifting their meanings is a slow, if never-ending, process.[11] At last, these perspectives are continuous reminders that knowledge represented in research texts is not an objective reality unfiltered through the researcher's gaze (Schwandt, 2000), that all researchers are positioned, and that knowledge is never more than *partial* (Clifford, 1986, p. 7, emphasis in original).

Seeking ways of ethically entering into youth lives, of prioritising youth perspectives, and of deepening my understanding of the researcher/researched relationship, insights arising from participatory inquiry (e.g. Reason & Bradbury,

---

[11] Overall, in this framework, I do not reject the idea that there dominant discourses which 'take on a hard objectified character' (Berger & Luckmann, 1967, in Filmer, Jenks, Seale, Thoburn, & Walsh, 2004), but I do use sociocultural theories to offer the idea that these discourses are constantly in flux as they are constituted of, and serve to constitute, the actions of people.

2001) were central in this study. A participatory view extends epistemology to include otherwise silenced and/or 'non-dominant, non-majority, non-Western ways of knowing' (Lincoln, 2001, p. 128), including the knowledges of young people. This opening of epistemologies underlines the idea that participatory research can aspire to be egalitarian research. In that spirit, I have tried to address power relations and break down the dichotomous relationship between the young people and myself.

Accepting that participants and I actively produced ethnographic knowledge, self-reflexivity or critical self-awareness was threaded throughout the process of formulating, collecting, and analysing data. For example, drawing on the writing of Irwin (2004), Springgay, Irwin, and Wilson Kind (2004), and Sullivan (2005), I produced a series of self-portraits using both still and video cameras during the study. Through the production of researcher-based images, I turned inward to critically examine, question, and continuously reprocess, reinterpret, and represent my understanding of the research process.[12] Moreover, throughout this book, I weave in aspects of personal narrative, making explicit my own position in the process. In fact, reflexivity enabled me to engage with the idea that as a researcher and educator, I, too, am produced in and through mediated action. I am made up of particular experiences. I am contextual, positioned, and located (Coffey, 1999). Because I grew up in New York (the primary research site) and lived in New York City for many years, I was pushed to consider my own status as possible insider – the local knowledges I understood and what this meant in terms of my relationships with youth and the data we produced. While this inquiry came about, in part, through a critique of the potentially ideological nature of certain educational perspectives, I soon came to believe through continuous reflection that there are no value-free or neutral choices in the research process and that my own inquiry itself promotes a particular ideology. For all my effort to bring youth voices to the forefront and to lessen (though never erase) the power relations between us, in the end, there is no escaping the idea that I ultimately shape the final accounts I present (Youdell, 2006, p. 61).

## *A Visual-Based Ethnography*

Over the course of this study, I brought together a series of methods including interviews, participant observation, and visual-based tools (see Appendix 1 for a detailed description of methods) in an effort to get at youth meanings, and as a means of accessing the space where youth lives, VMC and geography intersect in cultural practice.

---

[12] See 'Watching Myself, Watching Myself' (http://www.clarehall.cam.ac.uk/index.php?id=457).

As in visual anthropology, I had the dual purpose of studying the VMC used by youth in everyday life and employing visual media to study cultural processes (MacDougall, 1997). I made deliberate use of film (or video), photography, and other visual media (both mechanical and non-mechanical) to generate, make sense of, and represent ethnographic knowledge (Morphy & Banks, 1997). As MacDougall (p. 288) writes, in seeking to learn 'about a range of culturally inflected relationships enmeshed and encoded in the visual', researchers need a language, a way of knowing which, he argues, 'may be accessible only through non-verbal means' (p. 292).

Though post-positivist, phenomenological, and interpretive frameworks all employ visual methods, the ways in which they operate often go unexplained. Yet, as Pink (2001, pp. 2–3) writes, 'an awareness of the theoretical underpinnings of "visual research methods" is crucial for understanding how ... [they] are used to produce ethnographic knowledge'. In fact, I would argue part of the contentiousness of visual research might have to do with the idea that visual methods remain largely under-theorised and, at best, are only partially understood.

For the research presented in this book, instead of adapting 'frameworks that aim to distance, objectify, and generali[s]e' (Pink, 2001, p. 3), I drew on post-modern ethnographic work and visual researchers, theorists, and artists who posit a reflexive, collaborative, integrative view of the visual – who construe visual modes of research as potentially expressive, imaginative, participatory aesthetic practices. Rather than using the visual simply 'as a mode of recording data or illustrating text' (Pink, p. 11), I capitalised on the *subjective, expressive* (and sometimes ambiguous) nature of visual material forms in the production of ethnographic knowledge. 'Blurring genres' (Geertz, 1983; Denzin & Lincoln, 2000, p. 15), I brought together anthropological and artistic forms of knowledge and continuously drew on my own experience as a visual artist in the generation of ethnographic images. Using participatory visual methods, I engaged young people in the production of visual forms which pushed 'beyond the boundary' (Edwards, 1997) of simply docu-menting life and into an area where both the young people and I, as Hickman (2005, p. 103) might argue, were creating 'aesthetic significance': where to *create* connects to 'inventiveness', *aesthetic* refers to the senses, and '"*significance*" is associated with meaning and "signs" that are highly expressive and invite attention' (see Desai, 2002 for artists working as ethnographers).

I understood visual approaches as a form of social interaction between researcher and researched: through interaction and collaboration, there was no longer a subject-object dualism, but rather a 'continuity between subject and object' (Hastrup, 1992, p. 10). To further this, Banks (2001, p. 119) suggests all image-making in social research involves a collaborative element. Whether I was taking a photo or making a film with youth, or when I gave the camera to young people, my aim was to relinquish control and, in part, put the production of ethnographic knowledge in the hands of young people. I hoped that undermined in this collaboration was a distanced knowing, as well as hierarchies in the researcher/researched relationship.

Though these categories were not discrete, the visual methods used in both communities included the following: (1) Image-making by the researcher. The images I took during this study were meant to understand the visual systems in play, get a feeling of the physical and social landscape, explore issues emerging in the research, and record the production of participatory image-making. (2) Using pre-existing materials to generate ethnographic data, often referred to as photo- or film-elicitation, images, music videos, and magazines were used in casual discussion and interviews to elicit young people's perspectives, experiences, and other concerns arising throughout the study. Young people also created various images including digital self-portraits and collages which, in addition to being the catalyst for much casual discussion, served as the basis for photo- or film-elicitation in interviewing. (3) Participatory image-making: youth engaged in self-representational film-making, photography, and collage. For instance, young people wrote, directed, filmed, and edited a series of videos (I assisted in filming and editing). In both communities, for part of almost every day, I would work with different groups or individual youth filming and editing using basic digital cameras and free editing software. During production, youth did most of the filming, with one of them usually filming behind the scenes. Videos were approximately 3–12 min long and were screened for the community at the end of my time in each site. See Appendix 1 for a full description of all these visual-based methods.

## Representing Youth

'[R]esearchers', Denzin and Lincoln (2005) write, 'can no longer directly capture lived experience. Such experience, it is argued, is created in the social text written by the researcher' (p. 19). In this research, issues of power and hierarchy were threaded through the writing as I took young people's words and images, and, in many ways, 'impos[ed] my own interpretations on their actions' (Pilkington, 1994, p. 214). During analysis, as I started to pull the pieces together, I was not simply writing what I already knew, rather it was an active production (and construction) of knowledge and understanding (see Appendix 1 for analytic procedures). Feeling strongly about explicating the production of knowledge and seeking to 'evoke' (Tyler, 1986, p. 125), rather than suggest I could objectively represent, I reflexively gathered stories from fieldnotes which connected practices, relationships, and perspectives in the field with analytic points.

   As I started to write, I struggled: I skimmed multiple ethnographies from traditional to postmodern hoping to stumble upon inspiring frameworks and forms of writing. I was struck by words tucked into the preface of Margaret Mead's (1928/ 2001) *Coming of Age in Samoa*: 'I tried to couch it in a language that would be communicative to those who had the most to do with adolescents'. Mead believed in the usefulness of research, that if research is to be 'meaningful' to people, it 'must be written for them'. I took Mead's words seriously and have tried to produce a useful text which is accessible – capturing the detail of the world in which people live.

   Focusing on representation, power, subjectivity, and the production of knowledge, as well as to monitor my own voice, I have incorporated into the accounts presented in this book fieldnotes and personal narratives describing my interactions with the young people and my role in the research, fieldnotes that underline the situated and mediated nature of research, and fieldnotes that arguably helped me challenge my biases and beliefs (see Appendix 1 for participant observation and fieldnotes). While most of these fieldnotes are woven into the main text, others are woven into several 'boxes' in the analysis chapters. Fieldnotes in boxes have been edited for readability and are, in some cases, blended with my later reflections. I have also used boxes to offset important interview material.

Rather than forging (even forcing) artificial divisions between findings and my interpretations, importantly between the presentation of data and the theoretical assumptions and perspectives which have informed data generation, analysis, and discussion, throughout Chaps. 4, 5, 6, and 7, I move between theory and data in order to build a singular account of youth use of VMC in local places, as well as to consider central cultural processes underpinning the use of VMC. Underlining the indelible link between theory, data, and findings and making explicit my use of theories as well as the notion that all acts of analysis are interpretive (Coffey & Atkinson, 1996; Wolcott, 1994, 2001), rather than having a lengthy discussion at the end of the book, I include a discussion at the end of Chaps. 4, 5, 6, and 7 where I bring in conceptual tools to think about the mutual production of youth and aspects of their worlds (see also Appendix 1 for use of theory in data analysis).

Further, I have tried to extend the participatory inquiry into the final text as I (re) presented the voices of the young people (Lather, 1991). Hoping to ameliorate my own subjectivity, I have tried to stay as close to the data as possible and use, as much as possible, the words from young people themselves. I was also highly aware that in translating oral to written text, participants could be rendered inarticulate – which was hardly the case (see Luttrell, 2003, p. 42). I decided, therefore, to edit out some repetitions and short utterances (including 'uh' and 'um') which are part of everyday speech, but which have little to do with youth meanings. I use a series of ellipses to indicate omissions (see Notations). With respect to dialect, I tried to remain thoughtful in how I represented participants, and continuing to stay close to the data, I transcribed dialect when it was most pronounced; those words most strongly reflecting accents are spelled phonetically. I was also conscious of how I represented myself and applied the same rules I used to youth transcription and representation to my own speech (e.g. taking out unnecessary short utterances and generally keeping in my own dialect).[13]

To further highlight youth perspectives and emphasise the importance of individual experiences, I decided to focus most pointedly on key participants. Yet, returning to the Hope recently, I spoke to several of the central young people featured in this book (some of them now work at the Hope) – seeing how different they are now, how their perspectives have changed, and how they have moved on from who they were in 2005 and 2006 was a powerful reminder that the data and accounts I present in this book are a snapshot in time. In keeping with the importance of context – time

---

[13] I have also included a glossary of terms for slang used by young people and myself.

and place – and the situatedness of all research, I have used the past tense as much as possible rather than the 'ethnographic present' (see, e.g. Davies, 1999).

The situatedness of the research comes through in my writing style with respect to the chapters focusing on the Hope (Chaps. 4, 5, 6) and the chapter on Barlow (Chap. 7). While issues around confidentiality and anonymity have kept me from describing the youth in Barlow in much detail (see below), I am more apt to believe that my own experience as someone from the first research site (New York), experiencing Canada's North for the first time in the second site, as well as vast physical, social, and temporal differences between these sites, is at the heart of stylistic differences. For example, in the Barlow chapter (see Chap. 7), I spend considerable time describing place and my coming to know place. Moreover, for better or for worse, in the Barlow chapter, I feel my voice is stronger – though I was entangled in New York, my own experience in Barlow was almost transforming: with the youth, I searched for an identity – as researcher, as New Yorker, as a woman, as white – in (what to me was) a geographically extreme place.

While I am aware that multi-sited projects are not necessarily meant to compare sites or offer equal weight to each site in the writing of ethnographic texts, and though I originally went to Barlow primarily as a supplemental site and way to push the role of geography into relief, for me featuring Barlow in only one chapter of the book is not only a representational issue but arguably has become an ethical one (i.e. an issue connected to 'fairness' or the notion that all perspectives should be represented in the research process and product; see Seale, 2004). My concern is that in prioritising only one or two threads from the data in Barlow – threads that explicitly tied my work in Barlow to data generated at the Hope – I have inadvertently silenced important stories and voices from this community. Since leaving Barlow and writing this monograph, I am acutely aware that this site needs its own space, and am continuing to think of ways to get the rich data generated there and the perspectives of *all* the young people I spoke with and who gave me so much of their time, into the public domain.

With respect to terminology, except for general references to youth and young people in, for example, the literature in Chap. 2, when I use the terms 'youth' and 'young people' in the analytic chapters (i.e. 4–7), I am generally referring to youth who took part in this study. Using these terms, I aim to be as reflexive as possible, reminding myself and readers that there is 'no essence of youth' (Grossberg, 1989, p. 95) and that the terms 'youth' and 'young people' are socially constructed and, therefore, polysemic concepts (see Steinberg, 2006). By using the terms 'youth' and 'young people', I am not referring to a monolithic sociological demographic, but rather to complex individuals.

Further, central to this study is the idea that key identity markers such as race or gender are not static, essential categories but rather dynamic social constructions. Some researchers examining youth identities place the term 'race' in inverted commas, underlining the idea that race is socially rather than biologically produced (see, e.g. Archer, 2003, p. 19). While I do not use inverted commas with respect to race, I remain cognisant that identity markers are continuously constructed through cultural practices. With regard to racial terms and categories, I applied one rule throughout: I use the terms that the young people themselves used in the particular site I was working in. Youth in the study never mentioned the term 'ethnicity', but rather conflated it with race; therefore, I tend to use the term race rather than both race *and* ethnicity. This is particularly important for the Hope: though the United States Census separates a person's 'race' from their 'Hispanic' origin, young people at the Hope never spoke of a difference between being Latina/Latino and their race. Instead, conflating race and ethnicity, youth would often tell me that being Latina/ Latino is their 'race'; as Freddie, a participant at the Hope, put it, 'It's like your religion, man. It's your background, your race'. I refer, therefore, to Latina/Latino, black, and white as the three overarching 'racial' categories youth cited at the Hope. Connectedly, using the same terms as youth in my discussions, I generally use the terms 'white', 'black', and, at the Hope, 'Latina/Latino' (or Latino only, when speaking in general: a Latino family or, say, Latino business, where the family or business is neither male nor female), rather than Caucasian, African-American, or Hispanic (as used on the United States Census). In Barlow, many of the youth used the term 'Native' rather than First Nations, Aboriginal, or Indige-nous, and I have done the same depending on the context of my discussion. When writing about First Nations with respect to, say, history or demographics (e.g. in Chap. 3), I use the terms which were used interchangeably by people in Barlow including First Nations, Aboriginal, or, in some instances, Indigenous. In both communities, on those occasions when youth used different terms, such as African-American, I use the same terminology they did.

My final point has as much to do with issues around confidentiality and ano-nymity as it does with representation. Protecting the young people's identities was of significant importance to the participants. Knowing names would be changed that friends, parents, and/or teachers would not see their interviews, afforded youth great relief, and many seemed to open up about various issues after an assurance of confidentiality. Yet, confidentiality was not easy in a study using visual images – particularly self-representational images featuring the young people themselves.

Attempting to deal with these issues, I made the decision to leave out of this book the hundreds of images that reveal the identity of participants and/or the sites themselves. I have not included any images from Barlow and only very little descri-ption of individual youth as per discussions with the community leaders. Barlow is an easily recognisable town with a small number of youth, and descriptions of young people would jeopardise agreements of confidentiality. For the Hope, I ran into somewhat similar issues where the particular after-school club would be easily recognised if I included images of youth inside or just outside the school.[14] I do, however, include several images that youth from the Hope took, but do not cite their pseudonyms. Further, in my attempt to use as many images as possible without

---

[14] For the PhD dissertation, I had approval to include some images from the Hope and did include some images featuring the youth. In order to conceal the young people's identities, I blocked out faces and other identifying characteristics using various editing techniques. However, while I am able to show images in conferences and other live events, for wider print publication, I am unable to include these images. In addition, I did feel that the practice of blocking out the youths' faces took away from the participants' intentions and ownership of their cultural productions.

identifying youth and/or the field site, I have put several of the collages produced at the Hope and stills of the video titles from both communities in Appendix 2.[15] That is, I have inserted images at the end of the book and away from text that could reveal the identity of the young people.

## Aims and Overview of the Book

When I set out on fieldwork several years ago, my central aim was to use empirical data as a means of forging links between theory, pedagogy, and young people's lived experiences in visual art, culture, and design education. Years on, my aims have grown: while I still hope to forge links between theory, pedagogy, and youth experiences in education (now, more broadly conceived), I now want to rethink, theoretically and methodologically (and ultimately pedagogically), how we might understand contemporary youth experiences with VMC as they play out in diverse sociocultural contexts. Further, I want this research to go some way towards bringing youth themselves into a conversation which could ultimately shape an education relevant to all youth – including those youth not necessarily thriving in formal schooling – that is, an education which accepts, and seeks to understand and draw upon, VMC as a primary site of youth identity- and world-making. As Grossberg (1989, p. 114) puts it: 'we must allow ourselves to be educated by those we are attempting to understand, by the cultural forms they enjoy, and by the practices they engage with'.

Today, four aims stretching across theory, methodology, and eventually pedagogy underpin this book: (1) to bring the lives and voices of youth as contextual and active cultural agents into the discourse on VMC in education by providing empirical data which gets at the complexity of youth engagement with VMC. Connected to this: to provide a series of ethnographic accounts demonstrating *how* youth might be negotiating complex identities and authoring new cultural forms, using what is often considered 'global' culture, with/in and through local/global sociocultural-economic contexts; (2) theoretically, to offer a conceptual framework which at once envisions identities, VMC, and places as dynamic rather than static forms and describes and supports the examination of the relationship between youth, VMC, and local place; (3) methodologically, to begin demonstrating the possibilities of a multi-sited ethnographic approach as a means of understanding the local processes by which youth identity- and world-making is at once constrained and enabled by geography; and (4) to align conceptual thinking and practice in education broadly defined with contemporary youth cultural experiences: to consider the pedagogical possibilities of using participatory, visual-based ethnography as a tool to bring pedagogy into concert with youth identities and their practices with VMC across contexts.

---

[15] Though youth selected pseudonyms used in the videos, by the end of the study, everyone knew each other's names and I have changed the names again to strengthen confidentiality in the final text.

To further these aims, this book is broken into three parts: Part I provides a context for the study; Part II includes analytic chapters, and Part III offers implications for education. With respect to chapter conclusions, for Part I, the conclusions summarise general chapter content; for Part II, as noted, conclusions provide a more analytic discussion; and, for Part III, the concluding thoughts are presented in a narrative style.

So far, in Part I, I have highlighted some of the pedagogical, theoretical, and methodological issues and challenges to which this book responds. I underlined the importance of locality or place in understanding youth engagement with VMC, have argued for a more relational understanding of youth engagement with VMC, and described the new, multi-sited, participatory, visual-based ethnography used as a means of getting at the space where youth lives, VMC, and places intersect.

Moving forward, in Chap. 2, I locate this study, briefly looking across visual culture and art education, the field that inspired this research, and then more pointedly into those youth cultural studies that seek to understand youth lives, examine VMC, and young people as at once shaping and being shaped by local places. In the second part of Chap. 2, I introduce a conceptual framework which contributes a theoretical foundation to youth research in education as it overcomes various dualistic assumptions underpinning much educational research and pedagogy: it provides a more dynamic and relational understanding of the social world and of youth as active users of VMC, continuously constructing both themselves and their worlds.

In Chap. 3, I offer a context for exploring young people's use of VMC in the analytic chapters that follow. I draw on ethnographic, historical, and statistical information and note salient features of each site, including immigration and poverty rates in New York City and colonialism in Yukon, Canada. The focus is on the conditions for black and Latino families in New York and First Nations families in the Yukon. I draw on ethnographic fieldnotes that I hope provide for the reader a taste of my own sense of place, that is, my own sense of New York City and Barlow.

Part II of this book includes four ethnographic chapters. Beginning with Chap. 4, I describe early days at the Hope after-school club in New York, including impressions, activities, and feelings, before moving into the overarching theme of place. I flesh out the ways in which young people in New York City used VMC to describe, make sense of, and construct the various places (e.g. imagined communities) that intersected their lives and negotiate their own place-based identities. I conclude the chapter by arguing for the mutual constitution of place-making and place-based identities.

For Chap. 5, I stay in New York City and offer an analysis of the ways in which young people at the Hope used VMC to make sense of, maintain, and (re)construct racial identities and the racial boundaries or borders making up their worlds. Describing three intertwined cultural processes, I demonstrate how young people made sense of and constructed black, white, and Latina/Latino identities through the deployment of racialised VMC. I illustrate how youth used VMC to produce a particular form of authenticity and show how the unique intersection of authenticity, VMC, aspects of place, and youth experiences supported the crossing, blurring, reworking, or reconstructing of racial borders and, connectedly, the production of new racial identities.

Gender at the Hope is the focus of Chap. 6 where I argue that young people used VMC to negotiate local masculinities and femininities. Drawing on Bruner's (1990) narratives, I demonstrate how youth used forms of VMC to construct and make sense of the masculinities and femininities making up their world. In the second part of the chapter, I argue that young people's own gender identity work was a point of continuous negotiation. Drawing on the work of Connell (2002), I argue young people, working with/in and through the 'gender order' (composed of dominant gender ideologies), through particular material and sociocultural constraints, and in unison with their own lives, used cultural forms to not only rework and negotiate the values and ideals which comprised dominant gender narratives but to, in a sense, produce new gender identities.

Following the trajectory of the ethnography, in Chap. 7 – the final ethnographic chapter – I pick up on some of the themes discussed at the Hope and focus on place- and identity-making (racial and gender identities specifically) in Barlow, Yukon. After providing an ethnographic description of my early days in Barlow, I draw on cultural geography, particularly the work of Shields (1991), and underline the ways in which landscape and youth everyday experiences intersected youth place-making. Following this, I return to the themes of racial identities and authenticity described in Chap. 5, and using the example of the 'Original Gangstas' or 'OGs' (a group of First Nations boys who identified as black and drew heavily on the lexicon and performances of hip-hop artists), I describe the negotiations youth needed to make when drawing on urban hip-hop in the construction of their identities. I begin to shape the argument that *landscape* in addition to Appadurai's (1990, 1991) other 'scapes' (such as mediascapes) is not only a social and physical context affording and limiting their self-making, it is also a tool youth in Barlow used to forge credible identities.

Part III consists of Chap. 8 where I explore what these ethnographic accounts might mean for educational perspectives and educational research concerned with the ways in which youth are engaging with their visual material world and which aim to work with youth in this process. I review the central findings of this study; think about a local/global binary, which continues to structure youth studies research in education (McLeod, 2009); and consider the potential of multi-sited work. In the second part of the chapter, I flesh out an 'ethnographic pedagogy': a pedagogic mode driven by youth practices and perspectives. I suggest that this form of pedagogy could bridge disconnections between youth lived experiences and the theoretical and pedagogical approaches employed in forms of education seeking to bring the 'unofficial curriculum' into the official world of school. I also touch on some unique ethical concerns arising through this kind of pedagogical and research practice.

I want to close this chapter with Stuart Hall (1990, p. 222) who writes, 'Practices of representation always implicate the positions from which we speak or write'. This is a reminder to myself as much as to the reader: the story I tell here not only implicates my position, it is *'partial'* (Clifford, 1986, p. 7, emphasis in original), it is unique, and – like all cultural productions – it is situated, historic, and open to multiple interpretations.

# References

Appadurai, A. (1990). Disjuncture and difference in the global cultural economy. *Theory, Culture & Society, 7*, 295–310.

Appadurai, A. (1991). Global ethnoscapes: Notes and queries for a transnational anthropology. In R. G. Fox (Ed.), *Recapturing anthropology: Working in the present* (pp. 191–210). Santa Fe, NM: School of American Research Press.

Archer, L. (2003). *Race, masculinity and schooling: Muslim boys and education*. Maidenhead, UK: Open University Press.

Banks, M. (2001). *Visual methods in social research*. London: Sage.

Bennett, A. (1999). Hip hop am Main: The localization of rap music and hip hop culture. *Media, Culture & Society, 21*, 77–91.

Bennett, A. (2000). *Popular music and youth culture: Music, identity, and place*. London: Macmillan Press.

Berger, P., & Luckmann, T. (1967). *The social construction of reality*. New York: Anchor.

Bruner, J. S. (1990). *Acts of meaning*. Cambridge, MA: Harvard University Press.

Buckingham, D. (2003). Media education and the end of the critical consumer. *Harvard Educational Review, 73*(3), 309–327.

Burawoy, M. (2000a). Introduction: Reaching for the global. In M. Burawoy, J. A. Blum, S. George, Z. Gille, T. Gowan, L. Haney, M. Klawiter, S. H. Lopez, S. O. Riain, & M. Thayer (Eds.), *Global ethnography: Forces, connections, and imaginations in a postmodern world* (pp. 1–40). Berkley, CA: University of California Press.

Burawoy, M. (2000b). Grounding globalization. In M. Burawoy, J. A. Blum, S. George, Z. Gille, T. Gowan, L. Haney, M. Klawiter, S. H. Lopez, S. O. Riain, & M. Thayer (Eds.), *Global ethnography: Forces, connections and imaginations in a postmodern world* (pp. 337–350). Berkley, CA: University of California Press.

Burawoy, M., Blum, J. A., George, S., Gille, Z., Gowan, T., Haney, L., Klawiter, M., Lopez, S. H., Riain, S. O., & Thayer, M. (Eds.). (2000). *Global ethnography: Forces, connections, and imaginations in a postmodern world*. Berkeley, CA: University of California Press.

Clifford, J. (1986). Introduction: partial truths. In J. Clifford & G. E. Marcus (Eds.), *Writing culture: The poetics and politics of ethnography* (pp. 1–26). Berkeley, CA: University of California Press.

Coffey, A. J. (1999). *The ethnographic self: Fieldwork and the representation of identity*. London: Sage.

Coffey, A., & Atkinson, P. (1996). *Making sense of qualitative data analysis: Complementary strategies*. Thousand Oaks, CA: Sage.

Cole, M. (1996). *Cultural psychology: A once and future discipline*. Cambridge, MA: Harvard University Press.

Cole, M., & Engestrom, Y. (1993). A cultural-historical approach to distributed cognition. In G. Salomon (Ed.), *Distributed cognition* (pp. 1–46). Cambridge: Cambridge University Press.

Connell, R. W. (2002). *Gender*. Cambridge: Polity Press.

Davies, C. A. (1999). *Reflexive ethnography: A guide to researching selves and others*. London: Routledge.

Denzin, N. K., & Lincoln, Y. S. (2000). Introduction: The discipline and practice of qualitative research. In N. K. Denzin & Y. S. Lincoln (Eds.), *Handbook of qualitative research* (2nd ed., pp. 1–45). Thousand Oaks, CA: Sage.

Denzin, N. K., & Lincoln, Y. S. (2005). Introduction: The discipline and practice of qualitative research. In N. K. Denzin & Y. S. Lincoln (Eds.), *Handbook of qualitative research* (3rd ed., pp. 1–32). Thousand Oaks, CA: Sage.

Desai, D. (2002). The ethnographic move in contemporary art: What does it mean for art education. *Studies in Art Education, 43*(4), 307–323.

Dillabough, J., & Kennelly, J. (2010). *Lost youth in the global city*. London: Routledge.

Dimitriadis, G. (2001). *Performing identity/performing culture: Hip hop as text, pedagogy, and lived practice*. New York: Peter Lang.

Dimitriadis, G., & Weis, L. (2007). Globalization and multisited ethnographic approaches. In C. McCarthy, A. Durham, L. Engel, A. Filmer, M. Giardina, & M. Malagreca (Eds.), *Globalizing cultural studies: Ethnographic interventions in theory, method, and policy* (pp. 323–342). New York: Peter Lang.

Dolby, N. (2001). *Constructing race: Youth, identity, and popular culture in South Africa*. Albany, NY: State University of New York Press.

Dolby, N., & Rizvi, F. (2008a). Introduction: Youth, mobility, and identity. In N. Dolby & F. Rizvi (Eds.), *Youth moves: Identities and education in global perspective* (pp. 1–14). London: Routledge.

Dolby, N., & Rizvi, F. (Eds.). (2008b). *Youth moves: Identities and education in global perspective*. London: Routledge.

Duncum, P. (2001). Visual culture: Developments, definitions, and directions for art education. *Studies in Art Education, 42*(2), 101–112.

Duncum, P. (2002). Clarifying visual culture art education. *Art Education, 55*(3), 6–11.

Duncum, P. (2005). Visual culture art education: Why, what and how? In R. Hickman (Ed.), *Critical studies in art and design education* (pp. 151–162). Bristol, UK: Intellect.

Edwards, E. (1997). Beyond the boundary: A consideration of the expressive in photography and anthropology. In M. Banks & H. Morphy (Eds.), *Rethinking visual anthropology* (pp. 53–80). New Haven, CT: Yale University Press.

Eglinton, K. (2008). Using participatory visual ethnography to explore young people's use of visual material culture in place and space. In R. Hickman (Ed.), *Research in art and design education: Issues and exemplars* (pp. 51–65). Bristol, UK: Intellect.

Eisenhart, M. (2001). Educational ethnography past, present, and future: Ideas to think with. *Educational Researcher, 30*(8), 16–27.

Falzon, M. A. (2009). Introduction: Multi-sited ethnography: Theory, praxis and locality in contemporary research. In M. A. Falzon (Ed.), *Multi-sited ethnography: Theory, praxis, and locality in contemporary research* (pp. 1–23). London: Ashgate.

Faubion, J. (2001). Currents in cultural fieldwork. In P. Atkinson, A. Coffey, S. Delamont, J. Lofland, & L. Lofland (Eds.), *Handbook of ethnography* (pp. 39–59). London: Sage.

Filmer, P., Jenks, C., Seale, C., Thoburn, N., & Walsh, D. (2004). Developments in social theory. In C. Seale (Ed.), *Researching society and culture* (2nd ed., pp. 33–46). London: Sage.

Finney, J., Hickman, R., Morrison, M., Nicholl, B., & Rudduck, J. (2005). *Rebuilding engagement through the arts*. Cambridge, UK: Pearson Publications.

Fontana, A. (1994). Ethnographic trends in the postmodern era. In D. Dickens & A. Fontana (Eds.), *Postmodernism and social inquiry* (pp. 203–224). New York: Routledge.

Fraser, M. (1999). *Identity without selfhood: Simone de Beauvoir and bisexuality*. Cambridge, UK: Cambridge University Press.

Freedman, K. (2003). *Teaching visual culture*. New York: Teachers College Press.

Funge, E. (1998). Rethinking representation: Media studies and the postmodern teenager. *English and Media Magazine, 39*, 33–36.

Gablik, S. (1991). *The reenchantment of art*. New York.: Thames and Hudson.

Geertz, C. (1973). *The interpretation of cultures: Selected essays*. New York: Basic Books.

Geertz, C. (1983). *Local knowledge: Further essays in interpretive anthropology*. New York: Basic Books.

Grossberg, L. (1989). Pedagogy in the present: Politics, postmodernity, and the popular. In H. Giroux & R. Simon (Eds.), *Popular culture, schooling, and everyday life* (pp. 91–115). Granby, MA: Bergin and Garvey.

Guba, E., & Lincoln, Y. S. (1994). Competing paradigms in qualitative research. In N. K. Denzin & Y. S. Lincoln (Eds.), *Handbook of qualitative research* (pp. 105–117). Thousand Oaks, CA: Sage.

Hall, S. (1990). Cultural identity and diaspora. In J. Rutherford (Ed.), *Identity: Community, culture, difference* (pp. 222–238). London: Lawrence & Wishart.

Hall, S. (1997a). The local and the global: Globalization and ethnicity. In A. McClintock, A. Mufti, & E. Shohat (Eds.), *Dangerous liaisons: Gender, nation, and post-colonial perspectives* (pp. 173–187). Minneapolis: University of Minnesota Press.

Hall, S. (1997b). *Representation: Cultural representations and signifying practices.* London: Sage.

Hastrup, K. (1992). Anthropological visions: Some notes on visual and textual authority. In P. I. Crawford & D. Turton (Eds.), *Film as ethnography* (pp. 8–25). Manchester, UK: Manchester University Press.

Hastrup, K., & Olwig, K. F. (1997). Introduction. In K. F. Olwig & K. Hastrup (Eds.), *Siting culture: The shifting anthropological object* (pp. 1–16). London: Routledge.

Hickman, R. (2005). *Why we make art and why it is taught.* Bristol, UK: Intellect.

Hickman, R., & Eglinton, K. (2010). Exploring the ways in which youth engage with visual material culture in their everyday lives: A framework for inquiry. *Australian Art Education, 32*(2), 4–16.

Holland, D., Lachicotte, W., Skinner, D., & Cain, C. (1998). *Identity and agency in cultural worlds.* Cambridge, MA: Harvard University Press.

Holloway, S. L., & Valentine, G. (Eds.). (2000). *Children's geographies: Playing, living, learning.* London: Routledge.

Hörschelmann, K., & Schäfer, N. (2005). Performing the global through the local – Young people's practices of identity formation in former East Germany. *Children's Geographies, 3,* 219–242.

Ingold, T. (1994). Introduction to culture. In T. Ingold (Ed.), *Companion encyclopaedia of anthropology: Humanity, culture and social life* (pp. 329–349). London: Routledge.

Irwin, R. L. (2004). A/r/tography: A metonymic métissage. In R. Irwin & A. de Cosson (Eds.), *A/r/tography as living inquiry: An introduction to arts-based research in education.* Vancouver, Canada: Pacific Educational Press.

Jess, P., & Massey, D. (1995). The conceptualization of place. In D. Massey & P. Jess (Eds.), *A Place in the world? Places, cultures and globalization* (pp. 45–85). Oxford, UK: Oxford University Press/The Open University.

Kehily, M. J., & Nayak, A. (2008). Global femininities: Consumption, culture and the significance of place. *Discourse: Studies in the Cultural Politics of Education, 29*(3), 325–342.

Keifer-Boyd, K., Amburgy, P., & Knight, W. (2007). Unpacking privilege: Memory, culture, gender, race and power in visual culture. *Art Education, 60*(3), 19–24.

Kennelly, J., Poyntz, S., & Ugor, P. (2009). Special issue introduction: Youth cultural politics, and new social spaces in an era of globalization. *Review of Education, Pedagogy, and Cultural Studies, 31*(4), 255–269.

Kenway, J., Kraack, A., & Hickey-Moody, A. (2006). *Masculinity beyond the metropolis.* New York: Palgrave.

Kincheloe, J. L., & Tobin, K. (2006). Doing educational research in a complex world. In K. Tobin & J. L. Kincheloe (Eds.), *Doing educational research: A handbook* (pp. 3–13). Rotterdam, The Netherlands: Sense Publishers.

Kirsch, G. (1999). *Ethical dilemmas in feminist research: The politics of location, interpretation, and publication.* New York: State University of New York Press.

Lather, P. A. (1991). *Getting smart: Feminist research and pedagogy with/in the postmodern.* New York: Routledge.

Lather, P. A. (2001). Postmodernism, post-structuralism and post (critical) ethnography: Of ruins, aporias and angels. In P. Atkinson, A. Coffey, S. Delamont, J. Lofland, & L. Lofland (Eds.), *Handbook of ethnography* (pp. 477–492). London: Sage.

Lincoln, Y. S. (2001). Engaging sympathies: Relationships between action research and social constructivism. In P. Reason & H. Bradbury (Eds.), *Handbook of action research: Participative inquiry and practice* (pp. 124–132). London: Sage.

Lusted, D. (1986). Why pedagogy? *Screen, 27*(5), 2–14.

Luttrell, W. (2003). *Pregnant bodies, fertile minds.* London: Routledge.

Macdonald, S. (2001). British social anthropology. In P. Atkinson, A. Coffey, S. Delamont, J. Lofland, & L. Lofland (Eds.), *Handbook of ethnography* (pp. 60–79). London: Sage.

MacDougall, D. (1997). The visual in anthropology. In M. Banks & H. Morphy (Eds.), *Rethinking visual anthropology* (pp. 276–295). New Haven, CT: Yale University Press.

Maira, S. (2002). *Desis in the house: Indian American youth culture in New York City.* Philadelphia: Temple University Press.

Marcus, G. (1995). Ethnography in/of the world system: The emergence of multi-sited ethnography. *Annual Review of Anthropology, 24*, 95–117.

Marcus, G. (1998). *Ethnography through thick and thin.* Princeton, NJ: Princeton University Press.

Marcus, G. (2009). Multi-sited ethnography: Notes and queries. In M. A. Falzon (Ed.), *Multi-sited ethnography: Theory, praxis, and locality in contemporary research* (pp. 181–196). London: Ashgate.

Massey, D. (1993). Power-geometry and a progressive sense of place. In J. Bird, B. Curtis, T. Putnam, G. Robertson, & L. Tickner (Eds.), *Mapping the futures: Local cultures, global change* (pp. 59–69). London: Routledge.

Massey, D. (1998). The spatial construction of youth cultures. In T. Skelton & G. Valentine (Eds.), *Cool places: Geographies of youth cultures* (pp. 121–129). London: Routledge.

McLeod, J. (2009). Youth studies, comparative inquiry, and the local/global problematic. *Review of Education, Pedagogy, and Cultural Studies, 31*(4), 270–292.

Mead, M. (1928/2001). *Coming of age in Samoa.* New York: Morrow.

Mirzoeff, N. (1998). What is visual culture? In N. Mirzoeff (Ed.), *Visual culture reader* (pp. 3–13). New York: Routledge.

Mirzoeff, N. (1999). *An introduction to visual culture.* New York: Routledge.

Mitchell, W. J. T. (1995). Interdisciplinarity and visual culture. *Art Bulletin, 77*(4), 540–544.

Morphy, H., & Banks, M. (1997). Introduction: Rethinking visual anthropology. In M. Banks & H. Morphy (Eds.), *Rethinking visual anthropology* (pp. 1–35). New Haven, CT: Yale University Press.

Nayak, A. (2003). *Race, place and globalization: Youth cultures in a changing world.* Oxford, UK: Berg.

Nayak, A., & Kehily, M. J. (2008). *Gender, youth and culture: Young masculinities and femininities.* Basingstoke, UK: Palgrave Macmillan.

Petchauer, E. (2009). Framing and reviewing hip-hop educational research. *Review of Educational Research, 79*(2), 946–978.

Pilkington, H. (1994). *Russia's youth and its culture: A nation's constructors and constructed.* London: Routledge.

Pilkington, H. (2004). Youth strategies for glocal living: Space, power and communication in everyday cultural practice. In A. Bennett & K. Kahn-Harris (Eds.), *After subculture: Critical studies in contemporary youth culture* (pp. 119–134). New York: Palgrave Macmillan.

Pilkington, H., & Johnson, R. (2003). Peripheral youth: Relations of identity and power in global/local context. *European Journal of Cultural Studies, 6*(3), 259–283.

Pink, S. (2001). *Doing visual ethnography: Images, media and representation in research.* London: Sage.

Pink, S. (2006). *The future of visual anthropology: Engaging the senses.* London: Routledge.

Ramazanoglu, C., & Holland, J. (2002). *Feminist methodology: Challenges and choices.* London: Sage.

Reason, P., & Bradbury, H. (Eds.). (2001). *Introduction: Inquiry and participation in search of a world worthy of human aspiration. Handbook of action research: Participative inquiry and practice* (pp. 1–14). London: Sage.

Savage, M., Bagnall, G., & Longhurst, B. (2005). *Globalization and belonging.* London: Sage.

Schwandt, T. A. (2000). Three epistemological stances for qualitative inquiry: Interpretivism, hermeneutics, and social constructionism. In N. K. Denzin & Y. S. Lincoln (Eds.), *Handbook of qualitative research* (2nd ed., pp. 189–213). London: Sage.

Seale, C. (2004). Validity, reliability and the quality of research. In C. Seale (Ed.), *Researching society and culture* (2nd ed., pp. 71–84). London: Sage.

Shields, R. (1991). *Places on the margin: Alternative geographies of modernity*. London: Routledge.

Skelton, T., & Valentine, G. (1998a). Cool places: An introduction to youth and youth cultures. In G. Valentine, T. Skelton, & D. Chamber (Eds.), *Cool places: Geographies of youth cultures* (pp. 1–32). London: Routledge.

Skelton, T., & Valentine, G. (Eds.). (1998b). *Cool places: Geographies of youth cultures*. London: Routledge.

Springgay, S., Irwin, R., & Wilson Kind, S. (2004). A/r/tography as living inquiry through art and text. *Qualitative Inquiry, 11*(6), 897–912.

Steinberg, S. R. (2006). Why study youth culture? In S. Steinberg, P. Parmar, & B. Richard (Eds.), *Contemporary youth culture: An international encyclopedia* (Vol. 1, pp. xiii–xviii). Westport, CT: Greenwood Press.

Sullivan, G. (2005). *Art practice as research*. London: Sage.

Tyler, S. A. (1986). Post-modern ethnography: From document of the occult to occult document. In J. Clifford & G. E. Marcus (Eds.), *Writing culture: The poetics and politics of ethnography* (pp. 122–140). Berkley, CA: University of California Press.

Wolcott, H. F. (1994). *Transforming qualitative data: Description, analysis, and interpretation*. Thousand Oaks, CA: Sage.

Wolcott, H. (2001). *Writing up qualitative research* (2nd ed.). Thousand Oaks, CA: Sage.

Youdell, D. (2006). *Impossible bodies, impossible selves: Exclusions and student subjectivities*. Dordrecht, The Netherlands: Springer.

# Chapter 2
# Understanding Youth Culture, Visual Material Culture, and Local Places

## Introduction

Taking on board theoretical and methodological issues described in Chap. 1 with respect to the global postmodern, the significance of spatiality, and heightened mobility of youth, culture, and visual material culture (VMC), in this chapter, I continue to argue for a relational understanding of young people's engagement with VMC as I briefly map the terrain of visual art education (the field which originally inspired this study), concentrating on the ways in which youth engagement with VMC has been understood, studied, and theorised. Moving forward, I turn to perspectives outside of visual art education, focusing on youth culture approaches and, in particular, on what I have called 'local youth culture approaches'. Here, I note the promise of studies that bridge subcultural and post-subcultural theorising, use multi-sited ethnography to get at lived experience, and seek to access young people's perspectives and cultural meanings; I argue these approaches are most akin to my own understanding of phenomena and set in motion a theoretical and methodological starting point for inquiry. Aiming to theoretically reconceive, rethink, and wholly reimagine youth engagement with VMC in the production of selves and worlds, I knit together a theoretical framework that pushes past implicit dichotomous thinking described in Chap. 1, enabling the conceptualisation of identity-making from VMC as a dynamic and relational process.

## Non-relational and Relational Visual Art Education

In visual art education, where this research finds its roots, while the interpretation and production of meaning from images have been examined, studies exploring how young people use VMC in their everyday lives, as well as projects examining the ways in which youth might use VMC to make sense of and construct their

K.A. Eglinton, *Youth Identities, Localities, and Visual Material Culture: Making Selves, Making Worlds*, Explorations of Educational Purpose 25, DOI 10.1007/978-94-007-4857-6_2, © Springer Science+Business Media Dordrecht 2013

identities and the world around them, are rare (see in Mason, 2008). That said, if I open up this discussion to the examination of projects exploring various types of *engagement* with forms of VMC, there are more perspectives to look at. Engagement generally includes meaning-making, interpretation, and use, and includes studies and perspectives concerned with the general consumption and reception of VMC.

With respect to engagement, I would argue two approaches are generally used: non-relational and relational. In the first case, commonly employed theories underpinning pedagogy and research in visual art education remain implicitly non-relational (Gablik, 1991) and, connectedly, dualistic (Duncum, 2005a). By non-relational, I mean that young people, VMC, and contexts are conceptualised as largely unrelated entities, and by dualistic, I mean that the theories (e.g. aesthetic and developmental theories) underpinning and guiding the research and pedagogy often rest on a series of conceptual dichotomies or dualisms separating culture from mind, mind from body, individual from society, and so forth (Duncum, 2001, 2005a). As these points have been widely covered in literature (see, e.g. Efland, Freedman, & Stuhr, 1996; Freedman, 2001), I simply note that common aesthetic and developmental theories driving practice and research in visual art education are often based on aspects of modernism in art and cultural thought where the interconnected threads of expressionism and individualism (e.g. the notion of the acultural 'lone genius') and formalism and universalism (e.g. text or artwork judged by compositional aspects within the work or by a 'universal aesthetic' transcending context and history), which characterise modernism, underpin educational practices and shape the ways in which young people's engagement with VMC is understood (see discussions in Desai & Chalmers, 2007; Efland et al., 1996; see also Gablik, 1991). Moreover, in modernism, there is a turning 'inward' of art and artists; artists are considered isolated individuals, untouched by social and cultural influences (Danto, 1997, p. 6; Gablik, 1984, 1991). In modernist aesthetic theories (and practice and research), there is a sharp division between so-called fine art believed to be worthy of educational and empirical study and popular forms of VMC which are not on the theoretical, pedagogical, or empirical agenda (Tavin, 2007).

There are numerous empirical projects based on and supporting non-relational perspectives often focusing predominately on fine art and employing aesthetic and developmental frameworks derived from formalist aesthetics and/or theories of universal development. Rather than seeking to understand people's meanings, these studies aim to map a universal aesthetic development or, for example, aesthetic preferences; consistent with non-relational perspectives, many of these studies seek universals in human behaviour. In non-relational perspectives, culture is usually equated with a homogenised ethnic group (a 'type' of people), and contextual elements are considered 'independent variables' external to people (Rogoff & Angelillo, 2002, pp. 211–216; Rogoff, 2003). More explicitly, people, place, and culture are conceptualised as essential isolated entities, rather than as interrelated and inextricably linked.

Non-relational research is based on various dualisms. As Gamradt and Staples (1994, p. 36, emphasis in original) point out, the 'modernist tradition of arts research... relies upon a number of interrelated conceptual dichotomies', including 'nature *versus* culture', 'universal *versus* local', and, I add, individual *versus* society. This notion of dichotomics, or what I interchangeably call dualisms, is significant: the dualistic and non-relational nature of art education's research and theories are not only limited, but limiting. That is, seeking to understand youth engagement with VMC, these theories confine the 'view' or 'unit of analysis' to either the individual or, for example, social factors, rather than seeing them working, even bound, together.

Relational perspectives, on the other hand, might be referred to as postmodern or critical art education as they dispute a decontextualised, ahistorical under-standing of VMC, cultural producers, and engagement supported by modernist theories and instead highlight the relationship among people, VMC, and contexts. By postmodernism, I am referring not only to artistic movements breaking with the 'institutionalisation' of modernism (Featherstone, 1991, pp. 7–9; Gablik, 1991), but to movements beyond art, including the critique of meta-narratives or universal themes used to describe sociocultural phenomena, to the fracturing of objectivity, and to the promotion of sociocultural life as local, plural, multiple, contextual, and situated (Alvesson, 2002; Denzin & Lincoln, 2000, p. 17; Featherstone, 1991).

A relational perspective underpins the work of individual visual art researchers and educationalists (e.g. Darts, 2004; Mcfee, 1966; Neperud, 2000; Wilson, 2002) and is threaded through various approaches in art education including, for example, approaches to critical and contextual studies (Atkinson & Dash, 2005; Hickman, 2004a, 2004b, 2005), social and social reconstructionist perspectives (Efland, 1990; Freedman, 2000), visual culture art education (VCAE) (e.g. Duncum, 2002, 2005b; Freedman, 2003), and forms of multicultural art education (in particular 'social reconstructionist multicultural art education'; see Desai, 2003; see also Ballengee-Morris & Stuhr, 2001 for 'visual culture multicultural art education'). Several themes characterise relational pedagogical perspectives including expanding the contents of study to all VMC including popular culture; a focus on identity, culture, and context; and the employment of non-dualistic aesthetic and cultural theories. Critique and transformation are central to relational perspectives where pedagogy is often under-pinned by critical theories and where a critical pedagogical approach recognises the centrality of (popular) VMC in people's lives and posits the use of critique towards transformation and empowerment.

Generally, however, there is little relational empirical work in visual art educa-tion that examines young people's engagement with all forms of VMC (from fine art to popular forms including, say, fashion) and also places emphasis on the inter-section between VMC, young people, and local context. Projects at the intersection of context and culture in young people's engagement with all forms of VMC, and the influence of popular VMC on young people's cultural productions (most centrally 'art-making'), are often introduced in philosophical and position papers, and there are a few empirical studies that cite the importance of 'out of school' art learning or learning from the 'unofficial curriculum' of popular VMC (e.g. Anning, 2002; Bresler & Thompson, 2002; Duncum, 1997; Freedman, 1994, 1997a, 1997b; Hamblen, 2000, 2002; Thompson, 2002). Within relational perspectives that focus on critique (e.g. VCAE, see above), young people's engagement with VMC, and the intersection of VMC in youth lives, there are again numerous position papers and books advocating critique and offering various strategies for integrating all forms of VMC and aesthetic sites into the curriculum (e.g. Chung, 2007; Dias & Sinkinson, 2005; Freedman, 1997b, 2003; Freedman & Schuler, 2002; Heise, 2004; Keifer-Boyd & Maitland-Gholson, 2007; Tavin & Anderson, 2003; Wagner-Ott, 2002). But, overall, while anecdotal, instructional, and classroom-based projects abound, few engage in empirical studies (Hickman, 2008).

Of those that have conducted empirical projects (e.g. Darts, 2004; Pauly, 2003), a central focus is critical reflection: how and whether people are able to critique images or cultural sites as ideological texts. This focus on critique in empirical research is not surprising: postmodern and critical perspectives in visual art education and VCAE, in particular, draw heavily on media studies and education in the United Kingdom which often aims to offer youth the 'analytic tools' to 'enable them to function as autonomous, rational social agents' (Buckingham, 2003, p. 313). Yet, drawing on Buckingham (2003), it could be argued that these tools *continue* a 'modernist project' (p. 313; see also Buckingham, 1998a) characterised by non-relational perspectives, where, resonating with formalist aesthetics, the focus is *still* on uncovering the 'correct' meaning: in this case, the correct meaning or, more aptly, the meaning which reveals underlying power structures.

Moreover, in many relational perspectives, the concepts of culture and context remain problematic. For instance, Desai (2003, pp. 150–151) notes that the modernist conception of culture as, for example, a group's total 'way of life', a structure which people are 'born into', or a web which exists on the outside of people is still ingrained in much contemporary thinking in visual art education.[1] With respect to context, the concept remains under-theorised and somewhat ambiguous; moreover, I would argue, as the discourse of globalisation is brought to bear on visual art education, there appears to be an unquestioned acceptance of globalisation as a context that is a homogenising force moving in one direction (i.e. from the global to the local) (Pilkington & Johnson, 2003). Finally, many relational studies rely on techniques from literary criticism, which, in many ways, equate images with written texts. Arguably, studying people's 'reading' of images tends to discount the sensuous nature of all VMC (Mirzoeff, 1999; Willis, 2000); as Willis (p. 19) highlights; there is an undeniable physical quality to VMC: our relation to objects and images is immediate and tactile.

Taking these points into consideration, what needs to be asked is not how *capable* young people are at critiquing VMC, but rather, more simply, how do young people use VMC in their everyday lives? How do young people, as active participators in culture, use VMC to make sense of, construct, and/or negotiate aspects of themselves and their worlds? Research which examines these questions, that is, which seeks to understand from youth themselves, how they, as young people in a specific time and place, are using – living with, in, and through – VMC, can deepen theoretical understanding and ultimately support the various pedagogical projects that seek to work with young people in the complex area of VMC.

---

[1] Desai (2003) is discussing sexual diversity.

## Youth and Popular Culture

Though there are certainly deficits in visual art education with respect to understanding young people's use of all VMC, this area of study thrives, particularly the study of youth and popular visual material culture, across other academic sites and perspectives. In education specifically, Gaztambide-Fernandez, Harding, and Sordé-Martí (2004, p. 229) articulate three ways in which popular culture is considered: as a distracting force and/or hindrance to youth intellectual growth, as an approach to curriculum where popular culture is a means of engaging youth, and through a critical pedagogical approach (see, for instance, critical pedagogical perspectives: Giroux, 1994a, 1994b; Giroux & Simon, 1989; Girox & McLaren, 1994; Hayes, Steinberg, & Tobin, 2011; Kincheloe, 2004; McLaren & Kincheloe, 2007; Monchinski, 2008). In this final case, popular VMC is often explored as an epistemological site threaded through with power; there is often a focus on identities, resistance, reproduction, and transformation.

Sometimes, though not always, underpinned by critical pedagogical perspectives, there is a wide and varied literature in media literacy and education (e.g. see works by Buckingham, 2003, 2008; Buckingham & Sefton-Green, 1994; Kellner, 2002; Macedo & Steinberg, 2007; see Hobbs, 1998; Livingstone, 2004 for definitions, overviews, and debates in this field). Scholars from a diversity of backgrounds constitute what both Livingstone (2004) and Hobbs (1998) refer to as a confusing and contentious area of scholarship. Though foci vary, there is often a concern with youth production and consumption of media; citing Aufderheide (1993) and Christ and Potter (1998), Livingstone (2004, p. 5) writes, '[m]edia literacy – indeed literacy more generally – is the ability to access, analyse, evaluate, and create messages in a variety of forms'. Often, there is an emphasis on youth excluded from formal schooling, on sites of learning, and on ways in which popular culture is at once a vehicle of particular ideologies as well as a rich resource for identity-making.

Rather than rehashing debates and covering this wide literature, for purposes of the research presented in this book, it is better to dig beneath some of these perspectives and practices to understand the epistemological modes employed to understand young people's relationships to VMC. These modes span numerous theoretical positions, debates, and methodologies and generally fall under three interconnected categories: 'text' or 'text-based', 'reception', and 'lived experience' or 'youth culture' approaches. As a discussion of these three modes is a heavily covered literature, I point readers to thorough discussions in Dolby (2003) and Buckingham (1993a, 1993b; see also Valentine, Skelton, & Chambers, 1998). Offering a summary here, textual approaches centre on the 'text' including television, advertisements, or websites. Used empirically, these approaches examine texts through various methods, such as semiotics, and perspectives, such as feminism, and seek to understand the underlying structures of images, objects, and popular forms of media often considered 'vehicles of ideology' (Tobin, 2000, p. 3).

Textual approaches include pessimistic and populist versions (Tobin, 2000, pp. 4–6; also Buckingham, 1994).[2] The pessimistic position underpins, for example, the 'media effects paradigm', which suggests various forms of popular VMC are 'harmful forces' shaping youth lives (Tobin, p. 3). The populist stance is more optimistic about the power of youth to resist messages. Fiske (1989), for instance, argues that people continuously make their own meanings of texts and that while the producers of texts have 'semiotic power', people use 'semiotic resistance' to create their own meanings of popular culture. Gramsci's theory of hegemony is often used as a primary means of explaining people's meaning-making, consent, and struggle over cultural forms (Dolby, 2003; Bennett & Kahn-Harris, 2004).[3] Power is not simply impressed upon passive people, nor are people cut off from power; rather, in the way ideology works, through continuous consent and struggle, popular culture is negotiated. For the most part, textual approaches confine understanding to the text rather than on young people's meanings or perspectives. As such, these approaches are in danger of universalising youth into a coherent essential group and inadvertently ignoring the relationship between youth and texts (Tobin, 2000; Dimitriadis, 2001).

Reception approaches problematise the relationship between people and cultural forms, probe and question the notion of viewer as passive, and instead, looking at the interaction between aspects of the text and people, often underline the notion of popular culture as a site of struggle.[4] There is a great deal of empirical research within the reception tradition, and in visual art and media education there is a tradition of classroom-based projects examining the ways in which youth receive and make sense of media texts.[5] Of importance are reception studies that draw on postmodern and post-structural insights: these studies challenge the idea of young people passively receiving dominant ideologies and underscore the importance of local context and the fluidity of identities in the formation of meanings (see, e.g. Buckingham, 1994, 1998b; Grace & Lum, 2001; Tobin, 2000). While reception studies begin to highlight the changing nature of identities and underline the role of the local context, they do not explore the ways in which young people are using popular cultural forms in sociocultural practice. What is more, while ethnographic methods such as interviews are often used in reception studies, a full ethnographic

---

[2] Dolby (2003) describes '"pro-"' and '"anti-" populist' positions in defining popular culture.

[3] Hegemony means power 'can no longer be assured through domination but has to be won by consent' (Bennett & Kahn-Harris, 2004, p. 5).

[4] Reception approaches are referred to under various headings in the literature. Alexander (2003) breaks reception approaches into 'active audience approaches' and 'reception theory'. Where active audience approaches come out of cultural studies frameworks, reception theory draws on the work of literary criticism and is often referred to as 'reader-response' theories. Broadly, this division reflects a British tradition based on the work of Stuart Hall and an American tradition based on literary criticism (Alexander, 2003). All traditions share the idea of the viewer or receiver of cultural texts as an active meaning-maker.

[5] For example, though not specifically targeting reception approaches, see the collection edited by Buckingham (1998b).

approach including participant observation, so important to understanding youth cultural meanings and practices, is rarely employed (Dolby, 2002, p. 39; McRobbie, 1992).[6] On the other hand, the final approaches discussed, youth culture approaches, are in some cases characterised by ethnographic studies focusing on the lives of youth, the role of the local context, and on young people's everyday cultural practices.

## *Youth Culture Approaches*

A central focus of youth culture approaches is on how young people use popular cultural forms in their lives and how they resist, negotiate, and (re)produce cultural meanings in relation to local and global contexts. Almost mirroring the conceptual shifts, I described in Chap. 1, with respect to thinking about culture, identities, and spatiality, approaches in this tradition that move from subcultural to post-subcultural, to what I have called elsewhere 'local youth culture approaches' (Eglinton, 2009). Again, rather than reviewing a thoroughly documented and disseminated literature, I briefly describe the trajectory of this field here and its connections to shifting theory (see Bennett, 2000; Bennett & Kahn-Harris, 2004 for a comprehensive overview of these approaches; see also Muggleton & Weinzeirl, 2003).

Around the early to mid-twentieth century, empirical understanding of youth shifted to the importance of subcultures, suggesting, as Bennett (2000, p. 15) writes, 'that youth was, in effect, a "culture" or subculture in its own right'. The Centre for Contemporary Cultural Studies (CCCS) at the University of Birmingham expanded subcultural theory to the focus on style-based youth subcultures (ibid., p. 17).[7] Through the examination of youth cultural practices including behaviour as well as style, CCCS researchers examined subcultural resistance (Valentine et al., 1998, p. 13) and posited that the creative use and production of meaning from cultural forms at once shapes, but is nevertheless always constrained by, material conditions (Griffin, 1993, p. 47). Moreover, there was an intense focus on the macro-context of class (Bennett & Kahn-Harris, 2004, pp. 4–5).

Reflecting and constituting prevailing social and cultural theory, subcultural forms drew heavily on the idea of culture as a bounded object: subculture used as a kind of classification to study youth engagement with cultural forms carries with it the assumption that subcultural units are homogenous, bounded groupings of young people (see Bennett, 2000). The criticism here is that a bounded notion of culture cannot fully explain contemporary shifts in youth culture, which echo broader sociocultural movements; in this case, globalisation and, connectedly, proliferation of media have been linked to increased hybridity and fragmentation of youth culture (Bennett & Kahn-Harris, 2004, p. 2).

---

[6] With respect to understanding young people's active engagement with these forms, Dolby (2003, p. 265) believes reception approaches 'can only move the discussion and research so far'.

[7] Early style-based youth culture is most profoundly examined in the United Kingdom.

Responding to interconnected global processes, new theoretical tools have been considered and deployed including, for example, 'neo-tribes' (Maffesoli, 1996) and 'lifestyles' (Bennett, 2000; Featherstone, 1991), to study youth identities and engagement with popular VMC. These post-subculture concepts are open to articulated cultural formations, but envision groupings and identities forged primarily through 'creative' consumption rather than consumption based on class or, say, racial association (see Bennett, 2000; Pilkington & Johnson, 2003). Yet, while post-subcultural youth identities are understood as complex and multiple and while post-subcultural theorising seems to ask new questions in response to broad cultural shifts (see Dillabough, Rarieya, & Besley, 2007, p. 126), there are important criticisms. In particular, there is little examination of youth meanings; significant identity categories such as class and race are, in part, rendered theoretically irrelevant; and there is minimal sustained effort to understand the role of the 'local' in young people's cultural practices (see discussions in Kjeldgaard, 2003; Nayak, 2003a, 2003b; Pilkington, 2004; Pilkington & Johnson, 2003).

### Local Youth Culture Approaches

As noted in Chap. 1, more recently, youth culture scholars are rethinking a subculture/post-subculture binary and are putting localities, identities, and the everyday realities of youth at the centre of their research (e.g. Bennett, 1999, 2000; Dillabough & Kennelly, 2010; Dimitriadis, 2001; Dolby, 2001; Kehily & Nayak, 2008; Kelly, 2008; Kenway et al., 2006; Kjeldgaard, 2003; Nayak, 2003a, 2003b; Nayak & Kehily, 2008; Pilkington, 2004; Pilkington & Johnson, 2003; Salo, 2003; also see Pilkington & Johnson's special issue, 2003; a review by McLeod, 2009; discussion and edited collection Dolby & Rizvi, 2008). Bringing together the hybridity and fluidity that characterise the post-subcultural study of identities and those material structures and aspects of power that impinge upon youth lives as exemplified in earlier subcultural research, what I have called 'local youth culture approaches' focus on the ways in which youth use popular VMC to shape themselves and the world around them. Researchers in this area often use ethnographic approaches to get at both the meanings youth invest in global forms and the ways in which youth rework and reconstruct popular VMC through local discourses and cultural practices. Overall, these studies begin with a relational assumption of youth cultural production: they assume young people are active producers of culture who work with/in and through the local context using and creating meaning from cultural forms.

Dimitriadis' (2001) study in an after-school club and Dolby's (2001) research with youth in post-Apartheid South Africa are two important studies in this tradition as they place their focus directly on popular VMC, racial identities, and educational issues. Another excellent example of this kind of work is Willis's seminal large-scale ethnographic study of youth cultural production: *Common Culture* (1990a) (see also Willis, 1990b). Setting out to examine youth cultural practices 'from the point of view of their use and meaning for and by young people' (1990a, p. 6),

Willis (2000) understands cultural production as a continuous 'creative' work 'upon materials received from this cultural world, remaking them' (p. xv). Willis (2000) provides insights into the cultural processes underpinning youth use of VMC and describes a mutually productive relationship between self- and world-making through cultural production. Theorising the human-visual material culture relationship as living and dialectical, Willis (1990a, pp. 21–22) develops noteworthy concepts including the idea of 'grounded aesthetics' as those moments of symbolic engagement where we augment, appropriate, or, for example, personalise an object and in so doing 'change – however minutely – that cultural world'. Through 'symbolic creativity' (symbolic work) the makers/viewers – young people – are positioned as productive active agents shaping themselves and their cultural worlds. Symbolic work is located and sociohistorically situated, and, importantly, sociohistorical structures are resources for symbolic work: 'locations and situations are not only *determinations* – they're also relations and resources to be discovered, explored and experienced' (Willis, 1990a, p. 12, emphasis in original).

Yet, while the potential of these local youth culture approaches to understand youth identity-making from VMC is profound, as noted in Chap. 1, the global postmodern epoch demands researchers to reimagine both their theoretical as well as methodological (read: ethnographic) tools used to understand the social world (Dimitriadis & Weis, 2007; Marcus, 2009). Kennelly, Poyntz, and Ugor (2009, pp. 255–256, emphasis in original) write: 'No longer is it a question of *whether* globali[s]ation is having an impact on all aspects of human life; the more pressing question being asked today is *what* that impact entails' and, I would add, how do we *operationalise* these impacts and changes in educational youth research? Bringing together theoretical and methodological issues in youth culture approaches, Dillabough and Kennelly (2010) offer:

> There can be no youth identity which is merely global or local; rather a form of youth selfhood emerges that is intersubjectively constituted and contains a capacity for forms of self-ascription that must always been seen as differentiated through highly variable and material scales of change. Arguably then, it is only through comparative research that we can identify the persistent activities of cohesive subcultural groupings as well as rather less cohesive youth community groupings. . . (pp. 40–41)

Though not exactly comparative, there are a handful of multi-sited studies that focus on youth identities and culture, spatiality, and educational implications. Many of these projects are theoretically aligned with, and indeed constitute, the local youth culture approaches described earlier. Though in many cases the focus is not specifically on VMC, these studies inevitably examine youth engagement with popular media or VMC as an identity resource and as integral to lived experiences. Dillabough and Kennelly's (2010) '*spatial ethnography*' (p. 4, their emphasis), for example, brings into focus the ways in which disadvantaged youth living in and through what the authors refer to as the 'edges', 'margins', or 'urban fringe' of inner-city Vancouver and Toronto produce and negotiate new youth cultural formations often using VMC, against a backdrop of intense exclusion, and 'circulating forms of moral anxiety' at the global level (p. 197). Kehily and Nayak (2008; see Nayak & Kehily, 2008) also illustrate insights of multi-sited work in their exploration of femininities as they demonstrate how youth – in this article, primarily girls – draw on global media in the production of new feminine forms. In each of these studies, there is a primary focus on place, on local/global relations, on the impact of locality on identity performances and meanings, and on the importance of global media as a site of self-making.

While these multi-sited projects, and others in youth studies broadly, offer a way forward for educational research such as my own, which seeks to make sense of the distinct intersection where youth identities, VMC, and place and space meet, as Dimitriadis and Weis (2007) put it, 'work on popular culture and education has . . . been overwhelmingly single sited' (p. 335). What is more, as these authors and others (e.g. Desai & Chalmers, 2007) point out, the conceptualisation of culture as something that is 'bounded' continues to hold powerful sway in education and, I add, in educational ethnography.

## Conceptualising Culture, Locality, and Identity

Taking local youth culture approaches as both a backdrop and a starting point for discussions to follow, the second part of this chapter is dedicated to knitting together and describing a conceptual framework that at once envisions identities, VMC, and local places as dynamic forms and describes the relationship between these aspects. To develop this framework, I begin by describing ideas from 'reconstructive postmodernism' (Gablik, 1991), before bringing in insights from human geography, cultural psychology and sociocultural theories, and sociocultural anthropology. I argue that the relationship between people, place, and culture is productive where identities, culture, and places are not simply reproduced, but continuously remade. The concepts I describe here are extensively augmented, and new concepts are introduced in concert with the data (see Chaps. 4, 5, 6, 7).

### *Reconstructive Postmodernism*

Forms of postmodernism provide insights that enable a reconceptualisation of cultural products (i.e. VMC), producers/consumers (in this study: young people), and sociocultural context as 'interrelational' (Gablik, 1991). Using a more 'ecological' or relational perspective, I draw on Gablik's (1991, p. 22) 'two postmodernisms – a deconstructive and a reconstructive version' to start making sense of young people's use of VMC (see also McLaren, 1995; Sullivan, 1993). Where deconstructive postmodernism critiques and breaks down the art and 'cultural manifestations' of life, reconstructive postmodernism aims to repair cultural life: it is participatory, healing, and transformative (Gablik, 1991, pp. 24–26).

Reconstructive postmodernism recognises that context is central to engagement with VMC – to our producing, using, and creating meaning from VMC – and helps envise meanings as multiple, local, unfixed, and continuously changing through interplay between viewer/maker, VMC, and sociocultural context (Alvesson, 2002). In reconstructive postmodern, 'process' is central; Gablik (1991, p. 163) argues that we must overcome the *static* understanding of cultural production and instead focus on the world as 'process-oriented', constituted of 'dynamic interactions and interrelational processes'. Rather than seeing the viewer/maker, cultural forms, and sociocultural context as separate entities, the emphasis is on envisioning these as 'aspects' of sociocultural practice or activity (Wertsch, 1995).

## A Sociocultural Approach

To consider this interrelational process between people, place, and culture, I draw from sociocultural perspectives and cultural psychology. Concepts from cultural psychology and sociocultural perspectives that draw on the Russian school of cultural-historical psychology (specifically the work of Vygotsky, Leont'ev, and Luria) offer a relational, non-dualistic understanding of youth engagement with VMC; help explain the relationship between culture, people, and place (or context); and provide an understanding of young people's use and production of meaning from VMC as a sociocultural activity stimulated, enabled, and constrained by local places.[8] In this study, I drew on the sociocultural 'theory of mediation', 'cultural tools' or 'artefacts', and, in part, on the concept of 'context' (Cole, 1996; Cole & Scribner, 1978; Scollon, 2001; Wertsch, 1995; Wertsch, Del Rio, & Alvarez, 1995).

### Cultural Artefacts and Mediated Action

Described by Rogoff (2003, p. 51) as 'related though heterogeneous... proposals', sociocultural theories are united by the theory of tool or, more broadly, artefact mediation.[9] Developed by Russian cultural-historical psychologist Vygotsky and

---

[8] Depending on the version, sociocultural theories or perspectives are referred to as sociocultural-historical (Rogoff, 2003), cultural-historical (Cole, 1996), sociohistorical (see Wertsch's, 1991 discussion of Vygotsky), cultural-psychological, or cultural psychology (Cole) and situative approaches. Many of the terms for sociocultural theory are used interchangeably. Sociocultural theory is often called cultural psychology (particularly in the United States, see Cole, 1996; Cole, Engestrom, & Vasquez, 1997), and cultural-historical psychology is now commonly referred to as cultural-historical activity theory or CHAT.

[9] All sociocultural approaches assume an inextricable link between human mental processes and sociocultural-historical setting (Wertsch, 1991, 1995, 1998). Though sociocultural studies are interdisciplinary, there are common roots: two primary roots (which are, at the same time, strands) include cultural psychology (mainly the work of Cole, 1996) and Russian cultural-historical psychology. Using Marxist theory and perspectives from a variety of disciplines, Russian cultural-historical theorists sought to overcome a divide in psychology between those focusing on the study of behaviour (behaviourists) and those maintaining that psychology study human consciousness (subjectivists) (see Cole & Scribner, 1978 and Wertsch, 1985 for a review of Vygotsky's use of Marxist philosophy).

colleagues, this theory suggests that humans use tools or artefacts to mediate their (inter)actions with/in the world (including with each other) (see Cole, 1996; Cole & Scribner, 1978; Rogoff, 2003; Vygotsky, 1978; Wertsch et al., 1995).[10] Artefacts include all forms of VMC, tools such as hammers and scissors, sentient beings such as people (including, Scollon [2001, p. 4] writes, 'their bodies, dress, movements'), as well as language, scripts, ways of acting, recipes, narratives, signs, beliefs, and the like (see Bruner, 1990; Cole, 1996; Cole & Engestrom, 1993; Cole & Scribner, 1978). Artefacts are both *ideal* (psychological, symbolic, and conceptual) and *material*: material artefacts will carry with them symbolic meanings, and symbolic meanings are often manifested in material artefacts (Cole, 1996, p. 117, emphasis in original). All of our actions and practices including our thinking are mediated by cultural artefacts, and, further, mediating artefacts are layered and multiple. For example, on a basic level, writing this book is mediated by my keyboard, by language, by models of books I have read before, and by my own values, which themselves are artefacts I have 'internalised' from various sources including family and community (Vygotsky, 1978).

Artefacts or 'constituents of culture' transform people (in particular, human mental processes or the human mind) and the environment with/in which particular artefacts are produced and used (Cole & Engestrom, 1993, p. 9). That is, 'superseding' various dichotomies, artefacts (also called 'mediational means') are the means by which the sociocultural world and the individual are connected, (re)produced, and transformed (ibid., p. 10). Looking at the connection between the sociocultural and individual (here, the mind in particular), writing about 'mediated action' (i.e. human action mediated by cultural artefacts), Luria (1928, p. 495) writes 'instead of applying directly its *natural function* to the solution of a particular task, the child puts between that function and the task a certain auxiliary means' (in Cole & Engestrom, 1993, p. 5, my emphasis). Luria's reference to the 'natural function' is important as it is based on the Vygotskian (1978) concept of 'natural' or 'higher' mental processes. Higher mental processes are those processes of mind that are produced through cultural practice (through mediated action) – that is, those aspects of mind which are constituted of cultural artefacts. As a very basic example, the action of tying my shoe is mediated by, among other artefacts, the script for tying a knot. Knowing this cultural script transforms my thinking (i.e. my mental processes) and actions, and employing this script will change the environment: my shoe will now be tied. What is more, because the mind is made, in part, of these artefacts, which themselves are social in nature, according to sociocultural theory, the 'mind *is* social' (Cole & Scribner, 1978; Vygotsky, 1978; my emphasis).

Yet mediated action (people acting with mediational means or artefacts) does not and cannot happen in isolation. Cultural mediation only exists in relation to and

---

[10] Vygotsky uses Marx's social theory and an expanded version of Engels' tool use (Cole & Scribner, 1978). In this study, while the Russian cultural-historical school's notion of tools (particularly Vygotsky's psychological tools) forms a springboard for the concept of tools, I follow Cole (1996) and refer to tools as a 'subcategory' within a broader group called artefacts.

with/in context including physical place, social institutions, communities, and large discursive formations. In pulling together a unique framework to augment and open up understanding and to address theoretical gaps with respect to youth engagement with VMC, rather than drawing fully on the sociocultural notion of context, I bring into this framework concepts from human geography to conceive of context as locality or local place.


## A Relational Understanding: Locality, Identity, Culture

In human geography, locality or, more aptly, place (and space) has been considered through multiple perspectives (see Feld & Basso, 1996; Hubbard, Kitchin, & Valentine, 2004). I use the work of Massey (1993, 1998; also Jess & Massey, 1995), who argues that space consists of flows of social, cultural, political, and economic relations (see also Appadurai, 1990). In this model, place is intertwined with space – place is 'localised space' (De Boeck, 1998, p. 25) – and, as noted in Chap. 1, is conceptualised as the material space (i.e. physical space) as well as the 'meeting place' of social relations, global flows, and movements (i.e. sociocultural space) (Massey, 1993, pp. 65–66).

Globalisation does not automatically imply the homogenisation of local places, or the bearing down of global forces on local contexts, but rather places are formed and transformed at the 'global–local nexus' (Pilkington, 2004, p. 119). As a consequence, places are not coherent or settled, but rather they are always in process. They are dynamic, productive, and, importantly, as Massey (1993, p. 68) points out, particular and specific – a unique idiosyncratic mix of particular social relations constructed with/in a supra-contextual space that includes the overarching political, cultural, and social discourses constituting places themselves. Local places include, therefore, the physical context, but also social spaces including institutions, dominant narratives, political structures, and elements of power including power relations, exclusions, and the rules and regulations which shape and are shaped by cultural practices (Cole & Engestrom, 1993).

Culture, and cultural artefacts more specifically, can only be understood in relation to social, material, and historical contexts (i.e. in relation to place and space) (Cole, 1996; Mitchell, 2000, p. 63). In cultural psychology, Cole (1996) writes that all artefacts exist only in relation to context or, for the purposes of this research, place.[11] He points out that context is not simply something which 'surrounds' and, hence, shapes mediational means and actions of people but, rather, that context is 'that which surrounds *and* that which weaves together' (p. 143; my emphasis). Artefacts, therefore, *are* contextual, at once invested with meaning in local places *and* constitute and produce local places themselves. In other words,

---

[11] Cole (1996) refers to context as the 'supra-individual "envelope"' (p. 143).

while the social dimensions of places shape mediational means and actions, mediated actions and artefacts shape dimensions of place.

Implicated in the relationship between culture and place are people's individual and collective lives, experiences, histories, and, importantly, identities. People, in this case young people, construct their identities through mediated cultural practices using multiple available cultural artefacts such as local values, language, and VMC (Castells, 2004; Hall, 1996; Holland, Lachicotte, Skinner, & Cain, 1998). As people use cultural artefacts, giving them meaning in and through human (inter) action, these forms/meanings constitute mind – they are 'internalised' (Vygotsky, 1978) – at once (re)constructing various identities and (re)producing aspects of self and worlds (Castells, 2004, p. 7). In this framework, identities develop in concert with 'figured worlds' (Holland et al., 1998) that make up local places. Figured worlds can be described as intersecting permeable social spaces, which include loose knots of artefacts interpreted in roughly the same way by groups of people (Fish, 1980), for example, the figured world of school, the figured world of gender, and more broadly the figured world of youth in Barlow, Canada.

Through mediated action, identities, therefore, are always in the process of 'becoming', are dependent on time and place (i.e. are contextual), are multiple, and are enacted and produced in and through human (inter)action in everyday life (Castells, 2004; Holland et al., 1998; Meinhof & Galasinski, 2005; Rattansi & Phoenix, 1997). Moreover, we have an ever-changing web of identities made up of strong identity markers including, for instance, gender, race, disability/ability, religion, sexual orientation, and class. Connectedly, identities are not produced in isolation, but rather through difference and in relation to 'other' (Hall, 1996, 1997). That is, an identity, such as Latina girl from the inner city, will 'only acquire meaning and significance. . . in relation to what it is *not*' (Rattansi & Phoenix, 1997, p. 127). Indeed, because identities, such as racial identities, are contextual and formed through mediated action, they are relational (i.e. again, dependent on place, space, and historical time, on 'other', as well as produced in relation to other forms of identity such as gender or class), positional (e.g. in certain social spaces or figured worlds, women might occupy a lower symbolic position than men) (Holland et al., 1998), and, in part, performative (where, in a sense, action is constitutive of or produces the state of affairs) (Butler, 1990). What is more, identities, in a sense, *are* a kind of artefact; for example, the meanings of markers such as race, class, and gender are continuously drawn on and remade through social practice.

Significantly, the interconnection between place, people, and culture constrains and enables particular identities. That is, people, in this book youth, cannot construct any identity they wish. Describing the work of Bauman and writing about identity, Rutherford (2007, p. 9) describes the need to use the 'linguistic tools and cultural artefacts' provided by place and culture – tools, he writes, 'of our interdependency'. Not only do particular artefacts have to be available, but the use of artefacts and meanings invested in them are dependent on individual lives, histories, and collective experiences, as well as on aspects of local place – including aspects of power, rules, and values that bear down on use and meanings.

Culture then exists both outside and inside individuals: it constitutes our minds, mediates and produces our identities, and is the resource and product of the world around us (Cole & Engestrom, 1993). Finally, artefacts, their meanings, and individuals using them are not simply *products* of place, nor is action *determined* by place; rather, the relationship between people, place, and culture is productive. People do not simply reproduce identities, culture, and places, but rather the mobilisation of aspects including history and individual experiences in and through an always unique local–global nexus leads to the (re)construction of new cultural forms – including new places, figured worlds, and identities.

# Conclusion

I began this chapter by mapping the terrain of visual art education, concentrating on the ways in which youth engagement with VMC has been understood, studied, and theorised. I touched on the idea that a sustained focus on critique within relational perspectives implicitly drives forward a tradition of non-relationality which continues to separate theoretically, analytically, and pedagogically youth, culture, and context and obscures youth activity and everyday cultural practices. I repeated the need for studies which begin with youth perspectives and seek to understand the ways in which young people are actively using VMC in their daily lives. Exploring epistemological approaches to the study of youth and popular visual material culture specifically, I moved through textual, reception, and youth culture approaches, focusing on local youth culture approaches. I noted the promise of studies which bridge subcultural and post-subcultural theorising and which use ethnography, in particular multi-sited ethnography, to get at lived experience, access young people's perspectives and cultural meanings, and consider young people as active cultural producers shaping and being shaped by local context. I concluded that local youth culture approaches are most akin to my own understanding of phenomena and provide a theoretical and methodological starting point for inquiry. Coming back to the theoretical issues, I started to describe tools that support a relational non-dualistic understanding of young people's use of VMC. In particular, I discussed insights from reconstructive postmodernism and, most importantly, from sociocultural perspectives and human geography. I have brought these concepts together into a unique conceptual framework, which I suggest contributes to the education literature an inclusive, relational, and dynamic understanding of youth engagement with VMC.

# References

Alexander, V. (2003). *Sociology of the arts*. Oxford, UK: Blackwell Publishing.
Alvesson, M. (2002). *Postmodernism and social research*. Buckingham: Open University.
Anning, A. (2002). Conversations around young children's drawing: The impact of the beliefs of significant others at home and school. *Journal of Art and Design Education, 21*(3), 197–208.

Appadurai, A. (1990). Disjuncture and difference in the global cultural economy. *Theory, Culture & Society, 7*, 295–310.

Atkinson, D., & Dash, P. (2005). *Social and critical practice in art education: Social and critical practice*. Stoke on Trent, UK: Trentham Books.

Aufderheide, P. (1993). *Media literacy: A report of the national leadership conference on media literacy*. Aspen, CO: Aspen Institute.

Ballengee-Morris, C., & Stuhr, P. (2001). Multicultural art and visual cultural education in a changing world. *Art Education, 54*(4), 6–13.

Bennett, A. (1999). Hip hop am Main: The localization of rap music and hip hop culture. *Media, Culture & Society, 21*, 77–91.

Bennett, A. (2000). *Popular music and youth culture: Music, identity, and place*. London: Macmillan Press.

Bennett, A., & Kahn-Harris, K. (2004). Introduction. In A. Bennett & K. Kahn-Harris (Eds.), *After subculture: Critical studies in contemporary youth culture* (pp. 1–19). New York: Palgrave Macmillan.

Bresler, L., & Thompson, C. M. (2002). Context interlude. In L. Bresler & C. M. Thompson (Eds.), *The art in children's lives: Context, culture, and curriculum* (pp. 9–13). Dordrecht, The Netherlands: Kluwer Academic Publishers.

Bruner, J. S. (1990). *Acts of meaning*. Cambridge, UK: Harvard University Press.

Buckingham, D. (1993a). *Children talking television: The making of television literacy*. London: Falmer Press.

Buckingham, D. (1993b). *Reading audiences: Young people and the media*. Manchester, UK: Manchester University Press.

Buckingham, D. (1994). Television and the definition of childhood. In B. Mayall (Ed.), *Children's childhoods: Observed and experienced* (pp. 79–96). London: Falmer Press.

Buckingham, D. (1998a). Introduction: Fantasies of empowerment? Radical pedagogy and popular culture. In D. Buckingham (Ed.), *Teaching popular culture: Beyond radical pedagogy* (pp. 1–17). London: UCL Press.

Buckingham, D. (Ed.). (1998b). *Teaching popular culture: Beyond radical pedagogy*. London: UCL Press.

Buckingham, D. (2003). Media education and the end of the critical consumer. *Harvard Educational Review, 73*(3), 309–327.

Buckingham, D. (Ed.). (2008). *Youth, identity, and digital media* (John D. and Catherine T. MacArthur Foundation Series on Digital Media and Learning). Cambridge, MA: MIT Press.

Buckingham, D., & Sefton-Green, J. (1994). *Cultural studies goes to school: Reading and teaching popular media*. London: Taylor & Francis.

Butler, J. P. (1990). *Gender trouble: Feminism and the subversion of identity*. New York: Routledge.

Castells, M. (2004). *The power of identity, the information age: Economy, society and culture* (Vol. 2). Oxford, UK: Blackwell.

Christ, W. G., & Potter, W. J. (1998). Media literacy, media education, and the academy. *Journal of Communication, 48*, 5–15.

Chung, S. (2007). Media/visual literacy art education: Sexism in hip-hop music videos. *Art Education, 60*(3), 33–38.

Cole, M. (1996). *Cultural psychology: A once and future discipline*. Cambridge, MA: Harvard University Press.

Cole, M., & Engestrom, Y. (1993). A cultural-historical approach to distributed cognition. In G. Salomon (Ed.), *Distributed cognition* (pp. 1–46). Cambridge, UK: Cambridge University Press.

Cole, M., Engestrom, Y., & Vasquez, O. (Eds.). (1997). *Mind, culture, and activity*. Cambridge, UK: Cambridge University Press.

Cole, M., & Scribner, S. (1978). Introduction. In M. Cole & S. Scribner (Eds.), *Mind in society*. Cambridge, UK: Harvard University Press.

Danto, A. (1997). *After the end of art: Contemporary art and the pale of history*. Princeton, NJ: Princeton University Press.

Darts, D. (2004). *Visual culture jam: Art pedagogy and creative resistance*. Unpublished doctoral dissertation, University of British Columbia, Vancouver, Canada.

De Boeck, F. (1998). The rootedness of trees: Place as cultural and natural texture in rural southwest Congo. In N. Lovell (Ed.), *Locality and belonging* (pp. 25–52). London: Routledge.

Denzin, N. K., & Lincoln, Y. S. (2000). Introduction: The discipline and practice of qualitative research. In N. K. Denzin & Y. S. Lincoln (Eds.), *Handbook of qualitative research* (2nd ed., pp. 1–45). Thousand Oaks, CA: Sage.

Desai, D. (2003). Multicultural art education and the heterosexual imagination: A question of culture. *Studies in Art Education, 44*(2), 147–161.

Desai, D., & Chalmers, G. (2007). Notes for a dialogue in art education in critical times. *Art Education, 60*(5), 6–12.

Dias, B., & Sinkinson, S. (2005). Film spectatorship between queer theory and feminism: Transcultural readings. *International Journal of Education through Art, 1*(2), 143–152.

Dillabough, J., & Kennelly, J. (2010). *Lost youth in the global city*. London: Routledge.

Dillabough, J., Rarieya, J. F. A., & Besley, T. (2007). Extended review essay: Anoop Nayak's race, space and globalization: Youth cultures in a changing world. *British Journal of Sociology of Education, 28*(1), 125–134.

Dimitriadis, G. (2001). *Performing identity/performing culture: Hip hop as text, pedagogy, and lived practice*. New York: Peter Lang Publishing.

Dimitriadis, G., & Weis, L. (2007). Globalization and multisited ethnographic approaches. In C. McCarthy, A. Durham, L. Engel, A. Filmer, M. Giardina, & M. Malagreca (Eds.), *Globalizing cultural studies: Ethnographic interventions in theory, method, and policy*. New York: Peter Lang Publishing.

Dolby, N. (2001). *Constructing race: Youth, identity, and popular culture in South Africa*. Albany, NY: State University of New York Press.

Dolby, N. (2002). Youth, culture, and identity: Ethnographic explorations. *Educational Researcher, 31*(8), 37–42.

Dolby, N. (2003). Popular culture and democratic practice. *Harvard Educational Review, 73*(3), 258–284.

Dolby, N., & Rizvi, F. (Eds.). (2008). *Youth moves: Identities and education in global perspective*. London: Routledge.

Duncum, P. (1997). Art education for new times. *Studies in Art Education, 38*(2), 69–79.

Duncum, P. (2001). How are we to understand art at the beginning of a new century? In P. Duncum & T. Bracey (Eds.), *On knowing – Art and visual culture* (pp. 15–33). Christchurch, NZ: Canterbury University Press.

Duncum, P. (2002). Clarifying visual culture art education. *Art Education, 55*(3), 6–11.

Duncum, P. (2005a). Visual culture and an aesthetics of embodiment. *International Journal of Education through Art, 1*(1), 9–19.

Duncum, P. (2005b). Visual culture art education: Why, what and how? In R. Hickman (Ed.), *Critical studies in art and design education* (pp. 151–162). Bristol: Intellect.

Efland, A. (1990). *A history of art education: Intellectual and social currents in teaching the visual arts*. New York: Teachers College Columbia University.

Efland, A., Freedman, K., & Stuhr, P. (1996). *Postmodern art education: An approach to curriculum*. Reston, VA: NAEA.

Eglinton, K. (2009). *Making selves, making worlds: An ethnographic account of young people's use of visual material culture*. Unpublished doctoral dissertation, University of Cambridge, Cambridge, UK.

Featherstone, M. (1991). *Consumer culture & postmodernism*. London: Sage.

Feld, S., & Basso, K. H. (1996). Introduction. In S. Feld & K. Basso (Eds.), *Senses of place* (1st ed.). Santa Fe, NM: School of American Research Press.

Fish, S. (1980). *Is there a text in this class: The authority of interpretative communities*. Cambridge, MA: Harvard University Press.

Fiske, J. (1989). *Reading the popular*. Boston: Unwin Hyman.

Freedman, K. (1994). Interpreting gender and visual culture in art classrooms. *Studies in Art Education, 35*(3), 157–170.

Freedman, K. (1997a). Cultural association and communications: students' construction of meaning in response to visual images. *International Journal of Art and Design Education, 16*(3), 269–272.

Freedman, K. (1997b). Critiquing the media: Art knowledge inside and outside of school. *Art Education, 50*(4), 46–51.

Freedman, K. (2000). Social perspectives on art education in the US: Teaching visual culture in a democracy. *Studies in Art Education, 41*(4), 314–329.

Freedman, K. (2001). How do we understand art?: Aesthetics and the problem of meaning in the curriculum'. In P. Duncum & T. Bracey (Eds.), *On knowing – Art and visual culture* (pp. 34–46). Christchurch, NZ: Canterbury University Press.

Freedman, K. (2003). *Teaching visual culture*. New York: Teachers College Press.

Freedman, K., & Schuler, K. (2002). Please stand by for an important message: Television in art education. *Visual Arts Research, 28*(2), 16–26.

Gablik, S. (1984). *Has modernism failed?* London: Thames and Hudson.

Gablik, S. (1991). *The reenchantment of art*. New York: Thames and Hudson.

Gamradt, J., & Staples, C. (1994). My school and me: Children's drawings in postmodern educational research and evaluation. *Visual Arts Research, 20*(1), 36–49.

Gaztambide-Fernandez, R. A., Harding, H. A., & Sordé-Martí, T. (2004). *Cultural studies and education: Perspectives on theory, methodology, and practice*. Cambridge, MA: Harvard Educational Review.

Giroux, H. (1994a). *Disturbing pleasures: Learning popular culture*. New York: Routledge.

Giroux, H. (1994b). Doing cultural studies: Youth and the challenge of pedagogy. *Harvard Educational Review, 64*(3), 278–308.

Giroux, H., & Simon, R. (Eds.). (1989). *Popular culture, schooling, and everyday life*. Granby, MA: Bergin and Garvey.

Girox, H., & McLaren, P. (1994). *Between borders: Pedagogy and the politics of cultural studies*. New York: Routledge.

Grace, D., & Lum, A. L. (2001). 'We don't want no Haole buttholes in our stories': Local girls reading the Baby-sitters Club books in Hawaii. *Curriculum Inquiry, 31*(4), 421–452.

Griffin, C. (1993). *Representations of youth: The study of youth and adolescence in Britain and America*. Cambridge, UK: Polity Press.

Hall, S. (1996). Introduction: Who needs identity? In P. Du Gay & S. Hall (Eds.), *Questions of cultural identity* (pp. 1–11). London: Sage.

Hall, S. (1997). *Representation: Cultural representations and signifying practices*. Thousand Oaks, CA: Sage.

Hamblen, K. (2000). Local art knowledge: within children's art work and outside school culture. *Visual Arts Research, 25*(2), 14–24.

Hamblen, K. (2002). Children's contextual art knowledge art education: local art and school art context comparisons. In L. Bresler & C. M. Thompson (Eds.), *The art in children's lives: Context, culture, and curriculum* (pp. 15–27). Dordrecht, The Netherlands: Kluwer Academic Publishers.

Hayes, K., Steinberg, S. R., & Tobin, K. (Eds.). (2011). *Key works in critical pedagogy: Joe L. Kincheloe*. Rotterdam, The Netherlands: Sense Publishing.

Heise, D. (2004). Is visual culture becoming our canon of art? *Art Education, 57*(5), 41–46.

Hickman, R. (2004a). Meaning, purpose and direction. In R. Hickman (Ed.), *Art education 11–18: Meaning purpose and direction* (2nd ed., pp. 1–14). London: Continuum.

Hickman, R. (2004b). Diverse directions: Visual culture and studio practice. In R. Hickman (Ed.), *Art education 11–18: Meaning purpose and direction* (2nd ed., Chapter 10). London: Continuum.

Hickman, R. (2005). A short history of 'critical studies' in art and design education. In R. Hickman (Ed.), *Critical studies in art and design education* (Chapter 1). Bristol, UK: Intellect.

Hickman, R. (2008). The nature of research in arts education. In R. Hickman (Ed.), *Research in art and design education: Issues and exemplars* (pp. 15–24). Bristol, UK: Intellect.

Hobbs, R. (1998). The seven great debates in the media literacy movement. *Journal of Communication, 48,* 6–32.

Holland, D., Lachicotte, W., Skinner, D., & Cain, C. (1998). *Identity and agency in cultural worlds.* Cambridge, MA: Harvard University Press.

Hubbard, P., Kitchin, R. M., & Valentine, G. (2004). Editor's introduction. In P. Hubbard, R. M. Kitchin, & G. Valentine (Eds.), *Key thinkers on space and place.* London: Sage.

Jess, P., & Massey, D. (1995). The conceptualization of place. In D. Massey & P. Jess (Eds.), *A place in the world? Places, cultures and globalization* (pp. 45–85). Oxford: Oxford University Press/The Open University.

Kehily, M. J., & Nayak, A. (2008). Global femininities: Consumption, culture and the significance of place. *Discourse: Studies in the Cultural Politics of Education, 29*(3), 325–342.

Keifer-Boyd, K., & Maitland-Gholson, J. (2007). *Engaging visual culture.* Worcester, MA: Davis Publications.

Kellner, D. (2002). New media and new literacies: Reconstructing education for the new millennium. In L. Lievrouw & S. Livingstone (Eds.), *The handbook of new media* (pp. 90–104). London: Sage.

Kelly, J. (2008). Diasporian moves: African Canadian youth and identity formation. In N. Dolby & F. Rizvi (Eds.), *Youth moves: Identities and education in global perspective* (pp. 85–100). London: Routledge.

Kennelly, J., Poyntz, S., & Ugor, P. (2009). Special issue introduction: Youth cultural politics, and new social spaces in an era of globalization. *Review of Education, Pedagogy, and Cultural Studies, 31*(4), 255–269.

Kenway, J., Kraack, A., & Hickey-Moody, A. (2006). *Masculinity beyond the metropolis.* New York: Palgrave.

Kincheloe, J. (2004). *Critical pedagogy primer.* New York: Peter Lang.

Kjeldgaard, D. (2003). Youth identities in the global cultural economy: Central peripheral consumer culture in Denmark and Greenland. *European Journal of Cultural Studies, 6*(3), 285–304.

Livingstone, S. (2004). Media literacy and the challenge of new information and communication technologies. *The Communication Review, 7,* 3–14.

Luria, A. R. (1928). The problem of cultural development of the child. *Journal of Genetic Psychology, 35,* 493–506.

Macedo, D., & Steinberg, S. (Eds.). (2007). *Media literacy: A reader.* New York: Peter Lang.

Maffesoli, M. (1996). *The time of the tribes: The decline of individualism in mass society.* London: Sage.

Marcus, G. (2009). Multi-sited ethnography: Notes and queries. In M. A. Falzon (Ed.), *Multi-sited ethnography: Theory, praxis, and locality in contemporary research* (pp. 181–196). London: Ashgate.

Mason, R. (2008). Systematic reviewing: Lessons for art and design education research. In R. Hickman (Ed.), *Research in art & design education: Issues and exemplars* (pp. 35–50). Bristol, UK: Intellect.

Massey, D. (1993). Power-geometry and a progressive sense of place. In J. Bird, B. Curtis, T. Putnam, G. Robertson, & L. Tickner (Eds.), *Mapping the futures: Local cultures, global change* (pp. 59–69). London: Routledge.

Massey, D. (1998). The spatial construction of youth cultures. In T. Skelton & G. Valentine (Eds.), *Cool places: Geographies of youth cultures* (pp. 121–129). London: Routledge.

McFee, J. (1966). Society, art, an education. In E. Mattil (Ed.), *A seminar in art education for research and curriculum development* (pp. 122–140). University Park: Pennsylvania State University.

McLaren, P. (1995). *Critical pedagogy and predatory culture: Oppositional politics in a postmodern era.* London: Routledge.

McLaren, P., & Kincheloe, J. L. (Eds.). (2007). *Critical pedagogy: Where are we now?* New York: Peter Lang Publishing.

McLeod, J. (2009). Youth studies, comparative inquiry, and the local/global problematic. *Review of Education, Pedagogy, and Cultural Studies, 31*(4), 270–292.

McRobbie, A. (1992). Post-Marxism and cultural studies: A post-script. In L. Grossberg, C. Nelson, & P. A. Treichler (Eds.), *Cultural studies* (pp. 719–730). New York: Routledge.

Meinhof, U. H., & Galasinski, D. (2005). *The language of belonging.* Basingstoke, UK: Palgrave Macmillan.

Mirzoeff, N. (1999). *An introduction to visual culture.* New York: Routledge.

Mitchell, D. (2000). *Cultural geography: A critical introduction.* Oxford, UK: Blackwell Publishers.

Monchinski, T. (2008). *Critical pedagogy and the everyday classroom.* Dordrecht, The Netherlands: Springer.

Muggleton, D., & Weinzeirl, R. (2003). *The post-subcultures reader.* Oxford, UK: Berg.

Nayak, A. (2003a). *Race, place and globalization: Youth cultures in a changing world.* Oxford, UK/New York: Berg.

Nayak, A. (2003b). 'Ivory lives': Economic restructuring and the making of whiteness in a post-industrial youth community. *Cultural Studies, 6*(3), 305–325.

Nayak, A., & Kehily, M. J. (2008). *Gender, youth and culture: Young masculinities and femininities.* Basingstoke, UK: Palgrave Macmillan.

Neperud, R. W. (2000). Personal journey into the participatory aesthetics of farming. *Journal of Multicultural and Cross-cultural Research in Art Education, 18*(1), 67–73.

Pauly, N. (2003). Interpreting visual culture as cultural narratives in teacher education. *Studies in Art Education, 44*(3), 264–284.

Pilkington, H. (2004). Youth strategies for glocal living: Space, power and communication in everyday cultural practice. In A. Bennett & K. Kahn-Harris (Eds.), *After subculture: Critical studies in contemporary youth culture* (pp. 119–134). New York: Palgrave Macmillan.

Pilkington, H., & Johnson, R. (2003). Peripheral youth: Relations of identity and power in global/local context. *European Journal of Cultural Studies, 6*(3), 259–283.

Rattansi, A., & Phoenix, A. (1997). Rethinking youth identities: Modernist and postmodernist frameworks. In J. Bynner, L. Chisholm, & A. Furlong (Eds.), *Youth, citizenship and social change in a European context* (pp. 121–150). Aldershot, UK: Ashgate.

Rogoff, B. (2003). *The cultural nature of human development.* Oxford, UK: Oxford University Press.

Rogoff, R., & Angelillo, C. (2002). Investigating the coordinated functioning of multifaceted cultural practices in human development. *Human Development, 45*(4), 211–225.

Rutherford, J. (2007). *After identity.* London: Lawrence & Wishart.

Salo, H. (2003). Negotiating gender and personhood in the new South Africa. *European Journal of Cultural Studies, 6*(3), 345–565.

Scollon, R. (2001). *Mediated discourse: The nexus of practice.* New York: Routledge.

Sullivan, G. (1993). Art-based art education: Learning that is meaningful, authentic, critical, and pluralist. *Studies in Art Education, 35*(1), 5–21.

Tavin, K. (2007). Eyes wide shut: The use and uselessness of the discourse of aesthetics in art education. *Art Education, 60*(2), 40–45.

Tavin, K., & Anderson, D. (2003). Teaching (popular) visual culture in the classroom: Deconstructing Disney in the elementary art classroom. *Art Education, 56*(3), 21–24; 33–35.

Thompson, C. M. (2002). Drawing together: Peer influence in early art experiences. In L. Bresler & C. M. Thompson (Eds.), *The art in children's lives: Context, culture, and curriculum* (pp. 129–138). Dordrecht, The Netherlands: Kluwer Academic Publishers.

Tobin, J. (2000). *'Good guys don't wear hats': Children's talk about the media.* New York: Teachers College Press.

Valentine, G., Skelton, T., & Chambers, D. (1998). Cool places: An introduction to youth and youth culture. In T. Skelton & G. Valentine (Eds.), *Cool places: Geographies of youth cultures*. London: Routledge.

Vygotsky, L. S. (1978). *Mind in society: The development of higher psychological processes*. Cambridge, MA: Harvard University Press.

Wagner-Ott, A. (2002). Analysis of gender identity through doll and action figure politics in art education. *Studies in Art Education, 43*(3), 246–263.

Wertsch, J. (1985). *Vygotsky and the social formation of mind*. Cambridge, UK: Harvard University Press.

Wertsch, J. (1991). *Voices of the mind*. Cambridge, UK: Harvard University Press.

Wertsch, J. (1995). The need for action in sociocultural research. In J. Wertsch, P. Del Rio, & A. Alvarez (Eds.), *Sociocultural studies of mind* (pp. 56–74). Cambridge, UK: Cambridge University Press.

Wertsch, J. V. (1998). *Mind as action*. Oxford, UK: Oxford University Press.

Wertsch, J., Del Rio, P., & Alvarez, A. (Eds.). (1995). *Sociocultural studies of mind*. Cambridge, UK: Cambridge University Press.

Willis, P. (1990a). *Common culture: Symbolic work at play in the everyday cultures of the young*. Boulder, CO: Westview Press.

Willis, P. (1990b). *Moving culture: An enquiry into the cultural activities of young people*. London: Calouste Gulbenkian Foundation.

Willis, P. (2000). *The ethnographic imagination*. Cambridge, UK: Polity Press.

Wilson, B. (2002). Becoming Japanese: *Manga*, children's drawings, and the construction of national character. In L. Bresler & C. M. Thompson (Eds.), *The art in children's lives: Context, culture, and curriculum* (pp. 43–55). Dordrecht, The Netherlands: Kluwer Academic Publishers.

# Chapter 3
# Multi-sites: New York City, USA, and Yukon Territory, Canada

## Introduction

In this chapter, I describe particular geographical and social aspects of the two research sites: New York City (hereafter, used interchangeably with NYC, 'the city', or New York) and Yukon Territory, Canada. In New York specifically, I highlight visual material culture (VMC), including the built environment, as well as bring in demographic data describing, among other aspects, immigration and poverty rates. While my focus is most centrally on New York itself, I also touch upon some of the features of the Hope after-school club where I worked with youth during this research. For the Yukon, I underline the conditions for First Nations people and eventually focus much of my attention on Barlow, the community I worked in. For both sites, rather than championing the idea of an 'omniscient narrator' (Goodall, 2000, p. 121) objectively removed from the construction of this ethnographic text, I draw on ethnographic fieldnotes as well as my personal experience to make explicit my own positioning and offer a taste of my sense of place, that is, my own sense of New York City and Barlow.

## New York City and Hope After-School Club, 2005–2006

A mesh of noise, light, and movement and a web of multicoloured flesh, grime, and extreme measures of wealth and poverty and hope, New York City comprises five boroughs: Bronx, Staten Island, Queens, Brooklyn, and Manhattan, spread over approximately 321 square miles (517 km).

I grew up just outside of the city on Long Island, in a predominately white middle-class suburb of the city. I consider myself a native New Yorker and like to believe I am intensely liberal in most social, cultural, and political matters. In 2005,

K.A. Eglinton, *Youth Identities, Localities, and Visual Material Culture: Making Selves, Making Worlds*, Explorations of Educational Purpose 25, DOI 10.1007/978-94-007-4857-6_3, © Springer Science+Business Media Dordrecht 2013

when I started fieldwork, the population in the city was estimated at 8,143,197, making New York the most populated city in the United States and the 12th most populated city in the world.

Symbolic sites such as the Statue of Liberty and the Brooklyn Bridge make up the material landscape and appear to embody (American) discourses of liberty, freedom, democracy, prosperity, and progress (Zukin, 1995). Growing up just outside the city, I went there frequently. While my sisters and I played around in the back seat of the car, mom would tell us to 'lock the doors' as we drove through lower Manhattan; peeking out the car window, my eye would inevitably meet the cardboard boxes which sheltered the homeless.

As a teenager, friends and I would 'hop on the train' to the city where we would often spend the evening hanging out in Washington Square Park. Perched on low cement walls doubling as benches, we would smoke, talk to strangers, and watch street performers. Doing our best at 16 to look 21 (the legal drinking age in the United States), we would try to get into nightclubs or work on getting served cocktails in the Chinese restaurants – we usually failed, and many evenings were more simply spent admiring the black leather goods and other timely paraphernalia filling shop windows along St. Mark's Place.

The VMC of New York is a reflection and constituent of the temporal, social, historical, and economic factors making the city at once 'urban' and singular (Zukin, 1995). As corporate dollars imprint themselves in the landscape, the VMC changes with it. A good example is the gentrification of the East Village. When I was 21, after university and a stint in New Mexico, I moved to Manhattan, to the East Village specifically. At the time, the East Village was considered 'rough'. Drug dealers hung out on the corners, artists like myself lived and 'squatted' in storefronts and apartment buildings, and families raised their children. My building was occupied by several elderly Italian people who had been there since the 1950s; in a distinctive mix of Italian and English, they would talk to me about their lives, I would help them when they were ill, and they would give me overripe tomatoes which they grew on their fire escapes. Decades later as capital has made its way there, the East Village is materially, socially, and symbolically transformed and is now a place of upscale restaurants and high rents (Fig. 3.1).

The public transport system links hundreds of neighbourhoods, which themselves can be further broken into diverse communities, often held together through various identity categories including ethnoracial identification. The landscape of these smaller communities is tied together through 'ethnic' food stores and particular kinds of dwellings and shops. New York is a 'majority minority' (Lankevich, 2002, p. 256) where racially identified blacks and Latinos make up over 50% of the city's population.[1] For a variety of socio-economic reasons, groups seem to settle in

---

[1] Based on 2005 estimates, 44% of the population are white, 25.3% are black, 28% are Latino, 11.6% are Asian, .04% are American Indian or Alaskan Native, 0.1% are Native Hawaiian or other Pacific Islander, 17% are 'some other race', and 1.6% are two or more races. Source: http://www. nyc.gov/html/dcp/home.html. Accessed 16 July 2007.

**Fig. 3.1** New York City images clockwise from top: street scene downtown West Village, Brooklyn Bridge, buildings Lower East Side, abandoned shopping cart Lower East Side (*Brooklyn Bridge photo courtesy Christopher Palmer*)

distinct areas of the city. For example, the Bronx is 52.3% Latino, 29.9% black, and 12.2% white, while Manhattan is 47.5% white, 26.3% Latino, and 13.5% black (Fig. 3.2).[2]

Immigration patterns into New York are historically dependent on various social and economic dynamics. My family tree is typical for New York: bringing together religions (in my case Catholicism and Judaism) and made up of immigrants and people of various diasporas, the main roots of my family were transplanted from Italy and Eastern Europe in the first quarter of the twentieth century. Today, Latinos, notably Puerto Ricans and Dominicans, comprise a major immigrant group in New York. The Puerto Rican community is one of the strongest in the city; performances such as the Puerto Rican Day parade and the construction of new identities such as the 'Nuyorican' or 'NYrican' (i.e. the blending of New York and Puerto Rican identity) continue to rework the social and physical map of New York.

As much as the diverse ethnoracial fabric constitutes New York, blacks and Latinos in particular have faced extreme levels of discrimination, racism, poverty, and ghetto and segregated living conditions (Lankevich, 2002). In 2005 during fieldwork in New York, 19.1% of the population lived in poverty, and an additional 19% were 'near poor' where their income was approximately 100–200% above of the poverty level (in 2005, 9,973 USD per year per individual) – putting almost 40% of New Yorkers at poverty or near poverty status.[3] Child poverty is also a significant problem where in one community in the Bronx, 60% of children under five are living below the poverty level.[4] The great majority of people living at, below, or just above the poverty threshold in New York are employed.[5]

Poverty is divided along ethnoracial and geographic lines where 21.4% of blacks and 28.6% of Latinos are living below the poverty level compared to an average of 12.1% of whites.[6] The number of people living at or below the poverty level is most concentrated in areas of, for instance, the Bronx, Brooklyn, Harlem, and East Village and Lower East Side neighbourhoods in Manhattan; the Bronx is thought to be one of the most impoverished urban counties in the nation.[7] Income and net wealth disparity between the affluent and working poor is the highest in the

---

[2] Source: http://www.nyc.gov/html/dcp/home.html. Accessed 9 August 2008.

[3] Source: http://www.nyc.gov/html/om/pdf/ceo_report2006.pdf. Accessed 10 June 2007.

[4] In New York, at least 8.7 % of people are living below 50 % of the poverty threshold (that is, earning less income of less than 5,000 USD per year). Source: http://www.nyc.gov/html/om/pdf/ceo_report2006.pdf. Accessed 10 June 2007. The United States has *the* highest child poverty rate in the developed world. Source: http://www.stateofworkingamerica.org/news/SWA06Facts-International.pdf. Accessed 15 August 2008.

[5] See http://www.nyc.gov/html/om/pdf/ceo_report2006.pdf for the working poor in New York. Accessed 19 August 2008.

[6] In black and Latino households where the father is absent, poverty rates nearly double. Sources: http://www.nyc.gov/html/dcp/home.html; http://www.nyc.gov/html/om/pdf/ceo_report2006.pdf. Accessed 9 June 2007.

[7] Sources: http://www.nyc.gov/html/dcp/home.html; http://www.census.gov/. Accessed 11 July 2007.

**Fig. 3.2** Ethnoracial and religious diversity is part of the physical landscape (*Photos courtesy Amanda Barragry*)

nation and developed world (Elliot, Grote, & Levin-Waldman, 2001; Nepomnyaschy & Garfinkel, 2002). The wealthiest New Yorkers are predominately non-Latino white males; the poorest include people of black and Latino descent. For myself, since leaving home at 17 to study art at a university in Ohio, my income has varied from just below to 350% above the United States poverty threshold. Like most New Yorkers, even during those years when my income hovered around the poverty threshold, I was always in employment.[8]

Linked to the disparity between rich and poor, poverty, crime, and geography coincide: the most dangerous areas with the highest levels of crime in the city include the poorest parts of the Bronx, Brooklyn, and Manhattan.[9] New York City has gone through periods of spikes and lows in crime. The Hope after-school club where I carried out this study is part of a larger group of school-based community centres spread throughout NYC, initiated in response to a crime surge during the crack epidemic in the early 1990s.

Through a string of serendipitous events, it was my sister who, working for a community-based organisation in downtown NYC, provided me with information of a partnered organisation: the Hope. My communication with people at the Hope began in 2004 with some networking and led to a phone call with the programme director, Hana, in mid-2005. Hana had been running the programme for over 6 years; she was enthusiastic on the phone and described her strong commitment to enriching youth projects. Aiming to create safe spaces for youth and families during out of school hours, Hana later informed me in an interview that these after-school programmes offer young people 'a safe haven' keeping them 'off the streets' and engaged in educational activities.

Three interrelated components defined the programme for the adults: service to the community, recognition of the changing sociocultural worlds of youth and neighbourhoods, and an ethos and practice that responded to these changes. Hana stressed the importance of being there for parents and carers in the community:

Hana    Because they're so busy, they have so much on their plate… They have two
        jobs sometimes; they're on their own, a lot of single parents. So for them it's
        just like, oh thank God the [Hope's] there.

Providing community support also meant responding to changing social dynamics. Hana spoke about various social changes including the regeneration (i.e. gentrification) of the Greenwich Village area and changes salient since the September 11, 2001 attacks on the Twin Towers including 'a lot of anger' in youth, as well as 'parents having to move out of the neighbourhood because they can't afford the rent'. The programme sought to cultivate a feeling of community. Hana described

---

[8] Teachers' salaries were only approximately 250% above the poverty threshold when I was employed by the New York City Board of Education. Salaries now are 500% above the poverty level.

[9] Source: http://www.nyc.gov/html/nypd/html/home/home.shtml. Accessed 9 June 2007.

the importance of youth feeling like an adult cares about them, that someone was interested in their day, and wanting the programme to 'seem like a family'.

The Hope programme opened in 2000 and throughout the year could potentially serve over 1,300 youth from approximately seven surrounding schools. A large urban high school called the Greenwich Village High School (or GVHS) housed the Hope programme. Though all the youth went to school in the area, they lived throughout the city, often travelling to school in the morning with parents or carers who worked near the Hope. More broadly, there are 1,200 public schools in New York and a number of private and parochial or Catholic schools throughout the city.[10] While it would be financially impossible for many young people in New York to attend a private school, a good number of youth from low-income or poor families qualify for funding to enrol in one of the many Catholic schools. Enrolment in parochial schools reflects New York's 'majority minority', where in Manhattan and the Bronx, 85% of all children attending Catholic schools are black and/or Latino.[11] Indeed, many of the youth participants I had at the Hope attended one of the local Catholic schools.[12] Reflecting the earlier discussion on poverty, 65% of school children in New York, including those enrolled in Catholic schools, are eligible for a free or reduced price lunch (i.e. only those families living at, below, or just above the poverty threshold are eligible).[13] At the Hope, the youth I worked with, and the majority of youth in attendance, were eligible for free or reduced price lunch. I come back to the Hope, including my early days at the Hope and meeting the youth, in Chap. 4.

## Yukon Territory and Barlow, 2006

The second site I went to, Barlow, is in the Yukon Territory. The subject of poems and novels and the site of one of the greatest gold rushes in history, the Yukon is a space produced through an entanglement of histories including those of the First Nations people, white settlers and prospectors, government officials, missionaries, and travellers. The smallest of the three Canadian territories, the Yukon spans 300,501 miles (483,610 km) and is located on the western edge of Canada bordering British Columbia, the North West Territories, and Alaska. Replete with forests,

---

[10] Public schools are publicly funded through property taxes and state governments. Over 1,000,000 youth attend New York City public schools.

[11] Source: http://www.nysed.gov/. Accessed 19 August 2008.

[12] The demographic breakdown of youth attending public schools in 2004–2005 was roughly 38% Latino, 35% black, 15% white, 12% Asian/Pacific Islander, and less than one per cent American Indian or Alaskan Native. Source: http://www.cgcs.org/. Accessed 20 July 2007. The racial make-up of schools is related to geography and economics, where some schools in Harlem or the South Bronx have 100% black and Latino student bodies, and other schools in affluent areas of Manhattan will have a majority of white youth.

[13] Source: http://www.cgcs.org/. Accessed 19 August 2008.

mountain ranges, lakes, streams, and rivers, including the massive Yukon River flowing out to the Bering Sea, Yukon Territory's physical landscape is notoriously extreme and breathtaking. Several major roads including the Dempster Highway, which cuts through the tundra and crosses the Arctic Circle, and smaller winter roads connect an expansive landscape sparsely dotted with small communities (see Fig. 3.3).

A place of extremes, winter temperatures can drop below minus 50 °C and in the summer can go above 30 °C. In some areas, 24 h of sunlight marks the summer solstice, and months of darkness characterise the winter. Aurora Borealis or Northern Lights can be seen from the autumn. The biggest private industry in the Yukon is tourism. National parks, Northern festivals, First Nations' culture and heritage, gold rush history, and events including the Yukon Quest Dog Sled race continue to draw people to the Yukon; the Yukon has frequently served as a site and inspiration for numerous films, books, and other forms of arts and entertainment. Other important economic sectors include mining, government, forestry, fishing, hunting, trapping for the fur trade, and agriculture. Many of these sectors have a long, sometimes damaging, history with the First Nations people, with their traditions and subsistence practices. The mining industry, for example, though an important economic sector, has had a deeply negative impact on the First Nations' subsistence practices, lives, and health (Edelson, 2009).

The average population in the Yukon during my fieldwork in 2006 was 30,372: this number has since increased to approximately 34,747 in 2010.[14] In 2006, approximately 25% of the Yukon population self-identified as Aboriginal on the Canadian Census (according to the census, Aboriginal includes North American Indian – what I have been calling First Nation – Metis, or Inuit). In the Yukon, 83% of this 25% identified as First Nation specifically.[15] Across Canada, people identifying as Aboriginal (on this same census) constituted 4% of the population (i.e. over one million for the first time).

Employment is generally high in the territory, though seasonal. While the average household income is one of the highest in Canada, Edelson (2009) describes profound income disparities, with First Nations' households earning less than half of the average household income. Moreover, though the average household income is above the Canadian national average, the cost of living is high across the Yukon, and those First Nations families earning little, working for minimum wage, or receiving welfare are generally unable to meet basic needs.

Social issues, intense exclusions, and health problems often characterise the lives of many First Nations people and communities across the territory. Poverty is a continuing issue, and First Nations people are more likely than non-First Nations people to live in overcrowded housing or to have no housing; they are over-represented in prison, suffer from high rates of substance and domestic abuse,

---

[14] Source: http://www.eco.gov.yk.ca/stats/pdf/population_jun_2010.pdf. Accessed 10 March 2011.

[15] Source: http://www.eco.gov.yk.ca/stats/pdf/aboriginadata.pdf. Accessed 10 March 2011.

**Fig. 3.3** Yukon images clockwise from top: outfitter's cabins in Tombstone Park early spring, grizzly bear near the Arctic Circle up the Dempster Highway, testing the late spring ice on the Peel River, caribou antlers decorate a house (*Photos courtesy Katrine Kaarsemaker*)

and have a shorter lifespan than white people in the region (see Edelson, 2009). The Yukon has one of the highest rates of youth suicide in Canada, and nationally First Nations youth (commonly boys) are five to seven times more likely than white youth to take their own lives.[16]

Though high school dropout rates are improving, the Yukon, like the other two territories, has a higher dropout rate (15.5%) than the provinces. Educational disengagement is a common issue among First Nations youth; First Nations boys in particular have the highest dropout rate (see also Davison, 2004).[17] Across Canada, Aboriginal youth dropout rate is 22% as compared with non-Aboriginal 8.5%. As Davison underlines, educational attainment (or lack of) impacts a person's economic circumstances and mental and physical health.

Overall, in the Yukon, there are 14 First Nations spanning eight language groups. Though there is currently a drive to document and revive native languages, in 2006, only 12% of the Aboriginal population were fluent in their mother tongue.[18] The colonial history of First Nations people in the Yukon is a long, complex one involving exclusions and marginalisation, with the federal government, settlers and prospectors, and religious, often Christian, institutions all playing a part. This history includes early contact with traders, a massive influx of outsiders during the gold rush in the Klondike, relocation, and forced assimilation through the residential schools where thousands of First Nations youth were taken from their homes and sent to school miles away, sometimes not returning for a decade. Contemporary social issues impacting First Nations communities across the Yukon and Canada are often linked to a history of colonialism and to the interests of various parties in the resources of the land – through these interests, many First Nations subsistence practices, traditional customs, languages, and ways of life were denied value, denigrated, or lost (e.g. see Kirmayer, Brass, & Tait, 2000; Kirmayer et al., 2007; also in Edelson, 2009, pp. 14–17).

Since 1973, First Nations groups in the Yukon have taken steps towards self-determination and self-government.[19] After decades of negotiation with the federal and territorial governments, 11 of the 14 First Nations bands have settled land claims and are self-governing, allowing them to care for, support, and represent their community members.

Barlow, a small community located in the Yukon Territory, mirrors and comprises the contemporary and historical social issues and dynamics of the Yukon. A grid of dirt roads – where the closest traffic light is hours away – houses, cabins, trailers, and

---

[16] Source: http://www.hc-sc.gc.ca/fniah-spnia/promotion/suicide/index-eng.php. Accessed 10 March 2011.

[17] Source: http://www.statcan.gc.ca/pub/81-004-x/2010004/article/11339-eng.htm#c. Accessed 10 March 2011.

[18] http://www.eco.gov.yk.ca/stats/pdf/aboriginadata.pdf. Accessed 10 March 2011.

[19] In 1973, what was called the 'Council for Yukon Indians' presented to the Prime Minister Pierre Trudeau the document 'Together Today for Our Children Tomorrow' (see http://www.eco.gov.yk. ca/pdf/together_today_for_our_children_tomorrow.pdf. Accessed 10 March 2011. See also http:// www.gov.yk.ca/pdf/yukon_at_a_glance_web2.pdf. Accessed 10 March 2011.

shops are weather-worn, made of wood and corrugated steel, and often paint chipped. On dirt drives, piles of wood for fires lay next to old rusty cars, often missing wheels and doors and/or being used as extra storage space. The river edges the town – on the dike, people sit staring at the small boats, or at hills, or at the light, some play music and ride their bikes, and tourists take photographs; one day as I sat there reading, a middle-aged man almost landed on me as he swooped down from the sky on a massive paraglider. Historical tours are led by guides heavy in costume from the late nineteenth century. When I was there, the First Nations' Interpretive Centre was, at least to me, the most magnificent building in the town.

As I attempted to understand Barlow, I was struck by the mixture of people – First Nations and white, tourists and hikers, miners, bearded men, and weather-worn women. I was even more struck by the way the landscape – the social and physical space, as well as the VMC of place including the buildings, the muddy cars, and the pots of fake gold nuggets in gift shops – at once gave rise to, evoked, and incorporated a mesh of narratives including, for example, a First Nations narrative, a gold rush and colonial narrative, a narrative of untamed wilderness, and a narrative of place as Mecca for hikers and nature enthusiasts.

In 2006, when this study was carried out, the town had just over 1,300 residents (the population expands in the summer). Just over 100 of the residents came from outside of Canada, and over 1,100 were considered nonimmigrant population.[20] Approximately 250 of the residents were under the age of 18. The ethnoracial make-up of the population in 2006 included approximately 30% Aboriginal or First Nations, approximately 70% North American and European white and French Canadian, and just under one per cent 'visible minority' such as Chinese or black.

As in the Yukon broadly, a primary economic source in the town is tourism. Shops open in the summer and are boarded up by late September for the winter. Tourists stop in Barlow often on their way to and from Alaska. I started riding an old bike I bought up there. I'd pedal around town photographing the tourists sifting through troughs, getting a taste of mining for gold, the First Nations' Band Hall and Interpretive Centre, and the rickety fishing boats. Tourists told me that the town's First Nations' Interpretive Centre, history, landscape, lively art scene, and outdoor pursuits were the main reasons they came to visit.

While the largest source of employment in 2006 was the service and sales sector, more generally, 27% of the population in 2006 were not actively in the labour force (not unemployed, but not looking for or able to work, e.g. students or people taking care of their children), and approximately 13% of residents were unemployed.

Fireplaces warm houses, chopping wood is a typical way to get ready for winter, and outhouses are not uncommon. Residents live both in town and out, and before the winter cold and 24-h nights set in, some elderly residents move closer to the town centre. During my fieldwork, the Northern Lights started to appear in mid- to

---

[20] Source for all statistical and demographic references to Barlow: community profile in 2006 reported by Canadian Census. Accessed 26 September 2008. To ensure anonymity, web addresses are not provided here.

late September, and by the time I left Barlow in the second week of October, there was snow on the ground, and the Northern Lights could often be seen.

The self-governing First Nations community in Barlow is extremely active. They have worked with the federal government to secure land claims and self-government. Despite a history marred by displacement, colonialism, residential schools, exclusion, and abuse, they have come back strong. They are now the largest employer in the community, and there is a push to document their history and the importance of particular places, stories, dances, and the like. The First Nations community also actively organises 'culture camps', First Hunt, and First Fish for young people to take part in important traditional subsistence practices.

Youth in the town continue to go to the community day school throughout the winter, and schools close for summer by the end of May when the sun is in the sky for most of the night.[21] Some of the youth leave with their families for the winter, often taking up residence for a few months in Mexico and other warm spots. The school board includes First Nations leaders, Elders, and parents, and efforts are made to include First Nations language, tradition, and culture classes. That said, many of the First Nations youth (boys in particular) are disengaged from school, often excluded, and/or scholastically unsuccessful. Though improving, the high school graduation rate for First Nations boys is low – this statistic is mirrored nationally.

During my stay, I heard many stories about people who arrived in Barlow 30 years before as travellers or self-proclaimed 'hippies' and never left. The streets are safe, youth can (and do) play outside late into the night without problems, and there are social services in place to help with problems in the community. The people in the community care for each other; it felt familial – warts and all – and, though it was a small town, it seemed that room was made for me. My fieldnotes are full of entries about feeling 'accepted'. In fact, characteristic of the spirit of the people in Barlow, within weeks I had a group of friends to have drinks with, people knitting me scarves for the winter, others teaching me how to bead, some making me salmon salads, and others coming by my place just to chat. By the time the cold weather started to set in, many took pity on me: sometimes, I would come home to find firewood already chopped and lying by the door; other times, friends, community members, and youth themselves would pop by and build me a fire – each person teaching me their personal trick and assuring me that this was 'the best way to build a fire'.

Walking and riding the roads throughout July and August, I listened as tied-up dogs barked; my eyes stung and moistened from forest fires miles away, my feet grew dirty, and my face darkened from the sun. Over time, I was starting to connect to Barlow, to make sense of the North as a place both mythical and real – producing my own, as Shields (1991) writes, 'half-imagined and half-reality' understanding of Barlow – a Barlow I will come back to in Chap. 7.

---

[21] The school includes youth from 5 years up – from kindergarten (reception) to primary, junior, and high school years.

# Conclusion

Bringing together historical and statistical information, my own personal experiences, and fieldnotes, in this chapter, I have started to provide a general picture of the two sites featured in this study. While I had an overarching focus on social and economic conditions for black and Latino families in New York and First Nations people in the Yukon, I eventually narrowed my description to the Hope after-school club in New York and the community of Barlow in Yukon Territory. Throughout this chapter, I have tried to make explicit my own sense of place and my own positioning by articulating some of my experiences growing up in New York, as well as coming to know the second research site Barlow.

Overall, it was with/in and through the places described in this chapter, these sites of inequality and exclusion, on the one hand, and light, inspiration, thick colour, and verve, on the other hand, that young people at the Hope and in Barlow lived out their lives. It was with/in and through these places – sticky tangled webs tacked to history and spun with sociocultural threads – that countless young people, using available resources including VMC, participated in the cultural practices that constituted both themselves and their 'figured worlds' (Holland, Lachicotte, Skinner, & Cain, 1998). And, while the young people in this study used VMC in myriad ways, most salient were to make sense of the overarching themes of place, race, and gender. In Part II, I offer four ethnographic chapters where I explore these themes beginning with place at the Hope.

# References

Davison, C. M. (2004, September 15–18). Education and employment patterns among Northern Aboriginal youth: A study of resiliency, development and community health. In *Proceedings of the third Northern Research Forum, Yellowknife, NWT, Canada.* http://www.nrf.is/Publications/The%20Resilient%20North/Plenary%203/3rd%20NRF_Plenary%203_Davison_YR_paper.pdf. Accessed on 12 May 2011.
Edelson, N. (2009). *Poverty reduction policies and programs in the Yukon* (Social Development Report Series). Commissioned by the Canadian Council on Social Development.
Elliot, M., Grote, W., & Levin-Waldman, O. (2001). *Deepening disparity: Income equality in New York City.* Public/Private Ventures. http://www.ppv.org/ppv/publications/assets/90_publication.pdf. Accessed 12 May 2011.
Goodall, H. L. (2000). *Writing the new ethnography.* Oxford, UK: Rowman & Littlefield.
Holland, D., Lachicotte, W., Skinner, D., & Cain, C. (1998). *Identity and agency in cultural worlds.* Cambridge, MA: Harvard University Press.
Kirmayer, L. J., Brass, G. M., Holton, T., Paul, K., Simpson, C., & Tait, C. (2007). *Suicide among Aboriginal people in Canada.* Ottawa, Canada: The Aboriginal Healing Foundation.
Kirmayer, L., Brass, G., & Tait, C. (2000). The mental health of Aboriginal peoples: transformations of identity and community. *Canadian Journal of Psychiatry, 45*(7), 607–616.
Lankevich, G. J. (2002). *New York City: A short history.* New York: NYU Press.
Nepomnyaschy, L., & Garfinkel, I. (2002). *Wealth in New York City and the nation* (Social Indicators Survey Center Working Paper #02-02). New York: Columbia University School of Social Work.
Shields, R. (1991). *Places on the margin: Alternative geographies of modernity.* London: Routledge.
Zukin, S. (1995). *The culture of cities.* Oxford, UK: Blackwell.

# Chapter 4
# Representin' Place: Place-Making and Place-Based Identities

## Introduction

Holland, Lachicotte, Skinner, and Cain (1998) describe a 'figured world' as 'a socially and culturally constructed realm of interpretation in which particular characters and actors are recognised, significance is assigned to certain acts, and particular outcomes are valued over others' (p. 52). Imagined as knots, nexuses, and embedded conceptual spaces, created with/in and intersected by other worlds, the concept of figured worlds offers a useful theoretical and analytic heuristic. I envision certain figured worlds – such as the figured world of youth at the Hope – as dynamic cultural spaces: ever-changing spaces constituted of (localised) global flows of culture, including visual material culture (VMC) (Appadurai, 1990); on-the-ground unique local relations; sociocultural and physical conditions (Massey, 1993); and young people's individual trajectories as they intersect and are mediated by these flows, relations, and conditions.

Holding this particular conceptualisation of figured worlds in mind, in this chapter, I flesh out the ways in which young people used VMC to describe, make sense of, and construct the various places intersecting their lives as well as their own place-based identities. Specifically, after describing my early days at the Hope, I illustrate how young people drew on themes from VMC to construct the places that were part of their figured worlds; I suggest these places were akin to Anderson's (1983) 'imagined communities': communities formed at the nexus of young people's lived experiences, VMC, and material and social conditions of place itself; I demonstrate how, together with forms of VMC, these imagined communities served as mediating 'cultural artefacts' (Cole, 1996) which young people simultaneously produced and employed in the construction of their own place-based identities.

K.A. Eglinton, *Youth Identities, Localities, and Visual Material Culture: Making Selves, Making Worlds*, Explorations of Educational Purpose 25, DOI 10.1007/978-94-007-4857-6_4, © Springer Science+Business Media Dordrecht 2013

## Early Days at the Hope

When I arrived at the programme in early December 2005, the Hope had a family feel: the staff were more than colleagues – they grew up together, attended the same high schools, knew the same gossip. Most of the staff identified as black and/or Latina/Latino, and many of them spoke Spanish. There was a lot of hugging, touching, nicknaming, and familiarity not only among themselves but also between the staff and youth (many of whom were close in age).

I would show up to the programme each day around 2:45 p.m. Walking through the front doors that opened to a massive, brightly lit, multicoloured cafeteria, I would sign in with one of the female guards who sat at an entry desk.[1] The cafeteria at this time of day was an extension of the street – youth from the GVHS (the high school housing the Hope) sat on top of tables eating fast food, chatting, and waiting for friends. Many males wore black puffy coats, long T-shirts, and baggy pants with the waistline parked somewhere between their hips and their knees. Trucker hats or wide baseball hats and/or do-rags covered their heads. The girls varied between a 'tomboy' look (e.g. puffy coats and low baggy jeans and boots) or tight jeans, sneakers, and small form-fitting puffy coats. Heavy gold jewellery or bling hung from their ears, fingers, and necks. Music was everywhere: coming from MP3 players, mouths, and cell phones. Even the young people's talk had rhythm: walking through throngs of youth, I often could not distinguish between rapping and conversation.

Coming to the Hope after-school programme around 3:00 p.m., young people would spend a good part of the first hour in this cafeteria. Grouped by age, the youth would crowd together on long adjoining benches and tables eating snacks, doing homework, or more typically, shouting over everyone else's shouting before breaking up for group activities (e.g. basketball, chess, dance). Based on my research interests and practical concerns, the director, Hana, and I decided that I would work mainly with Timo's group which consisted of sixth, seventh, and eighth graders (students approximately 11–14 years old).[2]

The first days of the project consisted of my anxiously walking around, talking to young people and staff, and generally trying (most likely too hard) to fit in. Rather than discussing the project immediately with the youth, I attempted to get to know some of them first. Spotting Timo's group on the first day, I sat down next to what looked like four harmless girls in Catholic school uniforms. Feeling over-aged and painfully unhip, I asked their names; I soon learned they responded by switching their names and, in the process, made up a name for me – Darleen – which they said with a particular drawl and which somehow stuck.

---

[1] GVHS was the recipient of a project that went into schools to decorate and improve the physical sites. As part of this project, the walls of the cafeteria were painted in various pastels, including purple, red, and yellow.

[2] Timo was about 19 years old and the group leader. He grew up in lower Manhattan, often spoke his mind to other staff, and was quite strict with the boys in the group (whose behaviour was often considered 'problematic').

Many of the girls in Timo's group attended one of the local Catholic schools. The girls came in from all over New York; a few of them told me about the various funding they received to attend these Catholic schools. Though many of the 'Catholic school girls' (as they sometimes called themselves) would ultimately take part in the study, Shanti, Latoya, and Valentina became central participants.

Latoya's and Valentina's grandmothers were friends, and the girls had known each other since they were young. Latoya was 13, had dark brown eyes, and shoulder-length dark brown hair which she usually wore in a knot behind her head. She was always the first to volunteer what she called her 'background', 'heritage', or 'races', telling whoever was listening that she was part Colombian, part black, part Japanese, part Jewish, and several other parts. She usually finished by saying that she identified most with her black and Colombian roots.

Noticeably taller than Latoya, Valentina was 12 and identified as Puerto Rican and Argentinean. With a big smile, deep brown eyes, and dark brown hair, Valentina lived in Spanish Harlem with her mom and younger sister, excelled in sports (the older boys called her 'Shaq' after basketball star Shaquille O'Neal), wanted to be a doctor or a lawyer when she got older, but for now, 'lived for' her sister and her friends. One of those friends included 12-year-old Shanti, who lived in the East Village with her mom and various brothers and sisters who came in and out of her life (and apartment), depending on financial or social circumstances.

Part Indian, Puerto Rican, and black, Shanti often said, 'I'm a black Puerto Rican' or 'black *Boricua* [Puerto Rican]'. She was about the same height as Valentina, but with a wispier frame. With light eyes and hair, her friends would often tell her she should be a model. Though I had the hardest time getting to know Shanti and though my relationship with her was rocky in the beginning, when the project ended, I felt so close to her that I wrote in my fieldnotes that I felt like I 'abandoned' her. In Box 4.1 is an excerpt from a fieldnote illustrating some early tensions with Shanti.

Trying to 'get in' with the Catholic school girls, I would sit near them at the long cafeteria table and attempt to enter their conversations. Sometimes, they let me in, but mostly, for the first week or so, they gasped at my ignorance on matters of popular culture, teased me about my choice of words or, worse, ignored me. While getting in with the girls was difficult, acceptance (or tolerance) seemed easier with the boys. At first I wondered whether my gender or, in a more delusional fashion, my appearance had something to do with this; however, this fantasy was dismissed with a sobering glance in the mirror and rejected after a week when one of the boys commented on my skinny arms which 'could be used as jump-ropes'. Despite comments on my physique (that became the butt of many jokes), I felt at ease with many of the boys from the start.

I usually found the boys I worked with at the Hope, sharing the earbuds of an MP3 player, wildly chewing gum, and/or smacking each other on the back of the head and running away. Over time, several of the boys, including Freddie, became central participants. Freddie turned 12 during the study. Small, sinewy, and tightly wound, though he was, as he told me, '100 per cent *Boricua*', he sometimes referred to himself as 'white boy' because of his pale skin. According to the girls, he was

**Box 4.1** Early Tensions with Shanti

I sat outside with the girls as the boys played basketball. I brought in some magazines that Latoya and Valentina said they liked. Shanti asked if she could have a picture of Chris Brown [teen hip-hop artist] from one of the magazines. I foolishly replied, 'you can have it next week when we do collages.' Shanti pouted and told me she was dropping out of the project. It got really tense, and all of the other girls were sitting there. I guess I did not want them to think that I was desperate for youth to stay in the project, and/or that they could bully me (or use this as a weapon). So I said, 'fine, I have plenty of kids interested.' 'Good,' she snapped back. I felt like the other girls couldn't believe what I said; I think they assumed I would have begged her to stay. Maria [one of her friends] whispered in her ear, 'are you serious?' As Shanti nodded yes, I laughed and, tried to make light of what was a really negative moment, by touching her cheek and saying 'come on P—' calling her by the funny pseudonym she selected the day before. To my horror, rather than laughing, she wiped her face where I stroked it and shook her hand as if to flick away my filth.

We never spoke about the incident, and by the time we were making collages the following week, Shanti was participating.

(Source: FN010706)

'smooth', 'edgy', and a 'playa'. His notebook was covered with the nickname he acquired on his block in Spanish Harlem: 'Lil' F'; he had no problem speaking his mind – often spitting out a 'yo man that's bullshit' if he disagreed. He was usually dressed in baggy pants and T-shirt, and, though there was a 'no hats' rule at the Hope, when possible, he would wear his two-sizes-too-big New York Yankees baseball cap with the bill to the side.

Freddie spent much of his time with Malcolm from Queens, who was also 12. Malcolm's aunt drove him to Manhattan each morning on her way to work. During this drive, they would listen to soul music; Patti Labelle was someone Malcolm was 'just starting to get into'.[3] Slightly taller than Freddie, Malcolm identified as African-American or black; he had dark eyes and very short dark hair. He described himself as 'funny' and 'smart', and believed he knew more about music and celebrity gossip than most of his friends – a fact I can confirm after spending many months with him.

Numerous other boys including Gabe, Juan, and Louis were also involved in the project. Gabe identified as Spanish and Jamaican, was short, heavyset (what we might call 'husky'[4] in the United States); he lived in the Bronx and was into wrestling and Latin music. In the fieldnotes, I initially described how nervous Gabe made me. I wrote about 'tip-toeing around him as I would an "angsty" boyfriend', and 'laughing too heartily at his jokes'. Within a few weeks of meeting

---

[3] Patti LaBelle is a black soul singer from the United States.

[4] 'Husky' usually describes someone heavyset, small, and tough. There is more muscle than fat.

him, however, my writing changed, and I describe a growing attachment to him, 'how soft he really is', and how he was so interested in the project.

I went into the Hope as a volunteer, artist, and researcher; the youth understood I was doing research to learn about their lives and the ways in which they used VMC. The youth also knew I was an artist and had been an art educator before; however, it seemed that none of these factors necessarily translated into a particular role for me. Throughout the first few months of the project, in the process of figuring out my role (including my authority at the Hope), the young people would continuously test me: telling me outrageous things about friends (sometimes truthful, often not) and watching my face for a reaction, playing jokes on me such as hiding my bag to see if I would get angry, and breaking Hope rules when we were alone (such as wearing a hat). And I, for the most part, was continuously trying to learn my role – trying to balance between the demands of the Hope, my responsibilities as an adult in charge, as well as my responsibilities to the young people as participants, and the need for a deepening of relationships.

Through this difficult process, we all started to learn that I rarely got angry, played along with and often instigated jokes, was interested in outrageous stories, and would let them wear a hat if I knew we would both get away with it. My relationship with the youth at the Hope inevitably grew as the months passed, as we spoke for hours about what happened in school or what was happening at home, as I showed up day after day to hang out with them, as I dished out advice, bought them sodas, lent them small change for candy, snuck them food, took the blame when they got into trouble, critiqued notes from boyfriends, replied to their texts and Sunday afternoon calls, made them music CDs, took their photos, perfected my comedy routine, and took their lives seriously.

In fact, though I still do not know if this was the right thing to do, I generally let Hope staff do the disciplining, and the role which the youth and I slowly negotiated (and the identity which finally crystallised) was that of artist and researcher who was also a supportive friend and/or close auntie with particular benefits (e.g. I had access to beverages and food; I could get them out of certain Hope activities, would let them play music, borrow my phone, and was always willing to lend out digital media). In the end, while I will of course never know just how 'in' I was with any of them, I felt closeness to these youth that I never felt as an art educator in a classroom. Furthermore, though getting to know the girls and gaining their trust took more time, my relationships with the girls felt deeper than they did with the boys. While there might be any number of reasons why I felt closer to the girls, I think it is safe to suggest that my gender and, connectedly, my experiences afforded me greater 'access' to them, their stories, and emotions.

## Place-Making

One way of connecting with all the youth was through technology, and I had various camera equipment with me at all times for young people to use. Sitting at a long cafeteria table with the youth in early January, Malcolm picked up a video camera and started an impromptu interview with Freddie: 'So Freddie, how's your life? Does it suck?' We all laughed at the question, and Freddie quickly answered, 'Nah, c'mon, ya know, I'm here chillin' with my homies. We is in New York, ya know east side'. With the words 'east side', Freddie did a hand sign reminiscent of the gestures used by the rap artists I had seen on music television the night before.

Though I had a hunch about the importance of place before meeting the youth at the Hope, through fieldwork, I found that place and VMC intersected at two over-lapping points: (1) place or localities constrained and enabled the ways in which young people used VMC in their everyday lives, and (2) young people used VMC as a tool to make sense of and construct the places they traversed (where, going back to the first intersection, the construction of these localities was afforded and limited by aspects of place itself). At the Hope, one of the ways the youth made sense of and constructed the places intersecting their lives was by drawing on themes and cultural practices from forms of VMC. In the following sections, I focus on localities most salient for the youth and where the use of VMC featured most heavily, including New York and the five boroughs, conceptual spaces such as the 'ghetto' and the 'hood', and remembered places such as Puerto Rico.

## *'[I]n New York it's all about the hip-hop':*
## *Constructing New York*

New York was not described by the young people as a place of marked inequality, but rather, based on their own experiences and on the internalisation of common expressions and representations signifying New York; the youth made sense of the city through reference to embodied forms of cultural expression, including ways of acting, talking, style of dress, and aspects of hip-hop style. Each of these expres-sions was tangled with each other and with place. For example, style and behaviour were often informed by hip-hop's cultural practices and also by the physical and social conditions of New York, which itself served as a post-industrial context for the birth of hip-hop (Rose, 1994a, p. 73). Ten-year-old Latrice, who identified as Jamaican and Trinidadian and lived in Brooklyn, started to get at the overlapping nature of these forms:

Latrice: I have three main outfits that I like: I have one dedicated to New York, one
          dedicated to Trinidad, and one dedicated to Jamaica—
          . . .
K:        What's your New York outfit?
Latrice: My New York outfit is very loud. . . I have a shirt that's black and it has
          New York written all over it and everything—

Interconnecting behaviours and images, Latrice's words touch on style and the representation of places; they cite a common index of New Yorkers as loud and of New York as a notoriously noisy place – a quality of place which is neither fictive nor stereotypical, but part of the experience of urban living. Behaviour was almost always combined with style, where style both was informed by VMC and was itself a form of VMC. Shanti spoke to me about how people in New York act and dress:

Shanti: You see somebody, you know that's a New Yorker whatever.

. . .

Shanti: I don't know how you'll know, but you'll know. Like how they talk, how they dress.
K:     Like how do you think they dress in New York, the girls?
Shanti: They wear tight stuff.
K:     Tight stuff. And then the boys?
Shanti: They wear baggy stuff.

. . .

Shanti: All the way down to their butt and they show their boxers—

The style Shanti described here is a particular New York style that the youth at the Hope invariably articulated when making sense of New York and New Yorkers: a style born of hip-hop culture, where hip-hop style is connected to urban life, representing 'urban storms to be weathered' in hoodies and big coats (Rose, 1994b, p. 38). This is not to say that hip-hop style is not found in other areas of the city or across urban and non-urban communities around the world, but rather that youth would often draw on what seemed to be a natural connection between New York and hip-hop, and considered the cultural practices of hip-hop a distinguishing feature of their particular urban context (Forman, 2000). In a video Latrice made as part of this project, she spoke about the short-sleeved white top she had on with the words 'hip-hop' sprayed across it:

Latrice: Well you know in New York it's *all* about the hip-hop, so I bought this shirt dedicated to New York and to hip-hop.

Hip-hop's cultural practices including style, rap music, graffiti, and dance (primarily breakdancing) were the most common cultural expressions youth cited to make sense of the New York context, as well as the practices most frequently *claimed* for New York itself. Boys would often tell me about the geographies of rap: about where rappers were from in New York and the meaning of some of the lyrics with respect to specific localities constituting the city. Graffiti was claimed as distinctly New York, many of them superimposing their self-portraits onto a background with 'New York graffiti' (even if the graffiti used was found on the Internet and not located in New York). Latrice told me:

Latrice: That's how I remembered New York. Like when I go down to Delaware [US state] like I see graffiti and I'm like 'they tryin' to be like New York'.

Breakdancing and dances such as 'the Harlem Shake' were also considered a distinguishing feature of New York. Both boys and girls described the dancers they saw over the weekend on the streets, imitated them, and attempted the moves – often filming these attempts.

Cultural practices from hip-hop were often drawn on in tandem with popular media representations or narratives of New York found in forms of VMC such as television, film, and music. For example, popular narratives constructing the city as diverse and multicultural, innovative, a global centre of art and fashion, or a place of hyper-individualism constituted young people's talk about a place. As part of her video, Latrice did a freestyle poem about New York that brings together common narratives about the city and touches on both the affective and discursive aspects which make up the local for her:

Latrice: New York, New York is where all the fashion craze comes from
        New York is the city that never sleeps
        New York is the place where the cars go beep, beep
        New York is the place that I love the most
        New York is the place where nobody is a ghost.

Yet, the narratives used were not simply repeated by young people, but rather mediated and reworked through their own local experiences and individual biographies (see Gupta & Ferguson, 1997a, 1997b). Young people's embodied experiences of, for instance, diversity, urban closeness, and noise were mapped onto narratives in circulation and used to make sense of place.

Twelve-year-old Abigail provides a good example of how individual biographies might rework common discourses constituting New York. Most of Abigail's family was from the Dominican Republic, a few were from El Salvador and other parts of Latin America; she spoke fluent Spanish and was deeply connected to her Spanish roots. Describing 'being a New Yorker', she drew on the popular representation of New York as a 'melting pot' or place where people with varying identities live together in one geographical location:

Abigail: There's things you have to do to be a New Yorker... you need to be from
        different, I think you need to have at least more than one different
        background... this is the definition of New Yorker—
K:      So different backgrounds, does that mean you can't just be all Spanish?
Abigail: Well no not like that, you can't be like say you're Spanish or all Spanish or
        something, you can be all Spanish, but you can't be all like from Puerto
        Rico, you have to be also like Dominican or Puerto Rican or, you know,
        things like that—

Here, Abigail uses her own experiences of diversity to make sense of discourses circulated through various means, including VMC. Another important aspect of New York was not necessarily that it was a 'global city' (Sassen, 2007) but rather that it was made up of smaller localities, including the five boroughs.

## Making the Boroughs

Louis usually got to the club before the rest of the youth; he turned 14 while I was there and was part of Timo's group. The girls called him 'white', but he told me he was 'Cuban, Puerto Rican, and three per cent black'. Louis lived with his mom and older sister in what he and his friends, using hip-hop vernacular, called the 'dirty Bronx'. Travelling into Manhattan every day to go to one of the Catholic schools in Greenwich Village, he told Malcolm in peer-to-peer interviews that he was kicked out of his school in the Bronx for bad behaviour; it seemed he would often wear his school expulsion as a kind of badge of honour (see Appendix 1 for peer-to-peer interviews).

One day in April, as I was walking into the programme, he zoomed up behind me, tapped me on one shoulder, and then ducked behind me so I would not see him. As I quickly turned around, he popped up in my face and rapped (shouted) the lyrics from rap artist Busta Rhymes 'Touch it Remix' (a popular rap at the time). Holding up each one of his fingers, he recited directly from the song:

Louis: Got Staten Island on my pinkie, Queens on my thumb, the Bronx on my middle finger screamin' fuck you. Rock ice in Manhattan so there's the ring finger, you know I had to keep Brooklyn on the trigger finger, five boroughs of death, you don't understand—

Pushing his hand away, I teased him over the noise. 'What's wrong with you?! You're crazy!' He shouted back a phrase from the song: 'Touch it!', and, doing a hand sign, ran off into the building.

The significance of place in hip-hop's cultural practices cannot be overstated. Reworking themes from gangs, including territoriality and collective identities, Forman (2000, p. 70) describes rap's 'pronounced and explicit connection to specific locales and the articulations of geography, place and identity that sets the genre apart'. He writes of hip-hop as 'a geo-cultural amalgamation of personages and practices that are spatially dispersed' (p. 65). Rap music actively constructs localities – commonly, the five boroughs of New York City – through stories told through lyrics, mythic biographies, and fierce territoriality. The 'Touch it Remix', which Louis recited, provides an example of representations of the boroughs as either very dangerous (Brooklyn) or wealthy (in this rap, Manhattan is represented by 'ice' or diamonds on the ring finger).

That said, again, the youth did not take representations of the boroughs whole-sale and simply apply them to localities. Rather, in this case, young people spoke of a dialogue between VMC and the social conditions of locality itself. For example, Freddie spoke to me about the rap artist 50 Cent:

K:       So he's [50 Cent] a, do you think he is a proper gangster?
Freddie: Well he came from Jamaica Queens that's the, he came from the hardcore side—

In this excerpt, Freddie suggests a relationship between the toughness of 50 Cent as a rapper, his *authenticity* as a proper gangster (i.e. struggle on the streets is part of a rapper's credibility), and the 'hardcore side' of Queens. Here, the physical and social conditions of the locality construct the VMC itself. In the next excerpt, talking about New York localities, Freddie describes this relationship in the reverse:

Freddie: To be honest there's like the strongest side. I'm gonna say it that way... It's probably the west side and the east side... [that's] stronger.

K:        Are you talking Manhattan or are you talking all five boroughs?
Freddie: Well I think the hard, the hardest borough either be Queens or Brooklyn—
K:        Not the Bronx?
Freddie: Well yeah Bronx too because they got, you know they got, TS Terror
          Squad [rap group] and my man 50 [rapper] no not 50, Fat Joe [rapper]—

In Box 4.2 is a further example of the dialogue between aspects of place and
VMC. In this case, Gabe is talking about the struggle of one of his favourite rappers.

---

**Box 4.2**  Gabe Talks About Rapper Cameron

K:        What's his [rapper Cameron's] story?
Gabe:  Cameron? His story is like how he was raised in Harlem—
K:        He was raised in Harlem?
Gabe:  He went through a lot in Harlem. Harlem is no joke, and, I mean no
          joke! No joke. If they don't know you they'll shoot you. They will just
          stare at you with a mean face. They'll kill you.

---

Localities, here the boroughs, were constructed as dangerous, poor, or wealthy,
drawing on VMC, aspects of a local place, and connectedly, on the individual social
conditions which the youth lived in and through. The youth would often move
between representations of places found in rap music, films, and other media, and
their own lived experiences. For example, as Valentina described the Bronx as
dangerous, Shanti replied, 'It is not so bad, my sister live there'. Boroughs were also
constructed through a discussion of style:

K:        What do you think New York style is?
Abigail: Well it depends on what borough are you in.
K:        Okay for Brooklyn.
Abigail: Ghetto.
K:        Ghetto style and what about Bronx?
Abigail: Ghetto.
K:        Manhattan?
Abigail: It's not fair, it's so general,
K:        Lower East Side?
Abigail: Ghetto.
K:        And what about upper Manhattan?
Abigail: Classy.

Almost mirroring the words of Busta Rhymes in the 'Touch it Remix' recited by
Louis, Abigail's description of places through the medium of style is infused with
issues of class: not only is upper Manhattan dress 'classy'; her reference to ghetto
style is also significant. Specifically, the concept of ghetto and indeed ghetto style,
derived from hip-hop vernacular and signified through the baggy pants for boys and
tight dress styles for girls (as described earlier), is a fundamentally classed concept

where anyone claiming an authentic ghetto style will, for the young people, have to first experience difficult (usually poor) urban living. At the same time, class was ultimately tied to race: the poorer boroughs and areas of New York, where ghetto style was popular, were ubiquitously black and Latina/Latino – this was both a statistical reality (i.e. blacks and Latinas/Latinos inhabited much of Brooklyn, the Bronx, Queens, and the Lower East Side of Manhattan) and something propagated by rap narratives (Forman, 2000).[5]

Classing the boroughs and reference to the ghetto and ghetto style point to the complexity of place-making, where the 'imagined communities' (Anderson, 1983) created by the youth at the nexus of lived experience, social conditions of place, and narratives and cultural practices associated with VMC overlapped, informed, and constituted each other. Using VMC, communities including New York as a whole, the five boroughs, and smaller areas were, as Forman (2000, p. 83) writes, 'simultaneously real, imaginary, symbolic, and mythical'.

## *'My Neighbor-HOOD': The 'Hood and the Ghetto*

The youth drew on VMC not only to construct places you might find on a map but also to imagine conceptual places, including the ghetto and the 'hood. Both of these places found their way into the vocabulary and expressive practices of the young people, and, in part, find roots (and routes) in, once again, hip-hop's cultural practices. Used in the young people's daily vernacular, their constructions of these iconic places can be mapped onto meanings generated through representations of the 'hood and ghetto in VMC, most pointedly in hip-hop where the 'hood originated and where the 'ghetto' and 'ghetto style' have been 'commodified' (Quinn, 2005). Forman (2000) writes about the difference between the 'hood and ghetto in the context of rap artist Eazy-E's 'Boyz-in-the-Hood', which introduced the 'hood into rap's spatial discourses:

> [Rap] conceive[d] of the ghetto landscape as a generalised abstract concept, as space. The introduction of the 'hood, however, also adds a localised nuance to the notion of space that conveys a certain proximity, effectively capturing a narrowed sense of place… (p. 77)

Reworked through their own experiences, yet resonating with Eazy-E's construction, youth described the 'hood as *their* territory or place, where an immediate and/or extended family lived, where their homes, schools, and churches were. The 'hood suggested feelings of belonging or 'attachment' (Hall, 1997, p. 2) and 'loyalty to a place' (Lovell, 1998, p. 1). While I was at the Hope, a popular hip-hop song was 'My Hood' by rap artist Young Jeezy. The song's video features images of the artists 'doin' good for the 'hood'; black and Latina/Latino neighbourhood

---

[5] Louis, for example, expressed surprise when I told him I worked in both Harlem and the South Bronx. Laughing, he told me about how his sister lives in Harlem and he in the Bronx. He said whenever he sees a person like me (i.e. white) in the Bronx or Harlem, he 'thinks two things: they are either on crack or lost'.

**Fig. 4.1** Youth still photography; postcards illustrating participants' ''hoods' (Images used with permission from youth in this study)

youth dance in the streets; and cross-generational depictions communicate and construct the 'hood rap artists come from, 'represent', and serve. The youth drew on these themes from hip-hop as well as on their own experiences to construct the 'hood and make sense of their own locality.

A project the youth engaged in during the study was still photography, the product of which we sometimes referred to as postcards (see Appendix 1). Asked to photograph things illustrating their lives, all of the young people took images of their communities, apartments, local subway stops, playgrounds, pizza places, churches, and sites that represented and constituted their worlds (see Fig. 4.1). The youth would describe these images as their 'hood or – as Jeremy told me of the 'hood – their 'hometown'.

Though Freddie's 'hood would sometimes switch from the Bronx where he used to live to Spanish Harlem where he now lived, he had two photographs which he referred to as his 'hood. One featured graffiti on a wall in his apartment building which said 'Harlem' and the other was a photograph out his bedroom window which he titled for the final exhibition, 'My Neighbor-HOOD'. I asked him about the 'hood in an interview:

K:          One of your pictures was called 'My Neighbor-HOOD', what does the 'hood mean to you?
Freddie: Well like where you live and... like where you know a lot of people, Spanish Harlem.
K:          It's not a bad thing?
Freddie: No it's not.

In hip-hop, '[t]he 'hood is... regularly constructed within the discursive frame of the "home"' (Forman, 2000, p. 72). The youth too would refer to the 'hood as the place where they felt the most connection, where people knew them. For instance, despite coming to school every day in Manhattan, 13-year-old Ramona, who identified as Puerto Rican and spoke fluent Spanish, described her 'hood as the Bronx where she lived and went to church every Sunday. It was in the Bronx that people knew her and where, at church, old family acquaintances would hug her tightly and say in Spanish, '*Tu eres mi corazon, mi amor*' or as she translated for me, 'You're my heart, my love'.

Though the youth sometimes conflated the ghetto and the 'hood, when asked pointedly the difference, the ghetto was considered an abstract, sometimes a violent place. Speaking to me about the distinction between the two, Latoya told me that 'the 'hood is like a lot, like people, average people, doing normal stuff, but sometimes people get into fights'. The ghetto, on the other hand, she referred to as 'gangsta town' where 'it's worse, they fight almost every single day'.

For the young people, the ghetto carried meanings of poverty, criminality, gangs, and violence – meanings which can be traced back to the commodification of ghetto in the hip-hop genre of gangsta rap, where the imagery and lyrics are 'ghettocentric' (Quinn, 2005, p. 3)[6] – centred on the social difficulties, physical environment, and tough survivalist character of the ghetto and its inhabitants. Used abstractly and symbolically, 'ghetto' was a pervasive spatial idiom and an organising tool the youth used to make sense of their world. I will continue to come back to the idea of ghetto in the chapters to come, but for now, underline that at the Hope, 'ghetto' was deployed as a noun, adjective, and verb; it described places, styles, behaviours, people, food, images. It was raced as black and Latina/Latino, classed as poor, and changed shape, depending on the usage. Overall, the ghetto was a powerful narrative, a concept whose material roots spawned an imagined community, but whose branches have stretched beyond any recognisable form of community – however far we stretch our imaginations.

---

[6] Quinn (2005) notes the term 'ghettocentric' was first used by Nelson George in his 1991 article for the *Village Voice* called 'ghettocentricity' later reprinted in 1994: *Buppies, B-Boys, and Bohos: Notes on a Post-Soul Black Culture* (New York: Harper Collins).

## *'In Puerto Rico You Just Go Free': Constructing Homeland*

'Homeland', another spatial concept threaded through the data, was often linked to racial identities (see Chap. 5) and was constituted of family, memories, and forms of VMC that originated in a particular place. Two main concepts that continued to come up in young people's talk about homeland included cultural expression and freedom. In the first instance, the youth primarily conceived of their homeland through forms of cultural expression, for example, dance, music, and connected material forms that found their roots in a particular place. Latrice, for example, spoke about *Soca* music from Trinidad:

Latrice: I love Reggae, love Soca, and it really makes me, pisses me off [angers me] when I'm like listening to the radio and everything and they're like what are you listening to and I'm like Soca—

K:       Who says that?

Latrice: A lot of people. Some people at my school and this one girl in particular and I'm like 'it's Soca' and she's like 'what?' And I'm like 'you claim to be Trinidadian and everything but you don't know what Soca is?'

K:       Where did you hear the music first?

Latrice: Um, my mom. . . cause my mom she's Trinidadian so she plays it a lot and I got attached to it, I love it—

Youth homelands were often equated with 'their culture', a concept the youth conflated with race, and, often, with embodied VMC (rap artists, actors, and the like) that they claimed 'represented' their culture. For example, in a discussion with Freddie about his collage, which he made as part of this study, he connected 'his culture' and Puerto Rico (place) through forms of VMC, telling me that the rap artist Fat Joe 'represented' his culture. After telling me this, he pointed to an image on his collage and said, 'and now that we brought up Puerto Rico this is Daddy Yankee [rap artist]' (see Appendix 2 for sample collages). Freddie's reference to Daddy Yankee and Puerto Rico highlights *Reggaeton* (Latino rap music) as a popular form of VMC which was part of Latina/Latino youths' constructions of both Puerto Rico and the Dominican Republic. As Freddie explained, Reggaeton began, in part, with the work of Daddy Yankee and reminded him of Puerto Rico.

Other forms of cultural expression which, for the youth, represented belonging and loyalty to a place included flags and other symbolic forms of VMC; sitting with young people drawing, images would often turn into Dominican or Puerto Rican flags – these flags at once representing and constructing places. The youth described homelands as places filled with memories and experience, places where they belonged and where families remained. Freddie spoke about how photographs of his cousins reminded him of Puerto Rico. VMC such as photos of family and friends were not simply ways to remember people but served as reminders (and constituents) of homelands.

As mentioned, homeland was also expressed through the idiom of freedom, which included being trusted, being safe, and a feeling of freedom that the youth connected with the physical landscape. Within the context of freedom, the youth constructed homelands in opposition to New York. Freedom was connected with the affordances of the physical and sociocultural landscape. Valentina spoke in depth about the feeling of freedom she had in Argentina, where much of her family lives.

Valentina: Over there I feel like I have more freedom because over here [New York] I can't go anywhere by myself, and over there I can go anywhere by myself.

Certain freedoms were allowed in certain places. Ramona described how the physical landscape contributed to her feelings of freedom:

Ramona: Yes. Every time I go to Puerto Rico, I feel free. Like New York is free, but like things are happening so much that I don't trust it that much. My parents, nobody trusts it. Like so many things have happened, but Puerto Rico the heat with the beautiful trees and the water, the sand. Every time I've think about it, I think of freedom.

The physicality of places also afforded and constrained the use of forms of VMC such as style – landscapes were, in a sense, 'inscribed onto bodies' (Lovell, 1998, p. 10). For the girls in particular, the construction of homeland and the expression of freedom that defined it were often associated with what they could and could not wear in certain places. Ramona, who generally dressed in either tight jeans and a T-shirt or a loose velour sweatsuit, associated components of place and style:

Ramona: Here [New York] you have to wear your sneakers, you have to wear your shoes, like in Puerto Rico you just go free. Like you don't have wear your shoes. And the streets is clear, streets are very clear.

Girls spoke about the clothing they would wear when they were in their homeland. Latoya, who was part Colombian, spoke about fashion and its relation to place; she told me how, in Colombia, 'they dress anything, shorts, capris, sneakers, sandals'.

Together with forms of VMC, it seemed these imagined communities – these symbolic, material, and abstract places – including New York, the five boroughs, the 'hood, the ghetto, and the homelands were, in part, the cultural artefacts that mediated aspects of the young people's identities: as young people produced these imagined communities, they simultaneously used them to make sense and produce their *place-based* identities – identities which were dependent on the physical and sociocultural conditions of place itself.

## Place-Based Identities

The youth not only used various forms of VMC to produce and make sense of the imagined communities which made up their world, but in the process of this construction – in the process of representation – it could be argued that young people constructed place-based or place-specific identities. By place-based identities I mean identifications with certain imagined communities where one feels a sense of attachment or loyalty and/or feelings of belonging (Hall, 1996; Lovell, 1998; Savage, Bagnall, & Longhurst, 2005). By using the term place-based identities, I am not suggesting that identities are completely 'rooted' in place, nor do I mean to suggest that places are necessarily 'bounded' communities (Edwards & Usher, 2000; Savage et al., 2005). Rather, I use the term within the conceptualisation of places as dynamic sites (Massey, 1993) that stretch as far as the discourses and practices which continue to construct and define them.

At the Hope, almost all of the young people I worked with identified as New Yorkers, and all were born in New York or came to the city at a young age. New York was their place, a place they actively created and identified with, and a place with family and friends, personally significant neighbourhoods and institutions. In the following section, I illustrate aspects of place-based identity construction, including 'representing', and the expression of place-based identities through cultural practices, including the production of visual forms through participation in this study.

## *'You gotta represent': Expressing (and Creating) Place-Based Identities*

The youth drew on VMC, in particular from various hip-hop practices, in the construction of their place-based identities; a primary practice the youth engaged in was 'representing' or 'representin'.

Ten-year-old Jeremy knew a lot about music, rap artists' stories, fashion, and VMC more generally. Though he was often around, I did not work closely with him until a few months into the study.[7] Originally from Brooklyn, at the time of this study, Jeremy lived in an apartment near the Hope with five family members and a family friend. He had a twin brother and an older brother who 'taught him everything'. Short and heavyset with braided black hair, he rapped and danced and was feisty and friendly. Jeremy explained to me what it meant to represent:

Jeremy: [L]et's say any town that you was born and raised there, you'll always represent where you was from. You gotta represent. If you was from the Bronx you be like, 'Oh the Bronx is hot'. You know you be like that unless you move to Manhattan then you be like 'Oh Bronx is where I'm from' all the time.

---

[7] From the time I started at the Hope, I would see Jeremy hanging around, and he would often ask: 'Yo, come on Kris, can't I work wit you?' While I would have been happy to say yes, he was in a group much younger than Timo's, and I was not sure if I would have the resources to work with him on a video. I would usually say that he could hang around with me, but that I didn't know if we would have time to do a video together. Yet, he was persistent, and as we started to work together more closely, I came to recognise Jeremy as kind, mature, and one of the friendliest youth in the programme. Granted he was always getting into some kind of trouble, and though he told me at first he was 12 (and left back in school, and, therefore, in a younger group at the Hope) and later admitted he was 'about' ten (I believe he may have even been nine), to me he was irresistible.

Representing places is a distinguishing and well-established feature of rap music; hip-hop and rap is geographically mapped, and artists represent certain localities. Discussing the boroughs represented by various rappers, Freddie informed me, '50 Cent represents Queens, if I'm not mistaken the Game [rap group] represents Brooklyn'. Representing place and the performance of representin', particularly in the form of hand gestures and shout-outs (rappers, in performances, calling out the places they are from and owe tribute to) (Forman, 2000, p. 73), were a ubiquitous part of youth expressive practices. Reminiscent of rappers being interviewed on music television, when the camera was on, the youth would often jump in front of it and shout out to the imaginary audience 'Brooklyn!' or 'East Side'.

For his self-portrait, Jeremy superimposed himself against a community of rap artists and a wall of graffiti; as he stands among the artists, he is making a hand sign. I asked him about this and its relation to the importance of place:

Jeremy: This Eastside Ridaz [pointing to the hand sign he is making in the self-portrait] cause you know I'm on the east side right now.
K:       You live on the east side?
Jeremy: Yeah. But I am from Brooklyn I would have had a sign for Brooklyn but you know, I didn't figure out one.
K:       Do you think it's important to know like where people are from...
Jeremy: It's not important, but you know we have to represent our 'hood you know.

The Eastside Ridaz Jeremy mentions is one of the Cripp gangs in California and the name of a rap by artist Snoop Dogg. Hand signs are a part of rap aesthetics, appropriated from gangs and ultimately used by the young people in this study. Several salient points can be made about representing with respect to place and place-based identity-making: first, it seems representing (e.g. doing a hand sign or giving a shout-out) was a performative act which constructed place-based identities – by drawing on this tool from VMC, young people were not only performing place-based identities but producing their identities by expressing membership and belonging to a social and material space. As described in Chap. 2, as artefacts, including cultural practices drawn from VMC, are used and internalised by individuals, they become part of their own means of engagement with the world, as well as part of selves.

Second, in representing, the youth were not naming 'real' or 'essential' places, but rather, the places they named were a gloss for the localities, the 'hoods – imagined communities – they continually produced and maintained at the intersection of individual and collective biographies, VMC, and material conditions of place. The Brooklyn that Jeremy represented and expressed belonging to was not the Brooklyn that my sister, who lived there for many years, might have represented (a place which took her away from crowded Manhattan living). Like my sister's Brooklyn, Jeremy's Brooklyn was created from the unique position of himself and his peers who, perhaps, have had similar sociocultural experiences: a Brooklyn imagined through forms of VMC, including style and hip-hop practices, and a Brooklyn where he may have lived in difficult conditions (or not). The imagined communities the youth shouted out such as 'Harlem' were themselves cultural artefacts: polysemic spaces, which, as fast as they were constructed, simultaneously mediated the construction of the youth's own place-based identities.

Finally, the youth did not take the hand signs and shout-outs straight from VMC, but drew on the representational practices and performances from hip-hop to create their own expressions. Jeremy would have liked to have represented Brooklyn, his 'hood, but could not 'figure one out' at that moment. What is more, the reworking of these forms was dependent on the material and social aspects of localities, and on those symbolically figured worlds the youth lived in and through. For instance, while young people in Barlow, Canada, where I later carried out fieldwork, also gave shout-outs, they did not repeat the New York localities of rappers (I never heard a young person in Barlow shout out 'Brooklyn'); rather, they drew on the global east/west division in rap music and put a local spin on it. Barlow youth often repeated the following shout-out with accompanying hand signs: 'east side, west side, —side' where the third place cited was the name of an important First Nations' heritage site. Moreover, in both sites, representation of place, and hence the means of place-based identity construction, was more than shout-outs and hand signs. Looking at the Hope specifically, young people engaged in various expressive practices in the construction of their place-based identities (including dance, style, and the like). These practices were directly linked to the constituent practices the youth cited in the production of places themselves.

Through participation in this study, including using visual media such as photography and video, these expressive practices were made more visible. All young people produced various images, raps, and videos that expressed and produced place-based identities. Jeremy often told me of his hopes to break into the rap business. He kept a book of raps and, similar to rap artists, he created a persona for himself: 'Nice'. His video was self-titled: Nice Raps – his play on words and self-promotion are a typical practice of rappers (Quinn, 2005).

Jeremy wrote a number of raps while I was there, many of which he performed in his video. A particularly salient one for this discussion follows:

Jeremy: I was born and raised in New York,
       you know that's where I'm from.
       Though Brooklyn style always keeps it crunk,
       you know I gotta stay fresh to death,
       looking good for my girl.
       I always gotta have my hair
       in some kinda curl.
       That's how New York do,
       we don't play.
       Mess around with me and my crew
       and we will come to your house
       and you gonna pay.

Jeremy's rap (and video) describes three themes or practices found in youth expressions of place-based identities: (1) representing 'hood and belonging – in Jeremy's work, this is evident in his claim to be from a certain place; (2) representing through action, description, or citation, the practices of the particular locality – Jeremy rapped about 'Brooklyn style' and noted 'that's how New York do'; and (3), using common expressive forms from hip-hop to produce identity and place – Jeremy used the form and performance of a rap in his own video where lyrics and content are based on various songs which he reworked into his own.

These three themes can be found woven through the visual forms the youth produced through this study. For example, looking at representing the 'hood and belonging, 11-year-old Tonya's video titled 'Nikki's Crazy Life' (a name she made up for herself) features her in what she calls her 'hood, 'being crazy', stopping in all the 'local' places such as the local McDonald's, the pizza place, and the video shop. Tonya, who identified as Puerto Rican and described herself as 'untameable, crazy, and wild', lived in the East Village with her mother and attended one of the Catholic schools in the area. Tonya's video around the East Village is at once a means of representing her local place, her 'hood which she calls home, an expression of belonging to place, and an act of representing, of paying tribute to, and of making claims to place. It could be argued that, in and through this video, Tonya expressed her place-based identity as well as made sense of and produced the 'hood itself, an imagined community produced, in part, through themes from hip-hop.

Touching on the second practice (i.e. representing through action the cultural practices of locality), the youth created numerous images of themselves, engaging in the same practices they used to construct the locality of New York, practices often drawn from hip-hop. Louis, for instance, was learning to breakdance from his older sister, and graffiti 'reminded him of the city'. For his self-portrait, he asked me to photograph him in a breakdance pose. He and I then superimposed this photograph onto a background of graffiti from the East Village in Manhattan. In this portrait, Louis put himself in the imagined community of New York youth produced, and at the same time, through engagement in the practices which constituted place (here, breakdancing and graffiti), he was performing his own place-based identity.

Latrice's video work also represented belonging and was an amalgamation of the cultural practices that described or represented the imagined communities important to young people, including, for example, New York and their homeland. Her video is threaded through with various themes, focusing on place: she did two freestyle poems (one about New York and the other about Trinidad), gave the audience 'tips for girls living in New York', and told an imaginary audience – 'Oh and we have this thing that we do in New York' – before breaking into a localised version of a particular dance step to the words of a popular hip-hop song at the time – 'Lean wit it, Rock wit it'. Examining the third theme (i.e. using expressive forms from hip-hop itself such as raps), in Latrice's video, she not only cited and engaged in the cultural practices of locality; she simultaneously drew on forms from hip-hop, including freestyle poems and dance, as tools which arguably constructed and enabled her to perform and express her own place-based identity.

In the creation of these projects, and in the process, creating a narrative of self in place, young people used expressive means of identification drawn from forms of VMC, which, at the Hope, included dance, rap, video pastiche, music clips, and stylised editing found in music videos (Holland et al., 1998). As Hannerz (1983,

p. 356) theorises with reference to identity, all of these expressive practices that youth recorded, including style, dance, naming, and interacting in your 'hood, were not simply products or recordings of self and place, but were unique cultural forms and 'account[s] of a process' of self- and place-making.

## Imagined Places, Imagined Selves

In this chapter, I have described ways in which the youth used VMC, in particular, themes and cultural practices from hip-hop to construct the places intersecting their lives, as well as to produce and perform their place-based identities. Drawing on Holland et al.'s (1998) figured worlds and Anderson's (1983) imagined communities, I began to suggest that the places the youth created, traversed, and belonged to were not essential or primordial, but rather processual: constructed through mediated practice using available cultural artefacts such as VMC. I have also thought about imagined communities as a kind of cultural artefact the youth at once constructed and used in the creation of place-based identities – identities that belonged to the places they imagine. Finally, I have started to illustrate that VMC is lived and performed (Dimitriadis, 2001): through representational and performative means the youth expressed identification with imagined communities as well as produced places themselves. I end by probing this final point: thinking about the mutual production of place and place-based identities using VMC.

In the last section on place-based identities, I alluded to an 'interpenetration' (Robinson, 2000, p. 431) of self and place mediated through representational means and through engagement in cultural practices informed by VMC. Massey (1993) describes links between human relations, space, and place: places are 'malleable, temporal, and complex' (Robinson, p. 431), produced by active agents; place and identities are wholly interrelated. People construct and (re)produce places, and the places we produce are unique – dependent on people, physical geography, and social conditions. Further, places and people are in continual transformation: social (inter)actions are constitutive of place, and places constrain and enable the social (inter)actions that take place. This interconnection between place, space, and people is central to Henri Lefebvre's work, which brings together 'cultural practices, representations, and imaginations' (Hubbard et al., 2004, p. 5; see also Soja, 1999). Places are unique spaces 'created through acts of naming as well as the distinctive activities and imaginings associated with particular social spaces' (Hubbard et al., p. 5). In this sense, places, arguably, are also a 'locus for identity' (Hubbard et al., p. 5). As Nayak (2003), also discussing Lefebvre (1974/2001, p. 162), writes, 'the multiple ways in which spaces are imagined represents a means of living in those spaces'. He further states that '"place" shape[s] youth identities, but also youth identities shape and influence the character of places' (p. 28).

It could be argued that this shaping is done, in part, through the body: through the body we live, make sense of, and create place. Indeed, Lefebvre's and Nayak's works point to this lived and performative use of VMC and support an understanding of the mutual constitution of place and place-based identities: as the youth in this study used certain forms of VMC to imagine localities, as they performed and lived the various forms through behaviour, actions such as shout-outs, and style, they at once produced the imagined communities that defined them and defined the imagined communities that produced them.

That said, while these perspectives allow me to conceive of the youth as active producers of place, sociocultural theories and perspectives help deepen an understanding of the role of VMC in this process. Holland et al. (1998, p. 251) describe a 'codevelopment' between people and their figured worlds. This codevelopment is made possible through the use of (webs of) mediating cultural artefacts such as VMC, discourses, narratives, and language (Cole, 1996). That is, artefacts connect people and place, including the figured worlds making up places. As people use cultural artefacts, they at once create themselves and aspects of their worlds.

In sociocultural theories, person, place, and culture (i.e. cultural artefacts which include cultural processes and practices and their products) are mutually constitutive and in continuous transformation (Cole, 1996). Cultural artefacts, including VMC, are internalised by people, reused, and reworked. In this research, it seemed that in place and place-based identity-making, cultural artefacts included forms, themes, and practices from VMC that were picked up by the youth and lived and performed in everyday practice. In this performance, in this use, there was a mutual construction and constitution of localised social space (place), including figured worlds and place-based identities. For example, as Jeremy represented his 'hood through shout-outs and hand signs derived from VMC, he not only produced his place-based identity, but through his (mediated) action, he constituted the world around him. Practices drawn from VMC, in this case shout-outs, served as the glue and the medium between person and place. At last, youth in this study did not simply reproduce communities but (re)constructed places and selves at the intersection of sociocultural and physical conditions of place, their own collective and individual biographies, and inspiration or 'possibilities' (Appadurai, 1991) found and lived through VMC.

# References

Anderson, B. (1983). *Imagined communities: Reflections on the origin and spread of nationalism.* London: Verso.

Appadurai, A. (1990). Disjuncture and difference in the global cultural economy. *Theory, Culture & Society, 7,* 295–310.

Appadurai, A. (1991). Global ethnoscapes: Notes and queries for a transnational anthropology. In R. G. Fox (Ed.), *Recapturing anthropology: Working in the present* (pp. 191–210). Santa Fe, NM: School of American Research Press.

Cole, M. (1996). *Cultural psychology: A once and future discipline.* Cambridge, MA: Harvard University Press.

Dimitriadis, G. (2001). *Performing identity/performing culture: Hip hop as text, pedagogy, and lived practice.* New York: Peter Lang Publishing.

Edwards, R., & Usher, R. (2000). *Globalization and pedagogy.* London: Routledge.

Forman, M. (2000). 'Represent': Race, space and place in rap music. *Popular Music, 19*(1), 65–90.

Gupta, A., & Ferguson, J. (1997a). Culture, power, place: Ethnography at the end of an era. In A. Gupta & J. Ferguson (Eds.), *Culture, power, place: Explorations in critical anthropology* (pp. 1–29). Durham, NC: Duke University Press.

Gupta, A., & Ferguson, J. (1997b). Beyond 'culture': Space, identity, and the politics of difference. In A. Gupta & J. Ferguson (Eds.), *Culture, power, place: Explorations in critical anthropology* (pp. 33–51). Durham, NC: Duke University Press.

Hall, S. (1996). Introduction: Who needs identity? In P. Du Gay & S. Hall (Eds.), *Questions of cultural identity* (pp. 1–11). London: Sage.

Hall, S. (1997). *Representation: Cultural representations and signifying practices*. London: Sage.

Hannerz, U. (1983). Tools of identity and imagination. In A. Jacobson-Widding (Ed.), *Identity: Personal and socio-cultural. A symposium* (pp. 347–360). Atlantic Highlands, NJ: Distributed by Almquist & Wiksell International/Humanities Press [distributor].

Holland, D., Lachicotte, W., Skinner, D., & Cain, C. (1998). *Identity and agency in cultural worlds*. Cambridge, MA: Harvard University Press.

Hubbard, P., Kitchin, R. M., & Valentine, G. (2004). Editor's introduction. In P. Hubbard, R. M. Kitchin, & G. Valentine (Eds.), *Key thinkers on space and place*. London: Sage.

Lefebvre, H. (1974/1991). *The production of space*. Oxford, UK: Blackwell.

Lovell, N. (1998). *Locality and belonging*. London: Routledge.

Massey, D. (1993). Power-geometry and a progressive sense of place. In J. Bird, B. Curtis, T. Putnam, G. Robertson, & L. Tickner (Eds.), *Mapping the futures: Local cultures, global change* (pp. 59–69). London: Routledge.

Nayak, A. (2003). *Race, place and globalization: Youth cultures in a changing world*. Oxford, UK: Berg.

Quinn, E. (2005). *Nuthin' but a 'G' thang: The culture and commerce of gangsta rap*. New York: Columbia University Press.

Robinson, C. (2000). Creating space, creating self: Street-frequenting youth in the city and suburbs. *Journal of Youth Studies, 4*(4), 429–443.

Rose, T. (1994a). A style nobody can deal with: Politics, style and the postindustrial city in hip hop. In A. Ross & T. Rose (Eds.), *Microphone fiends: Youth music & youth culture* (pp. 71–88). New York: Routledge.

Rose, T. (1994b). *Black noise: Rap music and Black culture in contemporary America*. Hanover, NH: Wesleyan University Press.

Sassen, S. (2007). *A sociology of globalization. Contemporary societies series*. New York: W. W. Norton.

Savage, M., Bagnall, G., & Longhurst, B. (2005). *Globalization and belonging*. London: Sage.

Soja, E. (1999). Thirdspace: Expanding the scope of the geographical imagination. In D. Massey, J. Allen, & P. Sarre (Eds.), *Human geography today* (pp. 261–278). Cambridge, UK: Polity Press.

# Chapter 5
# (Re)constructing Race: Racial Identities and the Borders of Race

## Introduction

Figured worlds, those cultural spaces we construct, and are constructed by, are not only intersected by and constituted of various places where life is played out, but also by powerful sociocultural themes and discursive formations. Themes such as race, gender, sexual orientation, and social class can, in a sense, be construed as figured worlds in themselves as well as key identification categories – uniting and dividing us, shaping, framing, and colouring our everyday (inter)actions. In this chapter, I focus on race and describe three intertwined cultural processes suggested by the data: (1) young people made sense of and constructed racial identities and difference through the deployment of 'racialised' forms of VMC, including those cultural artefacts and practices the youth associated with particular racial groups. (2) In order to maintain difference and reinforce 'boundaries' or 'borders' (used interchangeably) of racial identities, the youth used VMC to construct, claim, and invoke a particular form of authenticity. (3) The unique intersection of authenticity, VMC, aspects of place, and youth experiences supported 'borderwork' or the crossing, blurring, reworking, or reconstructing of racial borders, and, connectedly, the production of new racial identities. I conclude with a theoretical discussion using the work of Homi K. Bhabha, linking together these interconnected processes of racial identity formation with the productive nexus where the youth, place, and VMC intersect.

## Constructing Racial Identities

The significance of race in the United States is magnified in New York City, where people claiming numerous racial identities dwell, work, and interact. At the Hope, it was not long before I recognised the salience of race in the lives of the youth I worked with: within the first week, 11-year-old Sonja, who attended one of the

K.A. Eglinton, *Youth Identities, Localities, and Visual Material Culture: Making Selves, Making Worlds*, Explorations of Educational Purpose 25, DOI 10.1007/978-94-007-4857-6_5, © Springer Science+Business Media Dordrecht 2013

local Catholic schools, told me she was part Puerto Rican, part Native American, part black, and 'something else, just a little pinch, but I can't talk about it'. When I asked her what, she whispered the word 'white'. Darting her eyes to the left where her neighbour sat, she followed with, 'But don't tell her'. When I asked her why she didn't want anyone to know, she exclaimed, 'Cause we was slaves! We was enslaved by them!' This time, she followed with, 'It was my grandma's daddy who was white, we pretend like she don't even have a daddy'.

The single biggest theme coming out of the data, my fieldnotes and trans-criptions are filled with thousands of references to racial types, links to VMC, and anecdotes. Also threaded through the data are entries about my own whiteness; in Box 5.1, I offer some reflections on my race as a researcher at the Hope; these reflections are drawn from several fieldnotes.

Exploring 'folk' theories of race and the intersection of class, Jackson (2001, p. 5) describes the biological, sociological, and performative constituents of race cited by black residents in Harlem, New York City. Biological aspects include physical characteristics such as skin colour; sociological aspects are associated with issues of inequality and discrimination, and performative aspects refer to ways of acting (see Warikoo, 2007, p. 390). Jackson writes about performance:

> You are not black because you are (in essence) black; you are black (in the folk logic of racial difference) because of how you act – and not just in terms of one sphere of behavio[u]r (say, intellectual achievement in school) but because of how you juggle and combine many differently raciali[s]ed and class(ed) actions (walking, talking, laughing, watching a movie, standing, emoting, partying) in an everyday matrix of performative possibilities. (p. 188)

While I found that the youth at the Hope also constructed race using biological and sociological themes, performance was the most commonly referred to constit-uent of racial identity. Youth would often describe someone as 'acting' black or white because of a particular gait or use of particular vernacular.

Intricately tied to performance, the primary sources the youth cited and used to produce and articulate the racial identities of both themselves and others were 'racialised' forms of VMC.[1] The most commonly cited racialised cultural artefacts and practices drawn on were from broad forms of VMC such as hip-hop and from 'embodied' and/or 'iconic' forms of VMC such as rap artists (see also in Dolby, 2001; Warikoo, 2007). Generally, for youth at the Hope racialised forms of VMC included styles and performances that young people associated with certain racial groups. Arguably, the association of these forms with particular racial groups was an outcome of the intersection of the youth, place, and VMC itself. For example, forms

---

[1] While race has been variously theorised and while some knowledges, such as scientific discourses that essentialise and fix race to static notions of culture, tend to wield power and dominate our everyday conceptualisation of social categories (Hall, 1997; Solomos & Back, 2000), young people continuously cited racialised forms of VMC as the main constituents of race. This is not to say that young people did not also draw on common discourses found in schools such as 'unity in diversity' (see also Archer, 2003) or, for example, on themes of racism and white superiority – as Freddie told me, 'it's racist to be white' – but rather that VMC was one of the primary ways youth constructed race as well as asserted their own racial identities.

**Box 5.1** Notes on My Racial Identity at the Hope

I am not sure why, but when I used to work in Harlem and the South Bronx, I was often mistaken for Latina. Just before Christmas break at the Hope, I was comfortably engaged in conversation with a group of girls. Flora from Puerto Rico casually turned to me and spoke in Spanish. I must have looked stunned because she immediately asked me, 'Aren't you Spanish? Don't you speak Spanish?' The moment she asked me, I felt like everything went into slow motion; I imagined all of the youth pointing at me shouting 'Gringa! Gringa! Gringa!' While the crisis seems comical now, at that moment, I felt like my connection to the young people would fall apart. I finally let out a shaky 'no.' 'What are you?' she asked. 'You're Colombian, right?' Latoya interjected. Unable to keep them guessing I laughed and said, 'What are you guys talking about? I'm white!' There was some surprise, a few raised eyebrows, but things seemed to settle quickly. Or so I thought: a few weeks later, as we worked on some collages, Louis shouted, 'Yo whitey, come over here!' We were now many weeks into the project. The young people knew I was white but never talked about it. That day, however, it was like breaking a dam. Most of the youth in Timo's group heard Louis say this. Some quickly looked down at their work, and I said to him using a half-angry/half-hurt tone I never took in this study except on this occasion, 'Don't say that.' It seemed Louis felt bad for about a second, but his remorse quickly left him and he followed with 'Okay, whitey.' As this was happening, Latoya was making things worse by saying, 'Ohhh did you hear what he called you?! He said whitey! He call her whitey!' Rather than showing how upset I was (i.e. devastated), and not knowing what to do, I cracked some weak joke about being 'slightly pale', and said to him, 'So I'm white, relax and stop shouting at me.' Thankfully, there was some laughter in the room. After that moment, the youth openly talked to me about my being white and about what whiteness meant to them. Many youths spent time telling me what I could and could not say as a white person (e.g. the n-word or *nigga*) or teasing me about how white I sounded. The term 'whitey' stuck, though not in a negative way, rather, I think it illustrated their comfort with me. In fact, it seemed from that moment, my whiteness for me and the young people was a space of exploration, irony, and good-humoured teasing.

   Sources (FN121505; FN011006)

of VMC considered 'white' at the Hope were 'racially neutral' in Barlow, Yukon. Additionally, the character and history of particular forms of VMC lent themselves to particular racialisations. For instance, the racialisation of hip-hop as black was propagated by the form itself, where a hip-hop artist's credibility often hinged on his or her being able to claim a black identity (Hess, 2005).

   In this study, I conceptualised performances drawn from VMC, including ways of acting and behaving, as cultural artefacts or 'cultural scripts' (Holland, Lachicotte,

Skinner, & Cain, 1998) that mediated action. Racialised artefacts and practices that the youth cited such as style and dance were at once VMC in and of themselves and constituents of larger VMC forms such as hip-hop, depending on how they were used and what form they took. Because of this complexity, the terms 'VMC' and 'cultural artefact(s)' are often used interchangeably.

In the following section, I describe the ways in which the youth deployed racialised cultural artefacts to construct the white, black, and Latina/Latino identities of both themselves and others (these are the only three racial identities the youth at the Hope referred to during the study).

## *'Oh, I'll never be that white': Constructing White Identities*

By the time the video-making part of the study was in full swing, it looked as if my role was more like a production assistant than a research project facilitator. In early March, Tonya and Latrice decided to start filming their video. Walking through entanglements of cool young people nestled in corners of the stairwell, we found an empty classroom on the second floor where we could discuss their video. Latrice talked excitedly about how she would examine her 'hard shell', issues with her father, and the ways in which her identity has changed over the course of her life. Tonya, meanwhile, was doing her favourite monologue from the movie *Mean Girls* for the camera; together, the girls soon decided to film a scene that would find its way into both of their videos. In this scene, the girls improvised accusing each other of (potential) sexual involvement with a boy in the class. The clip ends with the girls on the floor, pretending to beat each other up.

After filming, we went outside where Tonya and Latrice ran up to a group of girls and started screaming about their video. The other girls listened as Tonya and Latrice gave an account of the filming; when it came to the fight scene, they begged me to show it on my camera. Twelve girls gathered around the tiny screen. When the fight was in full swing, they all started shouting and laughing. Tonya said that 'this was the most exciting thing' she had 'ever done', and then said matter-of-factly, 'Yeah, we were acting really dramatic, like white. We were acting really white'.

The youth in the study constructed white people as acting 'perky', 'happy', 'snobby', 'nerdy', or 'chilled', like a relaxed California 'surfer dude'. Forms of VMC were racialised and connected to white identities: many of the youth cited rock music and heavy metal as 'white' music. The 'surfer accent' and lexicon were used to describe white males, and the California 'Valley Girl' was described as a white female accent (hereafter, surfer and Valley Girl accents will be referred to as white accents).

Probing the construction of whiteness, I asked Latoya, Shanti, and Valentina what it meant to 'act white', a phrase I often heard the young people use. In the following excerpt, the girls draw on VMC, citing various racially identified cultural artefacts such as the behaviour and vernacular they associated with white identities.

In doing so, the girls describe a quintessential type of whiteness as it was constructed by most youth at the Hope:

Valentina: That's easy 'oh my God, oh my God whatcha doing?' [white accent].

. . .

Latoya:     If they're acting white? 'Oh my God, like Vale don't talk to me like that like—' [white accent]

. . .

Latoya:     'I'm having a bitch fit!' [Valentina and Latoya start screaming].
K:          But that's from *White Chicks*! [A movie in which two black FBI agents go undercover posing as white heiresses. All laughing].
Latoya:     Well they *are* white!

. . .

Latoya:     They talk perky, preppy—

. . .

Valentina: I say 'like' all the time, but I don't talk in a perky voice and I'm not always like 'let's go shopping!!' [white accent]

. . .

K:          Do you think all white girls act like that?
Latoya:     Some.
Valentina: Some. Cause I know some that don't.

Several interconnected points can be raised from this excerpt: first, the practices the youth at the Hope cited to index whiteness were not composed of essential biological traits – fixed and organic – but rather practices and artefacts drawn, in part, from VMC. As the girls described this performance of whiteness, there was the sense that it was akin to clothing one could put on or shed (see also Dolby, 2001, p. 2). The girls did not cite these performances as a gloss for all white people but acknowledged that only *some* white people acted this way. They were not necessarily creating stereotypes but were perhaps citing a frame of reference, an index of what it meant to 'act white' in their figured world.

Second, connected to this, it could be argued that forms of VMC were not only racialised but that VMC mediated young people's understanding of whiteness more broadly – provided a 'model' of whiteness. When representing whiteness, young people would often summon the iconic personalities of embodied forms of VMC such as the white heiress Paris Hilton, rather than simply describing, say, a white Hope staff member from their daily lives. Bringing these two points together, Tonya and Latrice spoke about the movie *Mean Girls*:

Tonya:   I know I love that movie. I love Rachel McAdams, she reminds me of myself because I know once I get in high school I'll probably be like that—
Latrice:  I know, I know I'll be like, 'Yo move!'
Tonya:   She's like, 'I love your bracelet where did you get it?' [white accent].
Latrice:  Oh, I'll never be that white... [repeats under breath] I'll never be that white—

As the girls described the actions and language that constituted a broad form of whiteness of the lead 'mean girl' played by white actress Rachel McAdams, Latrice reflected on her own racial performance. Latrice was happy to identify with the character played by Rachel McAdams when Tonya described how tough she was in high school; however, the moment Tonya changed her accent to 'white', Latrice would no longer identify. The racialised artefacts and broad models that the youth used to construct and index racial identities were powerful markers of race.

In addition to VMC itself providing the artefacts and model of whiteness, it also promoted the nature of racial identities *as* performances rather than as essential traits. Illustrating this point, Shanti, Valentina, and Latoya described the popular television show *Fresh Prince of Bel Air* about a poor black youth from Philadelphia who is sent to live in Bel Air, California, with his rich extended family:

K:        Do you have to be white to act white?
All:       No—
Latoya:    No, not really—
Shanti:    I've seen black guys on... like on, what's that show with Will Smith?
Valentina: *Fresh Prince of Bel Air*?
Shanti:    Yeah you know Carlton? He acts white.

As this excerpt might suggest, Carlton's performance of whiteness (Carlton is black) mediated the girls' understanding of whiteness itself as a performance. At last, as the girls continued to talk about the character Carlton, they began to touch on the important role of class in the construction of whiteness.

Latoya: He acts white, cause he goes to a white school.
          ...
Valentina: It's like [acting white] when you try to act like really rich.
K:        So you think that acting that way is like acting rich?
Valentina: And snotty—
K:        And a way of dressin'... moving?
Shanti:    Dressing, walking... They dress like all uptight and stuff.
Valentina: They like that [flicks nose up like a snob]—
K:        Snobby?
Valentina: Yeah.

In fact, speaking to the relationality and interconnectedness of identity markers, many of the youth conflated whiteness with 'being rich' or 'classy', as Latoya told me, 'White people talk so rich and professional'.

Whiteness was inevitably a local construction. Considering data from Barlow, a town where many of the youth identified as white, acting white was often described as 'doing well in school' and 'not using slang'. In Barlow, the high population of white residents meant young people there had a slightly more nuanced understanding of whiteness; the youth rarely drew on embodied VMC to make sense of white identities. Conversely, though the youth at the Hope would insist that not all white people acted the same, they had few experiences to draw on: none of the young people I worked with at the Hope identified as white, and only some of them attended schools or lived in areas with a high percentage of white residents.

## *'Everything about me is black': Constructing Black Identities*

One day in late April, Jeremy and I planned to do his video. He was already in the Hope office for misbehaving. Freddie wanted to come with Jeremy and me, and as I always found it hard to say no to Freddie, I told him to work with us.

Freddie, Jeremy, and I parked ourselves around the middle table in the office; Jeremy decided to write several raps for his interview and video. Whenever Jeremy wrote down a few words, I would read them out loud, and Freddie would say to me, 'You sound like a white girl'. 'I know,' I would answer back. 'But, you really sound white,' he would reply. 'Yes, I know,' I would repeat. As this went back and forth a few times, Jeremy appropriated words from a song by hip-hop artist Bow Wow called 'Fresh Azimiz' (pronounced 'as-I'm-is'). When he was finished writing, Jeremy, dressed in baggy pants, a long T-shirt, white ups or sneakers, and with a big diamond-like earring popped through his right earlobe, grabbed a basketball (and Freddie and me) and flew out the door.

The three of us ran up the dark stairs to the second floor where we decided to work in an empty hallway. Before the official video-making started, Jeremy insisted on a short interview. Leaning against a wall, he told Freddie and me that he was 'a little bit of Spanish' and 'black, from Jamaica'. Asking what he identified with the most he replied:

Jeremy: Mostly black. Everything about me is black.
K:      Like what?
Jeremy: My dress style, the way I be acting, I'm ghetto.
K:      You think you act ghetto?
Jeremy: I am.

A particular theme from VMC called on to construct black and Latina/Latino identities was 'ghetto' (gangsta was also used). The idiom, drawn from hip-hop practices, was always raced as black or Latino (though most commonly as black) and was the most frequently used expression in the construction of black racial identities (see also Chap. 4). When the youth accused white people of acting black, they would say, as Shanti often did, that the person 'think they all ghetto'. Describing a black identity, ghetto referred to the deployment of racialised artefacts drawn from VMC, including wearing loose baggy pants, walking in a relaxed way (a swag with a kind of 'bop'), and using a particular lexicon including the contentious word *nigga* or any variation on this epithet (Quinn, 2005; Rose, 1994).

And, though the youth had a wide understanding of types of black identities, they invariably cited a ghetto performance and style as the quintessential black identity. Abigail told me about a particular instance of a 'white guy' acting black:

Abigail: There was a white guy who was dressing all ghetto. He had baggy pants. . .
         he had a big t-shirt with a cell phone. He goes, 'Yo, what's up my *nigga*?'
         I go [shocked face] and all of a sudden—
K:       And he was white?

Abigail: Yeah. He goes, he goes, 'Hello, what the fuck?' And I'm like, [shocked face] all my friends were like just staring at him and... we're like all staring at him and we're like, 'What's happening? Are we on *Punk'd* [TV programme showing practical jokes] or what?'... All of a sudden he goes, 'Are you deaf, mother fucker?'... It's like it's weird.

While Abigail included many of the common artefacts the youth used to construct an archetypal black identity, when the youth used racialised VMC to produce their *own* racial identities, they cited a myriad of artefacts that they connected with their racialised selves. Jeremy spoke to me about what it meant to act black; as he described particular racialised cultural artefacts, he began to articulate his own racial identity:

K:       What does it mean to act black?
Jeremy: Act black? Hold on, act black, all right you see how I'm turned around? You see anything wrong with my pants? [Turns so his backside is facing me].
K:       They're a little low.
Jeremy: Thank you, and being black they be walkin' around, 'yo wha' up homie' [demonstrates slouchy walk].
K:       So it kind of like ghetto?
Jeremy: Ghetto people... they just regular you know... they be doing like this walkin' [demonstrates same slouchy walk]. And ghetto is like gotta stay fresh.

Arguably, as Jeremy deployed these artefacts, as he walked around saying to his friends, 'Yo, wha' up homie', as he drew on these racialised scripts and tools from various forms of VMC (in this case, from hip-hop practices), he internalised, enacted, and constructed aspects of his racial identity. As discussed in Chap. 2, people internalise artefacts in the process of using them – at once constructing and articulating their identities. That is, aspects of himself were produced in action, where '[b]ehavio[u]r', as Holland et al. (1998, p. 31) write, 'is better viewed as a sign of self in practice, not as a sign of self in essence'.

Many of the youth spoke about the racialised cultural artefacts they used or connected with; for these youth, countless 'artifacts of the popular [took] on specific, raciali[s]ed meanings within their lives' (Dolby, 2001, p. 11). For example, Malcolm, who identified strongly as African-American or black (he used the terms interchangeably), spoke to me about how he was recently getting into soul music and about black music artists such as Patti Labelle and Gerald Levert. Speaking about other music he liked including rap and R&B (rhythm and blues), I asked Malcolm how these forms of VMC related to his African-American roots:

Malcolm: Like what it is to be a rapper, like be poor, like not have that much money, struggle and issues and stuff like that.

As Malcolm spoke about these forms, listened to them, and learned about them, he at once asserted aspects of his racial identity and what it meant to be black more broadly.

The various projects the youth participated in through the study also illustrate young people's use of VMC to articulate and assert racial identities. For example, working with Latrice and Tonya, I asked them if they wanted to write a script for anything in their videos; they said no, that they do everything freestyle. Because time was precious, the girls started doing freestyle poetry from the first day of filming. Latrice went first. Sitting on a stool in front of the camera, she began:

Latrice: Okay, this is [Latrice] comin' at ya live from [room number] and I'm gonna get real deep right now okay. [Turns away from the camera, openly composes self and quickly turns back to camera, her body is facing to the left but her head is turned to the camera].
You are you, but I am black.
I see a baby, sitting on a bench, you are you but I am black.
I see a pigeon resting on a nearby bus stop. You are you but I am black. . .
I see my best friend shopping at Strawberry's [clothing shop], you are you but I am black. I see a Chinese girl eating pork-fried rice. You are you but I am black.
This might not seem special to you, but it is to me.
Some people say 'oh who cares';
You are you, but I am black.

Latrice, in this case, drawing on hip-hop practices using freestyle poetry, performed, defined, constructed, and developed aspects of her black identity.

## '[Y]ou need to speak Spanish to be Spanish': Constructing Latina/Latino Identities

I took the opportunity to work at the Hope over the school holidays. On one of the last days of February vacation, Angie, Shanti, Abigail, and I were tired of the Hope's planned projects. Grabbing the digital camera, the girls and I went into a small space between the outside and inside doors to the large cafeteria. For the next 2 h, this cold, wet, dark space served as the perfect photography studio. Angie went first. Fourteen years old, she identified as Dominican and lived with her family right near the Hope. She had long, straight, shiny dark hair, dark brown eyes, was of medium height and weight, and wanted to be a model.

Hair up in a slick ponytail off her face, that day, she had her typical outfit on: a tight pink T-shirt, snug jeans, and sneakers. Telling us to 'hurry take my picture!', she tried out a few of the poses that she saw on *America's Next Top Model* (reality television programme). Abigail went next: she knew exactly how she wanted to be photographed and imitated a set of poses she saw in a magazine featuring her favourite character, Mia, from *Rebelde*. In fact, I had only known Abigail for about 5 min before she told me about *Rebelde,* a Mexican telenovela (television serial drama) that she watched five nights a week with her mother and sister. The show, Abigail informed me, is about 'rich kids in a boarding school in Mexico'. Abigail's role model Mia was *Rebelde's* main protagonist.

With olive skin, shoulder-length brown hair, and a fringe parted down the middle, Abigail was liked by everyone. She was a great dancer, loved a good joke, and was up on all the latest music. Abigail looked at the images as they appeared on the back of the camera and started screaming, 'I look good!' Early that evening, Abigail emailed her photos to some of Hope staff as well as to me. Later in that night, she called and told me to look on her MySpace (social networking) site. She had removed the photo of Mia from *Rebelde*, which she had had as her own photo, and put in a photo of herself taken that day. The next day at the Hope, Abigail and I digitally altered one of the portraits. She selected the image she thought looked the most like Mia in and superimposed it onto a large photograph of Mia from a Spanish magazine we had scanned into my computer. On the top corner, she added Mia's famous line: '*Que difícil ser yo*' [it's hard to be me].

Abigail's self-portrait touches on many of the markers the youth at the Hope cited to construct a Latina/Latino identity, including language, performance, homeland VMC, and style. Differing slightly from both white and black identity construction, the production of Latina/Latino identities did not necessarily have a commonly cited identity 'type' but rather consisted of oft-cited artefacts that the youth used to articulate their own Latina/Latino identities as well as to set a Latina/ Latino identity apart from other racial types.

For example, with respect to language, unlike the vernacular circulated by rap artists and picked up by countless youths in the assertion of a black identity, being able to speak Spanish in the case of a Latina/Latino identity was a strong marker of difference (and of belonging). As Abigail told me:

K: And how does someone act Spanish?
Abigail: You, you first of all, on top, of course, no nothing can change, on the top is
    you need to speak Spanish to be Spanish.

Young people's own identities as Latina/Latino often depended on whether or not they could speak Spanish; indeed, some youth would even use a particular accent if they could not speak Spanish as a means of claiming this identity. In some instances, participants described a Latino accent propagated by embodied forms of VMC (e.g. pop star Jennifer Lopez), friends, and family. See, for instance, Shanti's discussion with me in Box 5.2.

In fact, many youths who were 'part' Spanish at the Hope did not speak Spanish and needed to find alternative ways to claim a Latina/Latino identity. Shanti and Valentina told me that if you don't speak Spanish, it might be okay to claim this identity 'as long as you know the main things'. For many of the young people, this meant knowing enough Spanish to be able to listen to Spanish music and/or talk about Spanish dance and entertainers. Freddie, who was Puerto Rican but did not speak Spanish, took great pride in (and asserted his Latino identity through) rattling off the names of Spanish dances and food. Shanti told me how she would watch Spanish television. Though she did not know Spanish, she recited lines from commercials and telenovelas, drawing on the cultural artefacts the youth cited as Latino.

The youth also drew on homeland VMC, including those forms that originated in parts of Latin America and Mexico, such as dance, as well as those embodied forms articulating a Latina/Latino identity, such as the Latina pop star Shakira, to produce a 'Latino style'. The girls talked at length about the fashions of embodied VMC

---

**Box 5.2** Shanti Talks About Speaking Spanish

---

Shanti: Well actually my grandfather is Indian so then that makes my mother Indian, but then well I guess I'm like little, little Indian from my grandfather but like most, the two big things is Puerto Rican, and I'm black

K:      What do you identify with the most?

Shanti: Black . . . 'cause its not Puerto Rican really 'cause if the reason I don't really think of myself as Puerto Rican that much is because I don't speak Spanish. Like if I spoke Spanish I would say I definitely was Puerto Rican.

. . .

Shanti: And sometimes my accent like when I speak fast and stuff like I'm like "what are you doin'" [using this particular 'Latina/Latino' accent], and stuff like that. Like my accent sometimes just comes out and like when I do know words in Spanish then I speak it good 'cause I know how to like roll my tongue and stuff and I have like the voice for a Puerto Rican or whatever in Spanish and stuff—

K:      So it's like a Spanish accent almost when you're speaking English?

Shanti: Not all the time like when I get caught up in my conversation a lot of times like when I'm speaking for a long time then I just get caught up in it, and lost in it, and stuff then I'll like start talking a little fast and stuff and then you'll hear a roll out of my tongue or something like that.

---

icons. For boys, for instance, Latino clothing was modelled after rapper Daddy Yankee. Freddie described his own style as 'expensive, cool, Latino' and talked about how he 'like[d] to mix' his everyday wear with 'Latin shirts' that he saw 'on Daddy Yankee first'.

VMC gave the youth a means of participation and a chance to assert their Latina/Latino identity; Abigail's use of *Rebelde* begins to illustrate this. Abigail did more than simply watch the show. She read the magazines, listened to the CDs, and joined the fan club. Joining *Rebelde* chat rooms, she told me how the show connected her to youth in the Dominican Republic. Abigail asserted and performed her racial identity in her video project, in which we staged the *Oprah Winfrey Show* with myself as Oprah (terrifying) and Abigail playing the roles of three of the *Rebelde* girls: Mia, Roberta, and Lupita. On camera, she spoke about the characters, their clothing, their relationships, and their morals. Looking at the camera, she told the 'girls out there that don't know the 411 [New York City directory enquires number]. . . for the girls [that is] that don't speak Spanish, *Que dificil ser yo* [it's hard to be me]'. She ends the video as herself singing one of the *Rebelde* songs in Spanish. When producing this video, Abigail used language, performance, and homeland VMC not only to construct and perform aspects of her own racial identity but also to construct and reinforce the markers of this identity category.

Overall, whether the youth used VMC to produce and assert white, black, or Latina/Latino identities, the continuous construction and performance of racial difference was important, and the maintenance of difference was key (Hall, 1996, 1997). Hall (1996, 1997) describes how meaning is created through difference and how we need 'Other' to create and sustain meaning: how difference enables us to order and classify people, places, and objects.[2] In the creation of difference, we are able to understand ourselves, able to give our own identities meaning – in a sense, push our identities into relief up against (an)Other. While the youth used VMC to define, produce, and perform different racial identities, the data suggest the youth were not only producing and articulating difference, they were, in a sense, building racial 'borders' or 'boundaries', boundaries that demarcated and articulated difference, and boundaries that were imperative to maintain. In the second half of this chapter, I focus on the second and third cultural processes articulated in the introduction of this chapter as I explore these borders and examine the ways in which VMC intersected with the maintenance, crossing, blurring, and reworking of racial boundaries.

## Maintaining and Reworking Racial Borders

I thought it would be a good idea to get some of the young people's work from the project printed out so that they could see how the images they were taking might appear in the exhibition planned for the end of the project. Selecting a series of self-portraits produced by the boys, I had them enlarged and brought them to the Hope; a group of girls ran up to me and tried to rip the photos out of my hands. The boys heard about the photos too and soon ran over shouting variants of 'let's see the pictures!' and 'C'mon Kris show us!' I showed Juan's first. Thin, short, 12 years old, and from the Dominican Republic, Juan did the breakdancing segments on Malcolm, Louis, and Freddie's video. His self-portrait had no words, just him, squatting down, staring at the camera. He was happy with the image. I was relieved. I then showed Louis his portrait, and he made some comments about how he wanted to change the background. Malcolm examined his own portrait and said, 'I look burnt.' Freddie laughed and teased, 'Well, you *is* black,' 'Yeah, well, I'm not that *black*,' Malcolm testily replied.

Moving to one of the long cafeteria tables, Louis and I started changing the background of his portrait. As we struggled to superimpose his breakdancing pose he performed for the portrait onto a background of graffiti, Abigail kept running over and telling me things about Mia from *Rebelde*. The boys got angry with her and a nasty fight erupted. Things settled. I finished working with Louis and started working with Malcolm. He said he wanted his skin lighter in the photo. He said loudly, 'I look like the guy in *Barbershop*' (a movie with a primarily black cast). All of the boys started laughing; a few of them started reciting lines from the film.

---

[2] Hall is drawing on linguistics, anthropology, and the work of Russian theorist Mikhail Bakhtin.

As we worked to lighten the image, Freddie said to Malcolm, 'You are black, just accept it man' I could tell the comment upset Malcolm, and he sharply replied, 'Well, whatever, you're white'. (Though Freddie was Puerto Rican, the youth – himself included – often called him white because of his light skin.) For a split second, Freddie's face contorted, and then looking Malcolm directly in the eyes, he called Malcolm a 'nigger'. I had an instant visceral reaction, and before I could formulate a halfway appropriate response, Freddie switched to the more popular epithet *nigga* drawn from rap vernacular. '*Nigga, nigga, nigga,*' he taunted. Malcolm looked shocked; he was angry and spitted back, 'You wish you were. You're a wanna-be. At least I can say that I am one'. At that point, Louis jumped in and started chanting to Malcolm, 'Protect your people! Black Power, Black Power!' I tried to end the exchange, and as I called out to Timo for help, the boys quickly stopped. As Malcolm and I continued to work on the photo, Freddie nastily whispered, 'You know I'm still sayin' it in my mind'. Malcolm shrugged his shoulders and replied, 'And I'm still sayin' it in mine'.

This anecdote is heavily laced with some of the tangled issues around racial identities and the construction of race more broadly, suggested by the data. As described in the last section, young people used forms of VMC, in particular, racialised cultural artefacts, to produce and articulate racial identities. Further, at the end of the last section, I touched on the importance of difference, in particular, how we need difference or 'other' to understand our own identities. I also introduced the concept of racial borders or boundaries and noted that the maintenance of these borders (the maintenance of difference) was essential.

I stay with this idea of borders and the imperative of difference and, drawing on the work of Dolby (2001), add that I understand borders as 'sites' of difference, spaces where difference is articulated.[3] In this study, borders, as I will demonstrate, were contextual, moveable, and linked to identities. Using this concept of borders, I suggest that the nature of VMC as a medium of difference – a medium of contested, contextual, malleable meanings – meant that the borders of racial identities were always changing, forming and re-forming through the unique combination of the youth, the place, and the localisation (and particular racialisation) of select VMC. For the youth, this continuous change meant that they were constantly engaged in the '"work" of identity' (Dolby, 2001, p. 10, citing Soudien, 1996): working to maintain difference and to continuously negotiate the boundaries of various salient identification categories, including race (see also Archer, 2003).

I further suggest that for the youth at the Hope who identified as black, maintaining difference appeared more imperative for them than it was for their Latina/Latino peers. Bringing in ideas from McLeod (1999), it is possible this is a consequence of living in and through a place saturated by forms of VMC racialised or indexed as black and urban, predominantly hip-hop. That is, black-identified VMC such as hip-hop, which young people used to construct racial identities, seemed to

---

[3] Dolby (2001) uses the work of Anzaldúa (1987) and Anzaldúa and Hernandez (1996), and writes of borders as an effect of Scott's (1995) 'enunciation of difference' (p. 79).

be in danger of being assimilated into mainstream culture – and once assimilated, perhaps could no longer be used as a marker of racial group identity and difference (ibid.). Malcolm, who identified as black, told me that 'acting black' and claiming to be 'ghetto' were 'becoming more and more [common]'. When I asked him why it was so popular to be black now, he cited the pervasiveness and popularity of black-identified VMC.

For the youth, as difference was fundamental to identity, as VMC as a medium of difference was constantly changing, and as particular cultural forms that marked difference were slowly being assimilated into mainstream culture, their racial identity construction from VMC was a multilayered and knotty process. In fact, young people's use of VMC in the construction of racial identities was more complex than the deployment of racialised cultural artefacts outlined in the first half of this chapter. It seemed that two additional interconnected processes characterised by power and productivity were at work.

Looking first at power: data suggest that the use of particular artefacts, and hence claims to particular identities, was constantly monitored by the young people. Attempting to police and maintain the borders of race and prevent 'border crossing' (in this study, using forms of VMC associated with a racial group different to your own, such as when a white person acted black), young people invoked a form of authenticity they understood and constructed through VMC (also in Alba, 1999; Dolby, 2001; Warikoo, 2007).

And, second at production: in the process of maintaining borders, authenticity as a localised constructed form, together with the unique combination of place, youth, and VMC, supported (paradoxically) the crossing, blurring, and reworking of racial boundaries, and, consequently, the production of new racial identities. I focus on these processes next.

### *'You wanna say the n-word, you gonna get popped':* *Maintaining the Borders*

One way of understanding border maintenance is through the work of Holland et al. (1998), who describe a difference between 'figurative' and 'positional' identities. While figurative identities are the 'generic characters' that make up a figured world, positional identities 'are about acts that constitute relations of hierarchy, distance, or perhaps affiliation' (Holland et al., p. 128). In positional identities, a person's style, actions, language, and general use of cultural artefacts are considered 'claims to and identification with social categories' (ibid., p. 127), including, I would argue, categories of race. Positional identities have to do with the artefacts one *can* use, for example, the words one *can* employ, and, hence, the claims one *can* make to certain identities; as Holland et al. write, '[p]ositional identities have to do with the day-to-day and on-the-ground relations of power' including 'entitlement [and] social-affiliation' (p. 127).

The authors' use of the word 'entitlement' is important: as it signifies rights or claims to particular artefacts, I argue that young people policed the borders of racial identities by constructing and invoking forms of authenticity where claims or entitlements to particular artefacts were made based on seemingly *natural* connections between particular youth, race and/or place, and forms of VMC. In an effort to describe the authenticity that the youth constructed and used to maintain the borders of racial identities, I begin with an example of youth invoking racial authenticity, before illustrating how young people used VMC to produce authenticity itself.

## Constructing Authenticity

The artefact drawn from VMC that stirred the most vehement invocations of authenticity was the word *nigga* and its variants, including the 'n-word'.[4] Drawn from rap vernacular, this expression was found in rap music, on TV, in sidewalk conversations, and spray-painted on walls.[5] For the several young people who strongly identified as black, use of the word raised powerful feelings.

Shanti: Cause you know how like us black girls say it, we like to make jokes a lot, like we crack on people and stuff so like we don't mind that we have different races hanging out with us, white people um Latinos, blacks, whatever, Indian whatever. Like we don't mind that you hang out with us, but when you try to act black and then you say that word in a joke it's not funny, somebody will pop you in your mouth. . . You wanna say the n-word, you gonna get popped [punched or shot].

When I asked Latrice if it was ever acceptable to say the n-word, she told me this story:

Latrice: Only black people can say it to each other. . . Cause there's this white boy, his name is P, and he's always saying the n-word, and I almost punched him one day and he said, 'Oh I'm not scared of you' and I said, 'Good' then I said I was going to slap him and he said, 'Slap me,' and I said, 'Come over here,' and he said, 'Why don't you come over here,' and the teacher was talking, and I got up and I got in his face and I said, 'What? I'm not scared of you. Get it.' And I slapped him and he said, 'Yo, what the hell *nigga*?!' and then I went off and I started beating him down.

---

[4] With the young people, I almost never used the word *nigga*; if the young person used the word and I was seeking a meaning or discussing rules and issues around the word, I would employ it once only so we had a common language. In this book, I use n-word and *nigga* interchangeably, depending on the context.

[5] In 2007, the year after this fieldwork was conducted, the New York City Council passed a resolution symbolically banning the n-word. The ban encourages people not to use the word but is not enforceable. Media controversy surrounding this word continues to grow today. Contemporary use of the n-word, current debates, and the history of this word are the subject of many scholarly articles and popular publications (e.g. Asim, 2007).

Touching on who can and cannot use this artefact, who is and who is not *entitled* to use it, both Latrice and Shanti allude to the policing of racial identities by appealing, in this case, to racial authenticity. In these excerpts, both girls underline the idea that only 'us black girls' or 'black people' (i.e. people who can claim an 'authentic' black identity) can use this expression. Malcolm also spoke to me about using the n-word:

K:          Do you think its okay to use the n-word ever?
Malcolm: No. Well like there's like this rule, I didn't make this up, but some people
            say that don't say the word *nigga* if you was never really considered
            one... Like if you weren't considered like a Negro or something don't
            call it to someone else cause you don't know what's behind that—

Malcolm's words not only point to the deployment of racial authenticity but begin to articulate some of the constituents of the authenticity the youth invoked and developed to maintain racial borders, including history and struggle. That is, 'not knowing what's behind that', not knowing, in other words, what it might be like to grow up black, go through a particular history, or live in a place where you are faced with unique struggles were all part of the authenticity the youth constructed and invoked.

More broadly, the authenticity invoked was socially constructed or 'fabricated' by the young people (Peterson, 2005). Authenticity was not an organic trait, 'inher [ing] in the object, person, or performance', but rather, as Peterson writes, authenticity was a negotiated 'claim... made by or for someone, thing, or performance and either accepted or rejected by relevant others' (2005, p. 1086, citing Grayson & Martinec, 2004). In this study, authenticity, or what counted as real, was constructed differently by different groups of the youth in different places (see also Warikoo's 2007, 2011 studies). Because authenticity was so varied, I focus here only on black racial authenticity produced by black youth at the Hope and then on a kind of 'urban' authenticity constructed and invoked by both black and Latina/Latino youth. This is not to say that there was not a Latina/Latino authenticity, but rather that the importance and urgency of maintaining the borders of racial identities for black youth was most prominent in the data.

In many ways, the authenticity the youth fabricated to maintain and police the borders of racial identities was similar to the core features of hip-hop's 'keepin' it real'. McLeod (1999, p. 136) notes that 'authenticity has been invoked by hip-hop fans and artists... in terms of being "true," "real," or "keepin' it real"'. For McLeod, 'keepin' it real' includes various psychological, sociocultural, racialised, and geographic facets, including 'blackness', 'the street', and 'staying true to yourself' (pp. 137–143). For the youth at the Hope, authenticity was fleshed out by the themes of *biology* (appeals to the body or physical characteristics), *history,* including black history or the black experience, and *struggle*, which included unique struggles associated with urban or inner-city living. The youth would often cite one or more of these themes when invoking authenticity. In Table 5.1, I expand each of these themes.

| **Table 5.1** Constructing authenticity | Type of authenticity | Themes |
|---|---|---|
| | *Racial authenticity* | *Biology: appeals to the body* |
| | | Skin colour |
| | | Hair texture |
| | | Body type |
| | | *History* |
| | | Slavery |
| | | Civil rights |
| | *Urban authenticity* | *Struggle* |
| | | Social injustices |
| | | Urban living: poverty, |
| | | crime, living on the 'mean' streets |

The dotted line cutting Table 5.1 between racial and urban authenticity is meant to signify two ideas: (1) The themes of biology, history, and struggle, at once, split and connect racial and urban authenticity, and together, racial and urban authenticity form an overarching authenticity for both black and Latina/Latino youth at the Hope. (2) Struggle is tied to and part of collective histories, and, it could be argued, to biology, where physical markers such as skin colour have intense material effects on people's lives. In all aspects, VMC was both a model for authenticity (through the importance of authenticity in hip-hop music) and a means to construct the themes that constituted authenticity.

With respect to biology, the youth often cited physical attributes, most commonly, hair texture and skin colour, as markers of authentic racial identities. Latrice and Shanti spoke about how their mothers told them to be proud of their hair, and all girls found spaces within VMC that articulated a difference between black and white hair textures. In addition, though dark skin was a marker of an authentic black identity, the youth with the darkest skin would tell me to 'lighten up' their self-portraits on the computer; the youth with the lightest skin would disparagingly label themselves as white. Yet, despite jokes and digital touch-ups, when it came to asserting an authentic black identity, dark skin was essential.

Together with physical characteristics, history and the connected theme of struggle were part of the authenticity young people invoked to maintain racial boundaries. The youth who identified as black often deployed narratives of slavery in the United States to claim an authentic black identity and to police those attempting to border-cross. Shanti told me, for instance, 'black is like slave people' and those who did not 'go through slavery' did not have the right to use the n-word. As she put it during an interview, 'They [white people] like, "Oh my sista I know where you comin' from." They do not. Take note, [to the camera] you do not'.

Hall (1990) discusses the production of cultural identities, the imagined histories constructed by people disconnected from their original homelands (see also Hall, 1993). Writing in particular about the Afro-Caribbean experience, he describes how people use popular images and forms of VMC to (re)imagine and (re)construct histories which can be used as spaces of belonging as well as, it could be argued, points of exclusion for particular racial groups. In this study, using VMC to (re) imagine histories, the black youth cited social and political events which were commented on, reworked, renarrated, and relived through VMC. These histories and experiences were then used as markers of authentic black identities. The youth at the Hope cited popular embodied forms of VMC, images, symbols, and slogans that commented on specific social injustices. For example, talking about hip-hop artist Chamillionaire's song 'Ridin' Dirty' (popular during this study), Shanti and Latoya describe the song's commentary on racial profiling:

Shanti: That's my song—
K:      Why do you love that song?
Shanti: Cause that's true, you know he goes, 'the NYPD. . . be hating and hoping
        that they gonna find me riding dirty' like—
K:      What does ridin' dirty mean though?
Latoya: You is riding dirty—
Shanti: Gettin' into trouble—
K:      Oh is that what it means? Gettin' into trouble?
Latoya: You *riding dirty*: you stole a car—
Shanti: Yeah, they try to, they try to catch you. Yeah [to Latoya] stealing stuff or
        on weed whatever like they always tryin' to catch the black people [pause]
        mmm-hmm [nodding head yes].

Remarking on the specific problem of racial profiling in New York City, this song and others like it seemed to contribute to the girls' collective history and sense of racial authenticity, as well as help them to construct and articulate difference.

Hip-hop artist Kanye West also appeared to help many youths (re)construct their past and present experiences and set themselves apart through imagined, predominantly black collective histories.[6] Malcolm spoke to me about Kanye's work:

K:       What do you think about Kanye West?
Malcolm: He speaks the truth, but I ain't that big of a fan of his music.
K:       What do you think he's speaking about?
Malcolm: Umm, the power, justice and all that.

Latrice described his messages:

Latrice: Kanye West, he's deep. . . I like his song 'Jesus Walks' and the second part
         to it is cool. . . Cause they have a poet or somebody; they speak while
         they're talking and says, 'That's why my words can confide to the ears of
         the blind, I too dream in colour, and they rhyme, so I guess I'm one of a
         kind' and something else.
K:       Why do you like that line?
Latrice: Cause it's talking about the struggle! [Puts up Black Power fist]

---

[6] Kanye West is an African-American hip-hop artist who often intermingles his work with black history and politics, including the marginalisation and social injustices that are part of the black experience in the United States.

K:       When you talk about the struggle, do you mean your struggle? Or do you
         mean the struggle of a heritage or background?
Latrice: The struggle of the background [i.e. African-American struggle].

Latrice's reference to 'struggle' is the third theme of authenticity young people used to maintain the borders of a black racial identity, as well as a primary aspect of an *urban* authenticity. While, for Latrice, struggle represented the difficulties of black people in the United States, including slavery and social exclusion, for other youths, the theme of struggle was also associated with the difficulties of urban living, including inequality, injustice, and social exclusion for both black and Latina/Latino youth.

In other words, struggle was a dimension of *both* a racial authenticity *and* an urban or place-based authenticity: part of the collective experience of both black and Latina/Latino youth in New York City, particularly those black and Latina/Latino youth at the Hope whose lives were often framed by social and material inequalities. Indeed, it seemed that the two forms of authenticity (racial and urban) were tightly knotted together, and struggle was the link between them. For example, living a tough life gave a person (regardless of racial identity) a certain credibility or right to employ particular black racialised forms of VMC; at the same time, having a black authentic identity meant having been through tough urban experiences.

Struggle as a theme and link between urban and racial authenticities is also supported and articulated by forms of VMC. Quinn (2005, p. 12) writes about how gangsta rappers construct and create their 'personas' where living through tough inner-city conditions adds to their credibility as the 'real thing': as authentic (usually black) rap artists. All participants (black and Latina/Latino) at the Hope appeared to identify with and use embodied forms of VMC to construct their identities and to make sense of their material circumstances – that is, to make sense of struggle. Particular rap artists embodied struggle for the youth, where they were 'the real thing' – fleshy embodiments of struggle. For example, iconic black rap artist Tupac Shakur, shot to death in 1996, embodied struggle for many of the young people. Tupac was everywhere. His music rang out from cell phones, his name was etched into tables, his portrait hung in the art gallery of the GVHS. Indeed, this portrait was the backdrop for Latrice's self-portrait, and further, she carefully selected this spot under his gaze for the segment of her video where she describes the struggles in her life. Malcolm told me about Tupac within the first days of meeting him. 'I know a lot about him,' he told me. Later in an interview, he added:

Malcolm: What I liked about is how his rapping talks about, you know how some,
         most rappers talk about drugs and sex and... I like about how he talk
         about his mom and how all the struggles he went through. See most
         rappers stake their thing on one thing and that's money and stuff... He
         talked about issues and all that.

For the youth, Tupac was authentic – sharing the collective history and experience of black youth, as well as embodying the struggle of both black and Latina/Latino youth who lived in and through an urban environment laden with difficulties.

It could be that because struggle was a theme of both black racial and urban authenticity rather than maintaining racial borders, struggle set the stage for border crossing – where living a difficult urban existence gave an individual a particular credibility and allowed for the use of black-identified forms of VMC regardless of race. The youth often demonstrated this point, remarking how rap artists were credible or the real thing regardless of race if they went through certain struggles. The white rap artist Eminem, for instance, was considered an authentic 'black' rapper because he went through a tough life (see Hess, 2005). For the youth, Eminem, who has drawn on black style, music, and artefacts to construct his identity, has successfully crossed borders *because* he has been through and now embodies struggle. 'Eminem,' Jeremy told me matter-of-factly, 'he is black.' When I asked Jeremy if he meant that Eminem acted black, he replied, 'No, he *is* black.' Taking this one step further, it could be that Eminem not only crosses borders, but *blurs* and *shifts* or *reworks* borders: in the production and maintenance of borders, authenticity deployed as struggle provided a medium for the reworking and (re) construction of racial borders. This possibility is the third and final cultural process described in this chapter.

## *'Like a black rican, a blackarican': Reworking Borders*

As a dimension of authenticity constructed primarily from VMC, struggle crossed racial boundaries and provided an idiom that the youth at the Hope deployed to justify their use of VMC not typically associated with their racial identity. As a dimension connected with, for example, socioeconomic class, inequality, and urban living, struggle was a point of identification for most of the black and Latina/Latino youth I worked with. In this sense, struggle appeared to be the most 'elastic' part of authenticity (Peterson, 2005): while Latina/Latino youth could not stretch a black racial authenticity wide enough to include them, struggle (particularly in association with urban living) was inclusive, plastic, and adaptable to a myriad of youth circumstances. Because the theme of struggle was so inclusive, embodied forms of VMC such as Tupac were sites of connection and identification with collective experiences meaningful across racial identities, rather than sites of exclusion.

Yet, I cannot argue it was *only* the theme of struggle which supported a reworking of racial borders, or that the theme of struggle *fully* supported border reworking. Freddie, who was Latino living through various urban struggles in Spanish Harlem, who, theoretically, *could* invoke an urban authenticity, was still called a 'wanna-be' by Malcolm when he claimed that his style was gangsta, a black-identified form of VMC derived from gangsta rap. Regardless of the life he lived or the urban authenticity he could claim, Freddie's use of black VMC was still hotly contested by his black and Latina/Latino peers.

It seems more reasonable to propose that it was a combination of authenticity's constructed nature, the elasticity of struggle, policing and power associated with border maintenance, youth experiences, and unique places that facilitated 'border-work'.[7] Alba (1999, p. 18) provides a good starting point for thinking about forms of borderwork. In Alba's discussion, 'border crossing' refers to 'individual-level assimilation', where the border stays intact. 'Blurring', for Alba, refers to a situation where borders become 'less distinct' (p. 19). And, finally, a 'reworking' of the border, what Alba refers to as 'boundary shifting', 'involves the relocation' of the border where 'populations that once lay on one side are now included on the other' (1999, p. 19).[8] Appropriating parts of Alba's framework, I do not imagine these facets of borderwork to be exclusive but suggest that borderwork will always involve elements of all three.

Illustrating an example of borderwork, it was Freddie who first mentioned the neologism 'blackarican'. Though the label has been recently used in urban slang to signify someone who is both black and Puerto Rican, Freddie came up with blackarican in reference to a local fusion of cultural artefacts and expressions racialised as black and/or Latino:

K:       So there's like this mix, like fusion of Latino and black hip-hop [style]?
Freddie: Fusion yeah!
            . . .
Freddie: Like black rican, blackarican!
K:       Did you just make that up?
Freddie: Yeah.
K:       I like it.
Freddie: Blackarican!

For the rest of the youth, this identity was more tacit: rather than describing the borderwork and naming this unique identity formation, they instead spoke to me about a 'bond' between Latina/Latino and black youth. For the youth, Latinos and blacks had a special connection in New York City: a connection based on struggle, on living through similar urban conditions, on identifications through class, and through being 'non-white'. Latoya told me about white identities (not) bonding with Latinos and blacks. 'White? They too professional they can't jump [and bond with blacks or Latinos]'. This bond opened opportunities for border crossing, where it was often (but not always) acceptable for Latinos to use the n-word. Tonya comments:

Tonya: Latinos are closer to blacks than whites that's why blacks. . . don't like it
            when whites call them *nigga*, they don't mind it when Spanish people call it
            cause that they close, they tight like that.

Moreover, this bond or connection was also reflected and reinforced in forms of VMC.

---

[7] Many refer to borderwork; see, for example, Thorne (1993) or Dolby (2001).

[8] Alba draws on Baubock (1994) and Zolberg and Long (1997).

Freddie: African American and Puerto Rican, like I said, they real close, and a lot of
black people... they taking the beats and they are actually getting close,
like they're becoming friends. Like Daddy Yankee [Latino rap artist] and
Norry [black rap artist], and P. Diddy [black rap artist] and Daddy Yankee,
they really close.

Citing the bond between blacks and Latinos, Freddie also spoke about the
articulation of this identity through style.

Freddie: To tell the truth, black people and Puerto Ricans they like the closest out
of everybody else. So I would say yeah this clothes [pointing to his outfit]
is like Puerto Rican as well.
...
Freddie: Hip-hop and Puerto Rican.
...
Freddie: Hip-hop culture and [pointing to shoes] like I have the Daddy Yankee
sneakers, they fresh.

In her book on the production of race in a post-apartheid South African school,
Dolby (2001) describes a 'shift in racial alliances' between coloured and black
youth, and 'attribute[s]' this shift to new combinations of 'affiliations in the world
of popular culture' (p. 91). At the Hope, Freddie's blackarican identity was an
outcome not only of new alliances in VMC between Latina/Latino and black rap
artists but also of a combination of aspects, including, a place and time where
black and Latina/Latino youth lived through similar circumstances, a bond they
formed as a result of collective experiences, and a bond through struggle as an urban
form of authenticity, that contributed to the production of a new racial identity. These
aspects not only permitted border crossing but also seemed to allow for a reworking
of the borders that demarcated black and Latina/Latino identities, and ultimately
for the production of a blackarican identity.

## Racial Spaces, Racial Selves

What I have described in this chapter are three interconnected cultural processes
which together articulate not only one possible way that the youth used VMC
to construct racialised identities but also one of the countless ways in which
the youth used VMC in their everyday lives. What I have described might be
thought of as 'moments' in an overarching process of racial identity construction:
moments which are not necessarily linear or progressive, but relational, constitutive, and simultaneous; moments which include the use of artefacts such as
performance and style drawn from VMC to make sense of, construct, and assert
racial identities; moments where place and youth experience bear down on how
VMC is employed in the production of identities; moments which bring into

focus the imperative of difference and the idea that people's lives are framed and intersected by places and interrelations that afford and exclude identities and identity claims; moments characterised by the building and maintenance of borders through the 'imperative of authenticity' (Hess, 2005); moments which include the invocation of an authenticity fabricated using VMC – where hip-hop's 'keepin' it real' provides an overarching model of authenticity, and where embodied VMC and their messages enable youth to imagine collective histories and struggles; and, finally, moments where struggle, as a place-based and malleable concept, made borderwork and the production of new identities potentially possible. Taken together, I argue it was during these moments that particular youth, in particular places, at a particular juncture in history, used VMC to participate in the active construction and reconstruction of racial borders and selves.

In this final section, I engage with the writing of theorist Homi K. Bhabha to broaden an understanding of how racial identity construction intersects with the nexus of youth, VMC, and place. This discussion reflects the three processes laid out in this chapter: construction of identities through racialised cultural artefacts, maintenance of difference through border policing and authenticity, and border-work in the production of new racial identities.

Starting with the nature of cultural artefacts, I noted that as the youth used cultural artefacts, they not only asserted particular racial identities, but they internalised these artefacts to produce racialised selves. Cole (1996) writes of artefacts as both material and ideal or 'conceptual' (p. 117) (see Chap. 2). For example, style such as the baggy pants worn by some boys at the Hope is material and, at the same time, carries symbolic meanings. Similarly, language and performance, appropriated from forms of VMC, are symbolic and have material referents (ibid., p. 117). Artefacts mediate actions: we employ particular artefacts to get particular results. On the most basic level, this could be a car to get us home, and on a more conceptual level, it could be using a specific vernacular to convey particular meaning or identity. In the construction and reconstruction of racial selves, arguably, VMC as artefacts – as both material *and* ideal, tangible *and* symbolic – offers a way to think about how VMC mediated action and how, through this mediated action, both racial identities and worlds were produced.

However, as I noted in Chap. 2, youth in this study could not construct any identity they wished. Places constrain and enable particular racial identities. The meanings of artefacts are place-dependent. Artefacts are 'localised': made to mean in places through cultural practice. As Massey (1993) underlines, places are at once shifting, anchored, and unique (pp. 66–69). The geography of places, physical environments, and politics add to the power of places as stable spaces which allow and deny particular meanings of VMC and, hence, identities. A place's 'specificity', Massey (p. 67) tells us, 'is not some long internali[s]ed history but the fact that it is constructed out of a particular constellation of relations, articulated together at a particular locus'. Particular identities will be possible and not possible with/in particular (dynamic) constellations.

Similar to the findings in the local youth culture approaches described in Chap. 2, as VMC intersected with places and with youth who lived through these places, it was taken up in cultural practice, and its meanings reworked (see also Massey, 1998). At the Hope, threaded through this process was power instantiated as rights and claims to particular artefacts in particular places. Claims, invoked through authenticity, further impinged on identities. Authenticity built borders, defined difference, and, as I noted, simultaneously opened up the shifting of borders. It was the particular nexus of youth, place, and VMC where power was located (deployed as authenticity) and where there was a continual reconstruction of racialised identity borders and simultaneously selves.

Appropriating the writing of Bhabha (1990, 1994), I conceptualise this nexus as a 'third space'. That is, a 'liminal' or 'in-between' space that 'initiate[s] new signs of identity' (1994, p. 2). A fertile space where identities in this study were produced, contested, negotiated, reworked, and reconstructed; where the borders of race, as Dolby writes in her youth study in South Africa, were 'reinscrib[ed]' (2001, p. 95). In third spaces, as artefacts – artefacts which are made to mean in particular contexts – are used by the youth, the edges or borders of identities are constructed, crossed, frayed, blurred, and ultimately reconstructed. Borders, as Thorne (1993, p. 84) writes, are not an 'unyielding fence' but 'many short fences that are quickly built and as quickly dismantled'. In this conception, borders and identities are knotted together: as quickly as identities are produced, borders are constructed; as borders are reconstructed, new identities emerge.

This intersection of VMC, place, and youth where race was constructed and reconstructed could be thought of as a space, Bhabha (1990, p. 211) writes, of 'hybridity', where 'hybridity... is the "third space" which enables other positions to emerge':

> The process of cultural hybridity gives rise to something different, something new and unrecognisable, a new area of negotiation of meaning and representation. (Bhabha, 1990, p. 211)

Using Bhabha's work, the blackarican identity could be thought of as neither black nor Puerto Rican, but rather as a unique identity not born of two separate 'essential' or primordial identities, but reconstructed using remnants of previous constructions – in this case, remnants of identities which themselves were produced through the use of particular forms of racialised and localised VMC. This is not to say that youth identities (or selves) were disconnected from history, material aspects of place, or significant individual and collective experiences; in fact, I would vehemently argue the contrary, rather, that for the youth, racial identity construction using VMC was a contextual and continuous process of (re)construction rather than an 'unearthing' (Hall, 1990, p. 224; see also Maira, 2002, p. 111) of an essential racial form. In this sense, Bhabha (1990, p. 211) argues that 'all forms of culture are continually in a process of hybridity', in the process of being made and remade. In third spaces, as places change, as people's experiences change in place, and as flows of VMC touch down, are contested, and made to mean, racial worlds and racialised selves are continuously constructed and reconstructed.

It was not only racial identities that were produced in third spaces; racial identities are part of 'identity constellations' which include combinations of identity categories such as gender, class, and sexual orientation (Youdell, 2007:2). In the following chapter, I continue at the Hope and explore how young people used VMC to make sense of, construct, and/or negotiate aspects of another identity category: gender.

# References

Alba, R. (1999). Immigration and the American realities of assimilation and multiculturalism. *Sociological Forum, 14*(1), 3–25.

Anzaldúa, G. (1987). *Borderlands/La frontera*. San Francisco, CA: Aunt Lute Books.

Anzaldúa, G., & Hernandez, E. (1995/1996). Rethinking margins and borders: An interview. *Discourse, 18*(1–2), 7–15.

Archer, L. (2003). *Race, masculinity and schooling: Muslim boys and education*. Maidenhead, UK: Open University Press.

Asim, J. (2007). *The N word: Who can say it, who shouldn't, and why*. New York, NY: Houghton Mifflin.

Baubock, R. (1994). *The integration of immigrants*. Strasbourg, France: Council of Europe.

Bhabha, H. K. (1990). The third space: An interview with Homi K. Bhabha. In J. Rutherford (Ed.), *Identity: Community, culture, and difference* (pp. 207–221). London: Lawrence & Wishart.

Bhabha, H. K. (1994). *The location of culture*. London: Routledge.

Cole, M. (1996). *Cultural psychology: A once and future discipline*. Cambridge, MA: Harvard University Press.

Dolby, N. (2001). *Constructing race: Youth, identity, and popular culture in South Africa*. Albany, NY: State University of New York Press.

Grayson, K., & Martinec, R. (2004). Consumer perceptions of iconicity and indexicality and their influence on assessments of authentic market offerings. *Journal of Consumer Research, 31*, 296–312.

Hall, S. (1990). Cultural identity and diaspora. In J. Rutherford (Ed.), *Identity: Community, culture, difference* (pp. 222–238). London: Lawrence & Wishart.

Hall, S. (1993). What is this 'black' in black popular culture? *Social Justice, 20*(1–2), 104–111.

Hall, S. (1996). Introduction: Who needs identity? In P. Du Gay & S. Hall (Eds.), *Questions of cultural identity* (pp. 1–11). London: Sage.

Hall, S. (1997). *Representation: Cultural representations and signifying practices*. London: Sage.

Holland, D., Lachicotte, W., Skinner, D., & Cain, C. (1998). *Identity and agency in cultural worlds*. Cambridge, MA: Harvard University Press.

Hess, M. (2005). Hip-hop realness and the white performer. *Critical Studies in Media Communication, 22*(5), 372–389.

Jackson, J. L. (2001). *Harlemworld: Doing race and class in contemporary Black America*. Chicago: University of Chicago Press.

Maira, S. (2002). *Desis in the house: Indian American youth culture in New York City*. Philadelphia: Temple University Press.

Massey, D. (1993). Power-geometry and a progressive sense of place. In J. Bird, B. Curtis, T. Putnam, G. Robertson, & L. Tickner (Eds.), *Mapping the futures: Local cultures, global change* (pp. 59–69). London: Routledge.

Massey, D. (1998). The spatial construction of youth cultures. In T. Skelton & G. Valentine (Eds.), *Cool places: Geographies of youth cultures* (pp. 121–129). London: Routledge.

McLeod, K. (1999). Authenticity within hip-hop and other cultures threatened with assimilation. *Journal of Communication, 49*(4), 134–150.

Peterson, R. (2005). In search of authenticity. *Journal of Management Studies, 42*(5), 1083–1098.

Quinn, E. (2005). *Nuthin' but a 'G' thang: The culture and commerce of gangsta rap*. New York: Columbia University Press.

Rose, T. (1994). *Black noise: Rap music and Black culture in contemporary America*. Hanover, NH: Wesleyan University Press; Published by University Press of New England.

Scott, J. (1995). Multiculturalism and the politics of identity. In J. Rachman (Ed.), *The identity in question* (pp. 3–12). London: Routledge.

Solomos, J., & Back, L. (2000). Introduction: Theorising race and racism. In L. Back & J. Solomos (Eds.), *Theories of race and racism: A reader*. London: Routledge.

Soudien, C. (1996). *Apartheid's children: Student narratives of the relationship between experiences in schools and perceptions of racial identity in South Africa*. PhD thesis, State University of New York at Buffalo, Buffalo, NY.

Thorne, B. (1993). *Gender play: Girls and boys in school*. New Brunswick, NJ: Rutgers University Press.

Warikoo, N. (2007). Racial authenticity among second generation youth in multiethnic New York and London. *Poetics, 35*, 388–408.

Warikoo, N. (2011). *Balancing acts: Youth culture in the global city*. Berkley, CA: University of California Press.

Youdell, D. (2007). *Impossible bodies, impossible selves: Exclusions and student subjectivities*. Dordrecht, The Netherlands: Springer.

Zolberg, A., & Long, L. W. (1997). *Why Islam is like Spanish: Cultural incorporation in Europe and the United States*. New York: International Centre for Migration, Ethnicity, and Citizenship, New School for Social Research.

# Chapter 6
# Negotiating Gender: Gender Narratives and Gender Identities

## Introduction

In this chapter I focus on the theme of gender (and on gendered identities more narrowly) at the Hope in New York City. I argue that young people used visual material culture (VMC) to make sense of, negotiate, and perform 'gender narratives' and local gender identities, specifically the production of local masculinities and femininities.[1] I suggest gender identities were continuously negotiated and performed at the intersection between youths' individual and collective experiences, localities, and forms of VMC. To make sense of this process, I draw on the concept of narratives: appropriating Bruner (1990), I conceive of narratives as gender models or stories of masculinity and femininity made up of interlocking and overlapping values, discourses, and ideals circulating places and instantiated in embodied forms of VMC. I suggest gendered identities are not only similar to, but are mediated by, these narratives. That is, gender narratives both describe identities (particular types of, say, femininity) *and* are cultural artefacts that, with forms of VMC, youth not only made sense of and used but also negotiated and performed in the construction of their own gendered selves.

Before beginning, I note two representational issues in this chapter: first, because identity categories such as gender and race are interlinked, trying to write about gender alone is impossible. Archer (2003) writes, '[I]dentities might be conceptuali [s]ed as integrally inter-meshed and inter-related – such that axes of "race", ethnicity, social class, and gender cannot easily be separated out from one another because they are combined in such a way that they "flavour" and give meaning to

---

[1] Parts of this chapter have been previously published and adapted from Eglinton (2010).

each other' (p. 21).[2] Therefore, while I have made every effort to stay focused on gender, the findings must be recognised as wholly integrated with and dependent on the many identity categories youth constructed. Second, though I strove for equal representation from boys and girls, for gender the girls' contribution was greater. This is most likely the consequence of a number of factors including that I worked with more girls than boys, and my own gender as female might have meant that girls were more comfortable than boys talking to me about sensitive topics such as intimate relationships. Further, it could be that available 'scripts' for boys to discuss gender were limited and/or so constraining that the boys did not have the tools to talk about particular aspects of gender (Tobin, 2000, p. 33).

## Conceptualising Gender and Gender Narratives

In her ethnographic work exploring gender and gender relations among primary school children in two areas of the United States, Barrie Thorne (1993) draws on the metaphor of play – where gender might be conceived as an active, performative, dynamic, and imaginative process or production rather than an essential trait fixed to biology. Expanding on this understanding of gender, I bring in the idea that at the Hope gender was a social concept, dependent on time and place, and actively produced and negotiated by youth through mediated social (inter)action using forms of VMC (see also Gottlieb, 2002; Jackson & Scott, 2002). Focusing on gender identities, masculine and feminine identities were not necessarily static forms tied to biological sex but were instead contextual, multiple dynamic forms of masculinities and femininities.[3]

This means that at the Hope gender identities were open to reworking and negotiation and, further, that youth had to make sense of multiplicity – to at once find and produce patterns, sites of commonality, spaces of difference – in order to understand their own identities. To do so, it appeared that young people constructed and/or impressed upon their world stories of gender and frameworks to organise

---

[2] Importantly, sexuality and sexual orientation are categories that gender works in relation to the expression and experience of identities. Gender and sexuality share a special relationship, where Jackson and Scott (2002) define this relationship as instantiated through the heterosexual/homosexual binary in sexuality which 'mirrors, and is interrelated' with gender (p. 14). In this chapter, rather than conflating gender and sexuality, with Tobin (2000), I imagine sexuality as an aspect of gender in the production of romantic and/or intimate relationships, as part of the 'gender order' where powerful narratives about sexuality constrain youth identities (see, e.g., Connell, 2002), as well as related to gender in much the same way that class, race, and, for instance, nationality are part of identity configurations (Jackson & Scott, 2002).

[3] Writing about the fluidity of gender, Gottlieb (2002) summarises: 'Gender identity . . . is not as fixed, determinate, predictable as we may assume . . . gender identity is so decisively shaped by cultural effort – the mandate of values, the whims of history, the weight of the economy, the power of politics – that it may be a talk doomed to failure to delineate where "nature" ends and "culture" begins' (pp. 168–169).

masculinities and femininities into good, bad, hot, and not. Bruner's (1990, p. 56) concept of narratives helps make sense of this process: Bruner describes how people use narratives to construct and understand self and others and as a means of 'framing' and 'organi[s]ing' experience. Narratives might be imagined as a 'tool of identity' (Hannerz, 1983), a medium people use to make sense of the world, of selves, of experience, of others.

I suggest youth used gender narratives in two connected ways: first, the gender identities of young people were akin to gender narratives – what Connell (2002, p. 81) might refer to as 'gender configurations' – which youth, using various resources including VMC, continuously produced, negotiated, reworked, and performed through expressive cultural practice. Second, the various resources or cultural arte-facts that mediated this process were, with VMC, available gender narratives them-selves or, more specifically and more often, the constituents of narratives which might include local values, ideals, and/or discourses (Bruner, 1990): local values and, for example, ideals, which represented, constituted, and conveyed particular (and sometimes powerful) knowledges about femininity and masculinity (see Cole, 1996, pp. 124–130 for narratives, scripts, and cultural models).

## Gender Narratives at the Hope: Gangstas, Girlie Girls, and Tomboys

Feeling vulnerable early on in the study, I decided to find one of the key participants 13-year-old Ramona, hoping she would be as kind to me as she was to the other adults in the programme. Searching the school for the better part of an hour, I finally found her 'just chillin' in a large sunlit classroom with several other youth. As the kids played Yu-Gi-Oh cards, listened to music, and pretended to do homework, I grabbed a seat next to her; she spoke to me about her family, including how her younger brother Raphael 'completely saved' her from being a 'girlie girl'. A few weeks later in an interview with Ramona and Angie, I mentioned Raphael. 'What is Raphael like?' I asked. She and Angie both started laughing. 'Oh, that skinny little boy?!' Ramona squeezed out through giggles. 'He think he all ghetto, he all gangsta.'

Though I did not know it at the time, Ramona's mention of girlie girls and gangstas was significant, and I soon learned that in the figured world of youth at the Hope, there were several overarching gender narratives or 'gender types' (Holland, Lachicotte, Skinner, & Cain, 1998; Luttrell, 2003) that youth cited to make sense of the multiplicity of gender identities. Specifically, it seemed youth drew on embodied forms of VMC to describe and produce a 'lexicon of types' (Holland et al., 1998) including 'girlie girls' and 'tomboys' for girls and 'gangstas' for boys. While these identity types were sometimes described as extreme performances, they were not necessarily stereotypes (see Hall, 1997).[4] Rather, as narratives, they

---

[4] In other words, they were not intended to 'fix difference' (Hall, 1997).

were orientating frames, 'points of identification', and 'difference' (Hall, 1996, p. 5) in a complex world and an immediate means of identifying and understanding a type of masculinity or femininity. I describe these types, focusing on the ways in which youth drew on VMC to make sense of and produce these narratives.

## *'Rappers Are All Gangstas': Making Sense of Gangstas*

Just after 3:00 p.m. in mid-December, I found Louis sitting alone at Timo's table. Waiting for Malcolm, Gabe, and Freddie to arrive, he was throwing paper balls at the back of the girl's head in front of him. On the table was a poster with rap artist 50 Cent advertising his G-Unit sneaker line. G-Unit, Louis informed me, was '50's [hip-hop] group'. I sat with Louis and looked at the poster that included images of 50 Cent engaged in various activities including one where he has a large pile or wad of cash in his hand. Louis pointed to the image of 50 Cent holding the money and offered, 'He a hustler'. I asked Louis what a hustler was. 'They buy something for like a dollar and sell it for ten', he replied.

Gabe, Malcolm, and Freddie soon showed up and were closing in on the poster – sitting on their knees up on the benches and leaning over the images of 50 Cent, the five of us were tangled in a mess of breath and loud gum chewing. Showing my ignorance, I asked them the difference between rappers and singers. Getting into the conversation, they all started talking (shouting) over each other. Louis shouted the loudest: 'Rappers rap and singers sing, plus like fifty percent of rappers are black'. Gabe, wearing a tight wool skull cap with 'Bronx' sewn across the front, said, 'Rappers are all gangstas; all they rap about is violence, sex, and drugs'. Laughing, Louis added, 'And they always have half-naked women dancing in their videos'. He followed with, 'They degrade women'.

As the boys continued talking to me about rappers, Louis took out his new iPod and, telling me the exact price his mother paid for it ('99 dollars and ten cents'), located a rap by 50 Cent and handed me one of the earbuds to listen. 'All I listen to is rap', he shouted to me over the music. Freddie challenged him: 'You is lying, you listen to Spanish music'. I asked if there were Spanish rappers. 'Yeah', Louis replied, 'they is better than American ones'. 'Yeah', Freddie agreed, '[Spanish rappers] don't want no beefs [fights] they just make music'. By this time, Latrice was sitting at the next table with some of the other girls eating Kentucky Fried Chicken.[5] Freddie spotted her and shouted out, 'Yo, Latrice, gimme a chicken wing!' Gabe hit Freddie's chest, exclaiming in a fit of laughter, 'That sounded so ghetto, man!'

Playing this scene over again in my mind as I wrote fieldnotes that evening, I started to think about types of masculinities: I wondered if there was a common lexicon of boys' identity types including, for example, 'the jocks' popular in films and laced through the literature (e.g. in Eckert's, 1989 ethnography), or something

---

[5] American fast food chain selling fried chicken (and other items).

more local such as Nayak's (2003a, 2003b) 'Real Geordies'. At the Hope, I kept myself open to these masculinities – these assemblages of scripts, styles, and performances. I listened, watched, and even pointedly asked, 'Are there "types" of boys, you know like jocks?' It was Malcolm who finally set me straight, telling me in an interview one day, 'Boys don't do that really'. He later added, 'There are some people that are like gangsta'. Malcolm was right; in fact, similar to boys in Barlow (see Chap. 7), the overarching narrative boys at the Hope consistently spoke about was the gangsta or ghetto type.

Drawn directly from VMC, for youth (both boys and girls), the gangsta narrative was based on and made sense of through gangsta rappers and hip-hop aesthetics more broadly. Gangsta rappers represented the archetypal gangstas whom bell hooks (2004, p. 27) calls the 'essence of patriarchal masculinity'. For youth at the Hope, gangstas were hypermasculine, invested in violence, and epitomised survival; gangstas were urban and invariably raced as black (see also Archer, 2003; hooks, 2004).

Writing about racialised masculinities, O'Donnell and Sharpe (2000, p. 3) articulate the themes of 'black macho', 'black cool', and 'black flash'. These themes arguably offer a loose frame for fleshing out the characteristics of the gangsta narrative constructed by boys at the Hope. For example, beginning with 'black macho', which the authors describe as 'hardness', boys such as Louis told me that 'gangstas act all big and bad'. For youth, gangstas were survivors: they had tenacity and were able to overcome adversity. Gangsta hardness also meant hyper-heterosexuality and sexist behaviour: this understanding was drawn directly from hip-hop and gangsta rap, where, for example, gangsta hardness is coded in rap artists' talk of violence and survival and in their treatment of women, sexist attitudes, and actions (Boyd, 2002, p. 117; hooks, 2004; Quinn, 2005).

Intertwined with hardness was coolness: Majors (1990) writes of '*cool pose*' that includes a particular walk, style, and attitude. Cool pose was a performance youth included as part of the gangsta narrative. It was a way of talking, walking, and being that mirrored the hardness and style of rappers. Part of cool pose was O'Donnell and Sharpe's (2000) 'black flash', connected with the exaggerated wealth of gangsta rappers. Freddie cited this flash gangsta style, drawing on his lived experience at home in Spanish Harlem:

Freddie: If you really want to go into the topic of gangsta, Harlem they wear like, I don't understand, but they think it's cool, but why do you still have to have the tag still on your hat, the tag still on your shirt?. . . I saw it the other day on the train. . . Some guy had it on his pants.
. . .
Freddie: They think it's cool. I don't think it's cool. Why you gonna leave the tag on?
K:       Who started doing that first?
Freddie: Well the rappers, and then people pick it up from the rappers.

Freddie's reference to rap artists in the context of his experience gets at the idea that VMC was not only the basis of the gangsta narrative where hardness, coolness, style, and flash were derived from and constructed through VMC, it was means of making sense of the local masculinities which intersected youth lives. That is, VMC was both a source and a resource for producing and making sense of gender narratives. While gangsta was the only overarching male narrative cited by both boys and girls, two types of femininity were cited by girls, including girlie girls and tomboys (boys did not appear to contribute to the construction of girls' narratives).

## *'Paris Hilton is the queen of the girlie girls': Making Sense of Girlie Girls*

The girlie girl was a narrative of femininity described invariably by girls at the Hope as a hyper-feminine form who performs and engages in practices typically coded as female including, for instance, dressing up, applying make-up, and worrying about manicured nails. Marked by vanity, an overt or 'exaggerated' heterosexuality (Renold, 2000), often performed through an obsession with boys, this identity was based on getting a boyfriend or looking good for men (also see Renold, 2008). Girlie girls were flirtatious and, as Abigail told me, were airheads (lacked intelligence). Talking about girlie girls, Latrice believed 'they feel they [girlie girls] have to make up for in looks what they don't have for brains'.

Reflecting the interdependence of social identities, girlie girls were commonly raced as white. Describing girlie girls, the girls would often cite the same performances, accent, and embodied VMC used to construct white identities (see Chap. 5). Tonya and Latrice spent a considerable amount of time describing girlie girls.

Tonya: A girlie girl is someone who is always wearing skirts—
Latrice: Always wearing tight pants, always wearing make-up and have their hair nice down and soft ... and always like perky all the time and always like 'oh my God!' [white accent] ... They always gotta look cute and everything.

Appealing to biology, Latrice constructed girlie girls as white, citing hair texture as soft and deploying a white accent (see Chap. 5). In Box 6.1, Latrice talks, in part, about the whiteness of girlie girls.

---

**Box 6.1** Latrice Talks About Girlie Girls

I know why girlie girls is white, I know, because like their complexion is like paper, so they can wear anything [laughter]. It is it's like paper. They can wear anything. They can wear any makeup so then they get attached being able to wear all that make-up and they just become girlie girls. They just need it [make-up] all the time.

---

Further emphasising the interdependence of identity categories, girlie girls were usually classed as wealthy. In particular, they were described as hyper-consumers of expensive clothing, as 'snobby', and as living in areas of the city and suburbs where white people lived.

Ramona: I live in the Bronx, but like in a part there's a lot of girlie girls.
K:       There's girlie girls there?
Ramona: Yeah, I'm in like a white area.

Embodied VMC was the central resource youth used to construct and make sense of this narrative. In an interview with Shanti, Latoya, and Valentina, Paris Hilton's name came up; Shanti told me, '*She* a girlie girl, like *really* girlie.' We continued the conversation:

K:                         So is Paris Hilton a true girlie girl?
Valentina and Shanti: Yes!
Latoya:                   Oh my God!
Valentina:                The number one, the *queen*!
                          [All screaming]
Shanti:     She is the ultimate—
Valentina: She is the role model—
Latoya:     Paris Hilton is the queen of the girlie girls.
Shanti:     Yeah, she the queen bee.

More generally, embodied forms of VMC, including white female entertainers who shared similar wealth, racial identity, and hyper-feminine practices, represented and constituted this narrative. For example, white actresses and singers such as Hillary Duff, Jessica Simpson, and Lindsay Lohan were all cited as girlie girls.[6] Yet girls did not always agree on the VMC embodying girlie girl scripts nor on the practices of girlie girls. A central area of debate was sexuality and relationships with boys. All girls agreed with Abigail, who told me that girlie girls were 'boy-crazy', that girlie girls often 'make bad choices' with boys, and further that their lack of intelligence was connected to their less than honourable behaviour with boys. However, whether girlie girls were actually engaging in sexual activity was questionable, and there was often a fine line between being boy-crazy and being sexual with boys: as Tonya put it, 'sometimes they [girlie girls] will go to the limit of being a slut.'

Moreover, embodied VMC such as Paris Hilton was not only used to construct this narrative, VMC was used to make sense of this narrative as it played out in their lived experience. For example, in the following excerpt, Latoya, Shanti, and Valentina describe Alex, a friend from school:

K:        And so this girl Alex would like to be like that [a girlie girl]?
Valentina: Yes, I think she will become—
Shanti:    Yes—
Latoya:    Like, [a girlie girl] to be—
          . . .
Valentina: I think she'll become Paris Hilton one day except with[out] the rich stuff.
Shanti:    And in high school she'll be like ghetto white—
K:         Is she white?
Shanti:    Yup!

---

[6] Hillary Duff is a white American actress and teen pop singer. Jessica Simpson is a white American pop singer and actress. Lindsay Lohan is a white American actress, pop singer, and model, known by youth at the Hope for her partying, sexual exploits, and role in the movie *Mean Girls*.

Valentina: No, she Spanish that's the weird part.

> . . .

Shanti:    Her skin, her skin colour's white but she's Spanish. . . And girlie girls do
           not, Spanish people do not act like girlie girls.

Describing Alex, the girls at once map VMC onto their lived experience and map
their lived experience onto models provided by VMC. In this case, the girls use
embodied VMC as an orientating point for understanding, making sense of, and
describing this local femininity.

### 'Missy Elliot, she has it going on, like she a tomboy': Making Sense of Tomboys

Resting at one end of what seemed to be a 'continuum of femininity', with girlie
girls on one end and tomboys on the other, the tomboy was loose collection of style,
performances, and actions including particular attitudes towards boys. Where
the archetypal girlie girl was the white, self-obsessed, wealthy Paris Hilton, the
tomboy model was the strong, black, heavy-set rap artist Missy Elliot. During an
interview about her collage, I asked Ramona about Missy Elliot:

Ramona: Missy Elliot?. . . She is so, she's the best. That's number one, Missy Elliot
           is number one.
K:         What about Missy Elliot do you like?
Ramona: Missy Elliot, she has it going on, like she a tomboy.

Javiera too spoke at length about both Missy Elliot and tomboys. Thirteen and
from the Dominican Republic, Javiera was heavy set, with a big smile and short
dark hair which she slicked back into a small ponytail. She often wore big gold hoop
earrings and a gold necklace with a pendant hanging from it with her name 'Javiera'
encrusted in diamond-like stones. Often dressed in baggy jeans, puffy-coat, Tims
(boots), or basketball sneakers and living with her family in the East Village, she
and her girlfriends would often play basketball at the local court. Javiera spoke to
me about why she liked Missy Elliot:

Javiera: Cause she, I don't know, she like me like she dress baggy sometimes and
           just her personality like she likes rappin' like I do.

Missy Elliot embodied the style, personality, and performance of tomboys,
where the tomboy did not wear what would be considered particularly feminine
and/or revealing clothing, was into sports, and enjoyed a friendship with boys.
Javiera spoke to me about tomboy style and actions in opposition to girlie girls:

K:         And what are they like [tomboys]?
Javiera: They cool, they fun, they like wear shorts; girlie girls don't really wear
           shorts—
K:         Why not?
Javiera: Like basketball shorts—

As Ramona told me, 'Tomboys dress like more, I don't know, like ghetto... and girlie girls they wear mini skirts'. In opposition to the feminine and form-fitting clothing of the girlie girl, the clothing marking a tomboy style was commonly described as a ghetto style worn by female (and male) rap artists including low-slung baggy pants, hooded sweatshirts, gold jewellery, puffy-coats, and work boots or sneakers.

Unlike girlie girls, tomboys were not there for the pleasure of boys (Renold, 2000), but rather tomboys were friends with boys; they could hang out with them without necessarily being romantic or sexual. Tonya and Latrice spoke about what they were like when 'they used to be one [a tomboy]':

Latrice: I used to be their [the boys'] best friend... I was their best friend they be like 'yo Latrice' I'd be like 'what up' [imitates them doing a handshake where they knock fists]—
 . . .
Latrice: Even though I was a girl, if you was to look at me in class I would be sitting at my desk on my chair like this [squatting in a 'tough pose']—
Tonya:  Right. You be like 'yo whaz up?'

In this excerpt, Latrice and Tonya not only mention their relationship to boys but articulate a performance of tomboys almost mirroring the gangsta 'cool pose' (Majors, 1990). In connection with this performance and their relationship with boys, tomboys were considered independent, tough, and possessing street knowledge. Tomboys were not dependent on boys but rather depended on themselves: speaking about Missy Elliot, Javiera praised, 'She just does her thing'.

As all narratives were shot through with class, race, and other identity markers, though race was never mentioned, the performances, style, and language youth used to describe tomboys were the same artefacts used to construct a black racialised identity described in Chap. 5. Yet, while I can assume that tomboys were raced as black and in some cases Latina and while it could be that for young people being black and/or Latina/Latino was racially neutral or the norm and, therefore, unnecessary for youth to highlight, racial and classed aspects of tomboys were never explicitly mentioned by girls.

## *Localising and Using Narratives*

While the articulation of these narratives – in particular girlie girls, tomboys, and gangstas – is not necessarily novel (Reay (2001), for example, describes several types of femininity found in a primary classroom in inner-city London including 'girlies' and 'tomboys'),[7] these narratives were highly contextual – impossible to

---

[7] Emma Renold (2000, 2007) also describes 'tomboys' and 'girlie girls' in her work, and in another example, Louise Archer (2003) describes a gangsta identity constructed by Muslim boys in the northwest of England.

tease apart from their social context. As I demonstrate in the following section, the girlie girls, tomboys, and gangstas youth described at the Hope were not global forms youth simply (re)cited but rather localised, gendered identity types youth actively constructed and made sense of using VMC in relation to their individual experiences as raced and classed youth in New York City.

Connected to this, for both boys and girls, the data suggest narratives were neither fully invested in nor fully rejected. Rather, gender identity work was a point of continuous negotiation where something more active, participatory, and relational seemed to be happening and, further, where elements of power in the form of limitations and constraints were threaded through this process. What I found was that gender narratives were part of and instantiated larger gender ideologies that constituted localities and championed what it meant to be masculine or feminine. Bruner (1990, p. 29) conceives of narratives as carrying with them the values, ideals, and, for example, scripts of communities. In this case, girlie girls, gangstas, and tomboys carried with them powerful ideologies which posited what 'real' manhood might look like and propagated a womanhood constrained by a series of dichotomies such as good/bad, passive/assertive, and innocent/sexual.

Drawing on and adapting the work of Connell (2002), I would argue that these powerful ideologies make up the 'gender order' – an aspect of all local places. Composed of the enduring structures of gender, the gender order is a dynamic layer of local places made of influential and dominant values and ideals of gender postulating, for example, the ways in which males and females *should* act and the roles they *should* take. These ideologies are often represented, conveyed through, and embodied in forms of VMC where a rap artist, for example, will embody the masculine ideal of 'toughness', a 'necessary' aspect of 'being a man' in a particular gender order. Yet, while particular narratives certainly provided models to which youth aspired, the dominant ideals of masculinity and femininity such as, say, toughness for boys, which constituted these narratives, could not easily be invested in by the young people, but rather, like all artefacts, their use was constrained and enabled by place – by the gender order of place – as well as by their own lives. I explore the complex process of negotiating masculine and feminine identities in the second half of this chapter.

## Negotiating Gender Identities

Connell (2002) writes of gender identity construction (i.e. 'gender learning') as '*gender projects*', produced through the 'constraints and possibilities of the existing gender order' (p. 82, emphasis in original). He notes the '*pleasure*' and '*difficulty*' (p. 78, emphasis in original) of 'doing gender' (West & Zimmerman, 1987) and of producing credible masculinities or femininities with/in and through the existing social structures. Examining this complex process, I argue that youth used VMC to understand, rework, and negotiate ideals of masculinity and femininity in concert with their own lives, as well as to perform local gender identities. I point out again that narratives of masculinity and femininity are comprised of aggregates of values and ideals, scripts, and, for example, styles. And, further, that in the negotiation of identities, youth worked at the level of these aggregates. That is, youth reworked and negotiated the constituents of narratives rather than the overarching masculinities and femininities more generally. While there are countless resources youth called on in the negotiation of their gendered identities including peer groups and family, I remain focused on VMC and on the significant role of VMC in this negotiation.

## *'[W]hy do you gotta go around with guns in your pocket instead of using your fists?': Negotiating Masculinities*

'Masculinities', Frosh, Phoenix, and Pattman (2002, p. 3) write, '[are] accomplished through the exploitation of available cultural resources such as the ideologies prevalent in particular societies'. As some ideologies and cultural practices are more powerful than others, in every community, some 'versions' of masculinity will be more dominant than other versions (Connell, 2002, pp. 81–83; Mac an Ghaill, 1994).[8] Further, as it is impossible to conceptualise gender apart from social context and from other social categories that give each other meaning (Archer, 2003, p. 21), versions of masculinity which hold particular sway for particular youth in certain places and times will depend on local circumstances as well as on categories such as race, class, or, say, sexual orientation.

Brought to bear on this study, where the black and Latino boys I worked with lived in and through various social inequities, the dominant or 'popular' (Frosh et al., 2002) masculinity was a classed and raced masculinity based on the gangsta narrative described in the first part of this chapter. Embodied as a black (and in New York sometimes Latino), hypermasculine form, the gangsta masculinity was drawn from both their lived experiences and VMC as well as by the local gender order. This masculinity was ubiquitous in the lived experience of youth in New York, where countless men employed a gangsta style and performed a gangsta 'attitude', and in VMC where embodiments of gangsta and gangsta aesthetics continued to be at the forefront of popular VMC. Moreover, as narratives carry with them the weight of community and history, the gangsta masculinity was not simply a creation of popular VMC. Rather, the gangsta masculinity was composed, in part, of enduring ideologies of the existing gender patterns in place which traditionally held 'real' men to be, for example, 'tough, emotionally unexpressive, detached, responsible, and occupationally successful' (Majors, Tyler, Peden, & Hall, 1994, p. 250).

---

[8] Though contested, the concept of 'hegemonic masculinity' drawn from Connell (e.g., Connell, 2002; Connell & Messerschmidt, 2005) is useful in imagining how forms of masculinity gain dominance not through force but through the transmission of ideals woven through the gender order and championed through community, through VMC itself, and through institutions such as schools (see Connell & Messerschmidt, 2005, for a summary of critiques on the concept of hegemonic masculinity). Archer (2003) helpfully writes of 'hegemonic masculinit*ies*' (p. 15) and further of 'local hegemony', 'developed and utili[s]ed to account for the ways in which particular discourses may be powerful, or hegemonic, within highly locali[s]ed instances' (p. 16).

Consequently, the gangsta masculinity for boys at the Hope was extremely powerful: it held popular and personal appeal for black and Latino youth living in an urban environment, as well as significant sway as it was connected to and bore the imprints of more powerful overarching Western models of masculinity. And yet, despite its significance, the boys at the Hope did not (and could not) fully invest in all the ideals of this masculinity. It seemed that while the boys' lives may have resonated with some of the social experiences of gangsta rappers (e.g. living through difficult material conditions, growing up black or Latino in the inner city) and though dominant ideals of masculinity that circulated in place were influential and pervasive, the boys remained corporeal beings with individual identity combinations, families, and trajectories. It was, in part, these individual and collective local experiences which seemed to not only constrain their investment in various ideals but which were brought to bear on what the boys themselves considered to be the most important ideals of masculinity.

Of the countless ideals and valued qualities of masculinity, drawn from both the gangsta narrative and the gender order more broadly, that boys revered, sometimes reworked, and consistently used in the negotiation and performance of their own identities, four were most profoundly evident: toughness; survival; community, friends, and family; and talent. While boys negotiated and constructed the valued qualities of masculinity through various forms of VMC, the primary form was embodied VMC. More specifically, reflecting the centrality of autobiography in hip-hop (Hess, 2006), boys drew most saliently on the lives and mythologised biographies of hip-hop artists and on other male entertainers more generally. Boys would often speak at length about rappers' 'stories', both real and fictive, and often it was the spun biographies of artists that served as a tool for evaluating, reworking, and negotiating masculinity.

Jeremy spoke to me about 50 Cent (i.e. the 'rapper's story' he 'liked best'); he described the part fictional, part autobiographical movie *Get Rich or Die Tryin'* starring 50 Cent:

Jeremy: I saw the movie, but they said it was a true story you know. After I saw that movie that movie made me think about how he [50 Cent] been doing his life . . . what he wished to become and what he wished to have and something like that . . . It was a good movie, and how his mom dies in it, and he only had his father, and he never found his father, and it's like, he only had his self . . . he was livin' with his aunt and grandmother and uncle and all of that, and his uncle was always mean to him and stuff like that, and so he had to do it on his own. And when he went to jail he had to find his own place after that cause his grandfather, and had to go to court and stuff, so he found his own place . . . then he got shot nine times that was sad. He still survived, and he had a baby too so his mother had to take care of the baby.

As Jeremy touches on how, through the crafting of a life story, forms of VMC might come to embody ideals of masculinity important to youth, embedded in this retelling are the central themes or ideals of masculinity (embodied by 50 Cent) that boys at the Hope negotiated and reworked in light of their own lived experiences, including, again, toughness; survival; community, friends, and family; and talent. I expand on each of these ideals here.

## Toughness

Found in both the gangsta narrative and in traditional constructions of masculinity, for the boys at the Hope, toughness was the most esteemed ideal of masculinity. In concert with their own lives, boys seemed to produce this ideal in *resistance* to a gangsta toughness, which postulated a hypermasculine 'hardness' asserted through violence, including gun use and getting into beefs or fights with other rappers. For instance, all of the boys rejected gangsta rappers' use of guns. Like many of the other boys, Freddie spoke about 50 Cent:

Freddie: Well I don't know cause I'm not gonna grow up like him he scared of everybody—
K:       Is he scared of everybody?
Freddie: Because well in my opinion, because why you gotta go around with guns in your pocket instead of using your fists? [Makes fists with hands]. You know like fists [punches the air].
         . . .
Freddie: I'm very against guns. If I ever got into a fight, just to let you know, whoever uses guns, they're cowards. I understand the cops that's a different story because they're protecting the world, but me? I would never use guns in my life. I would always use my fists.

As Freddie denounced the use of guns and labelled those who use them cowards, it could be argued that he resisted the gangsta connection between toughness and gun use without fully rejecting the ideal of toughness. Instead, negotiating between violence propagated in the gangsta narrative and a more traditional masculinity constituting the gender order in place which insists men stand up for themselves, Freddie at once reworked 50 Cent as a coward and, in a sense, reworked what it means to be tough more broadly, where carrying a gun is now cowardly and using your fists is tough.

Negotiating the meaning of toughness within the framework of their own lives, where their family experiences (e.g., Jeremy's older brother told him to never under any circumstances carry a weapon), age, and other factors kept them from desiring or obtaining weaponry, the boys drew on alternative forms of toughness also derived from VMC. For example, Freddie later told me that his role model, Daddy Yankee (a Latino rap artist), was 'cool cause he don't carry a gun on him'.

Another aspect of being tough was 'staying out of trouble', *not* getting into beefs with other rappers, and generally 'doing your own thing'. Almost in opposition to the hardness and violence propagated by many of the gangsta rappers, for the boys toughness was about being strong enough to *not* get into fights and to stay out of trouble. Bringing in his own experience, Jeremy told me:

Jeremy: Don't get in trouble, cause one time my brother got put in some place [juvenile home] that he told us not to go and you know I don't want to end up there someday if I misbehave or whatever.

Continuing to draw on hip-hop, the boys accessed forms of VMC they believed embodied a toughness that was different from the violence of the gangsta rapper (even though many of the artists they cited would still be considered part of this genre). Citing rapper Young Jeezy, Gabe spoke about staying out of trouble. In this excerpt he deploys the expression of 'respect':

Gabe: I got a lotta respect for him, you know, he's cool he doesn't look for no trouble he's just out there to make money the right way by makin' music he doesn't dis anybody

For boys, the idiom of respect was an organising concept deployed as a means of articulating and measuring valued qualities of masculinities. Used in hip-hop vernacular, 'respect' is a means of expressing honour, remembrance, or the outward expressive valuing of friends, family, and other artists (Boyd, 2002). Here Young Jeezy is respected for not looking for trouble.

Yet, while boys respected artists who stayed out of trouble, this did not mean that you did not stand up for yourself. For the boys, an aspect of toughness was not letting people 'step on you'. The boys spoke about embodied male VMC who stood up for themselves and their family and friends. Speaking about wrestler John Cena, Gabe remarked, 'John Sena. . . I know it's the business [wrestling] like to make the money, but to me, John Sena is like a person he never backs down. He's always there to stick up for himself'.

Finally, being tough was about having tenacity and determination. Drawn directly from gangsta rap and other hip-hop artists, this trait was not reworked by boys but rather understood through these forms. Tenacity was spoken about in the context of embodied VMC who had been through hard times and kept going, who always knew what they wanted, and who worked hard to get it. Jeremy compared 50 Cent's determination with his own: 'You know, he know his whole life that he wanna make music, and he did it, and I will do it too'.

## Survival

Survival was a revered quality of masculinity for boys at the Hope. Boys would often examine the biographies of artists and the trials they had to overcome, and respect was given to those embodied forms of VMC who pulled through various crises. Boys cited aspects of survival including overcoming drugs, poverty, and other social ills and fighting various social justices. Several boys used Young Jeezy's song 'Soul Survivor' as a way to understand and express the theme of survival. Freddie took time in an interview to talk about the song:

Freddie: Well Young Jeezy he came out with 'Soul Survivor' you know that's the song right there [hits his heart]—
K:       Tell me about Soul Survivor—
Freddie: Like in the video he was poor. . . Was making money the wrong way he was selling pot, weed, marijuana, all the kinds of drugs. . . And he made money, and he was getting famous in his place you know, then somebody wanted to buy something so they act like they gonna buy something, but they actually shot him and took all the money and—
       . . .

Freddie: It's not a true story, it is in the video. So they shot him whatever and the reason they got soul survivor is because he survived it from all the bullet shots from his head down to his stomach.

Though Freddie knows that this is not necessarily Young Jeezy's own story, the theme of survival embedded in this tale is powerful. Invulnerability, the idea of living a difficult life and of overcoming odds, was important to the boys at the Hope who themselves lived in and through difficult social and material conditions. For boys, survival was about dodging bullets and living on the streets. Many of the youth spoke about 50 Cent as being a survivor because he was 'shot nine times'; Hess (2006) writes that '50 Cent's own life experience includes surviving a gunshot to the face which ... authenticates both his struggle to become a rap star and his seeming invincibility to the forces of the street' (p. 1). There were, of course, incoherencies and contradictions inherent in the boys' negotiation of masculinity; in this case, though youth were against gun use as a form of toughness, surviving gun violence was still a profoundly valued quality for the boys; in fact, the rap artists boys denigrated as 'cowards' for using guns were momentarily redeemed if they had overcome impossible odds.

## Community, Friends, and Family

The theme of community, friends, and family was connected to survival and toughness and included, among other aspects, providing for family and protecting, standing up for, and taking care of loved ones and the 'hood. This ideal was made to mean through a negotiation between themes in VMC and the traditional models of masculinity. At once drawing on and working against some themes from gangsta rap, the boys cited forms of VMC who took care of family and friends, who were not individualistic, and who were charitable and community oriented. Embodied male VMC who possessed those qualities, who cared about where they came from, and who remained humble were the most commonly cited role models for the boys. Louis described his role model:

Louis: The running back on the Falcons [American football team] cause he gives back to his community—
K:     What does he do?
Louis: Gives money to them ... during [hurricane] Katrina he made every... football player give in like I think 10 million bucks [dollars]—

Boys constructed this ideal in relation to their own lives, where the 'hood, friends, family, and community were central components of their lived experiences. They drew on themes from hip-hop which included remembering where you are from and 'keepin' it real' or being authentic – true to self and community (see also Chap. 5). Freddie spoke at length about his role models. Citing Daddy Yankee, Eminem, and wrestler John Cena, Freddie used his own experience to think about these embodied forms of VMC and to invest them with meaning. He described how Eminem 'sticks up for his family' and further that:

Freddie: He's [Eminem] strict for his family. He wants the best family; he wants the best life for his children. And I understand that one hundred percent because when I grow up I want my children to actually have a life that I've never had . . . I'm not going to spoil them, but like I'm going to give them what they want. They got to earn it though.

Using VMC, touching on his lived experience, toughness, survival, and family as mediated through VMC, Freddie imagines his own possible future.

Connectedly, many of the boys rejected rap artists' objectification and denigration of women. Malcolm did not like the way 'they [rap artists] treat women, and talk about sex'; Freddie thought it was 'inappropriate'; and Louis told me that he liked Eminem 'when he is not degrading women'. As many of the youth were raised by their single mothers, boys often elevated women, in particular their mothers, to high status (see also Dimitriadis, 2001). Louis told me, 'I would not be alive if it weren't for my mom, she is always there for me'. Drawing on traditional models of masculinity from the local gender order, the boys took an oppositional stance to the treatment of women by rap artists; drawing on traditional constructions of masculinity, the boys saw it as their duty to protect women and community.

### Talent

The gangsta masculinity features physicality not just through sports but through dance and even sexual activity – with gangsta rappers often bragging about their (hetero)sexual conquests (hooks, 2004). However, it was not necessarily the rampant physical heterosexuality of the gangstas that the boys valued. Instead, it was the sportsmen and dancers (usually from hip-hop genres including breakdancing) who were the most respected forms of embodied male VMC (and forms of physical talent). The boys would cite young hip-hop artist Chris Brown as the 'hottest' because of his dance ability. Hours were spent trying to emulate the moves they saw in videos. Moreover, youth praised sports stars as well as their own personal talent in sports. The most popular answer to the question, 'What is best about being a boy?' was invariably met with: 'We are good in sports'. Sportsmen were cited as role models, their names sewn onto shirts, and their 'moves' often emulated either on the basketball court or, more commonly, through wrestling. Other talents included being a good rap artist, knowing how to rhyme and possessing talent in aesthetic forms of hip-hop including video making and/or graffiti.

Overall, the boys did not simply mirror the ideals as constructed by the popular gangsta masculinity or by the dominant gender patterns more broadly but rather drew on and against forms of VMC, bringing VMC into concert with their own lived experiences to ultimately negotiate a local masculinity.

## *'Good girls gotta get down with the gangstas':*
## *Negotiating Femininities*

Similar to the boys, the girls at the Hope did not simply take up popular narratives of girlie girls and tomboys but rather used available resources, including VMC, to negotiate local ideals of femininity. For girls, this process of negotiation was highly complex: the dominant gender order not only comprised the various ideals and models of femininity, but it also located girls within a series of 'binaries', most primarily that of '"good" and "bad" girls and their attendant meanings around sexuality, femininity, power and agency' (Aapola, Gonick, & Harris, 2005, p. 39, see also p. 132). Therefore, not only did the girls have to negotiate their femininity through a reworking of dominant ideals from VMC and from the powerful gender order (which postulated a 'traditional femininity' valuing, say, passivity), but this negotiation took place with/in and through these dichotomies, which powerfully positioned girls and further constrained their actions (Budgeon, 1998).

Tied to this, while girls' identities were constrained by persuasive models and enduring dichotomies, their identity negotiation was further complicated by the historic context where there is presently a burgeoning of 'choices' (i.e. discourses of femininity) available to girls. As many point out (e.g. Harris, 2004), Western girls today have more choices and freedoms than their mothers or grandmothers had. For example, girls can now draw on contemporary discourses of 'girl power', which propose a model of femininity articulating 'confidence, [and] assertiveness' (Budgeon, 1998, p. 139). Therefore, girls in this study had to negotiate identities with/in the constraints of powerful binaries as well as navigate the immense choice in between binaries, always against, with/in, and through the dominant gender patterns in place, where ways of being a girl were highly contradictory and conflicted.

In the following section, I describe this complex and multilayered negotiation by focusing on the overarching theme of self-respect evident in the data and, more pointedly, on five ideals of femininity nested within this theme that were most significant for the girls at the Hope: respecting your body, self-control and choice, heterosexuality, individuality, and strength. I suggest girls used resources including embodied VMC to navigate the dichotomies and contradictions composing the gender order and to simultaneously make sense of, invest meaning in, and rework ideals of femininity in light of their own experiences.

## Self-Respect

From their illnesses to their love lives, to their actions both on screen and off, the 'real' and fictional lives of embodied female VMC were used by the girls to think about their gender identities and those qualities of femininity they valued. To critique the actions and behaviours of these forms, the girls deployed the value of self-respect, which comprised five interlaced subthemes or ideals of femininity.

### Respecting Your Body

Respecting your body was a major aspect of respecting yourself. Abigail told me that respecting yourself meant that women 'shouldn't show off their body' or 'sell' their bodies. Similarly, Valentina noted that to respect yourself meant 'not doing drugs', and Shanti added that respecting yourself is 'about your body. If you don't respect your body you don't respect yourself'. Respecting your body included not abusing your body (e.g. having an unhealthy relationship with food) and not objectifying or otherwise degrading your body.

In particular, not objectifying the body was intertwined with sexuality, and girls invested meaning in this ideal by drawing most profoundly on rap videos, specifically on the scantily dressed female dancers whom rappers employed to dance in them (see also Weekes, 2004). As Latrice told me:

K:        What does it mean to respect yourself?
Latrice: Respect yourself means don't go shaking your tail in people's faces, which
         means don't be a prostitute, a slut, a ho or a video hoochie.

These highly eroticised female dancers or, in Latrice's words, 'video hoochies', were a source of great debate, confusion, and contradiction for the girls. Box 6.2, which features a discussion with Shanti, Latoya, and Valentina, captures some of this confusion. Arguably, these dancers represented for the girls what it meant to disrespect your body including (for the girls): showing off your body, simulating sex through dance, wearing 'small clothes', and letting people 'own', 'control', or 'use' you. Many of the girls believed the dancers had sexual relations with the rappers to 'get ahead' or were, in fact, prostitutes.

Exemplifying the multilayered process of negotiating particular values and ideals of femininity, the girls not only used VMC (i.e. the actions of these dancers) to invest meaning in the value of respecting your body, this value was part of a powerful and traditional model of femininity, and therefore, it not only mediated the meanings they made of VMC but also mediated their own expressive actions. It could be that one reason the dancers in the videos were a great area of conflict for the girls was because for the girls I worked with, dance was the most valued embodied form of cultural expression. As such, the dancers' overt sexuality seemed to fall in sharp contrast to the innocence the girls were meant to perform as young women (see Aapola et al., 2005, pp. 162–164 for dance).

I would argue that at the intersection of VMC, the girls' lived experiences and desires, and constraints of the traditional gender order, girls continuously reworked what it meant to respect your body. To do so, the girls again used VMC, this time to construct a space between dancers who disrespected and dancers who respected their bodies. For example, I asked Tonya and Latrice the difference between the girls in the rap videos and female pop stars such as Shakira and Beyoncé, who also wore revealing clothing and danced provocatively. Tonya believed that Shakira could wear what she wished and dance how she liked, however provocatively, because she had not 'done a little sompin' sompin' on the side' (i.e. engaged in sexual relations to get ahead). Shakira might have shared some of the same moves as the video dancers; she might have even performed a more overt kind of sexuality; however, Shakira worked her way to the top without disrespecting her body or 'doing something she did not want to do'. For the girls, respecting your body was modified to mean that you could dress however you wanted or dance however you liked provided you had ownership, self-control, and self-determination.

---

**Box 6.2** Shanti, Latoya, and Valentina Talk About the Video Girls

| | |
|---|---|
| K: | How do you feel about the rap videos that have women on them? |
| Latoya: | I don't like it. |
| Valentina: | I think it's kind of like disturbing. |
| Shanti: | Disturbing yes— |
| Valentina: | It is just disgusting cause how can they treat women like that— |
| Latoya: | I just, 50 Cent he has like the women there— |
| Shanti: | And then the women are gonna do that too— |
| K: | It's disturbing because— |
| Valentina: | Because the way they treat women— |
| K: | You think they treat women pretty badly? Why? |
| Latoya: | It's not just the women— |
| Shanti: | Cause they have them in like bikinis and shaking their butts and— |
| Latoya: | Some of 50 Cent's videos and Fat Joe's [rap artist] videos they have women in and Nelly's [rap artist] 'Grillz' [song title and video] they have women in these short shorts— |

. . .

| | |
|---|---|
| Latoya: | It's not just the rappers that are doing that it's the women also because their the ones that want to be inside the video— |
| Shanti: | Yeah, yeah— |
| Latoya: | And wear those kind of clothes and plus they're prostitutes— |
| K: | You think that the women are prostitutes? |
| Latoya: | Yes! Well, not really, but— |
| Shanti: | Some— |
| Latoya: | Short shorts, God you wear that in the summer not in the winta! |
| Shanti: | And plus it's in the swimming pool! |
| Latoya: | Exactly not outside— |
| Shanti: | Like they don't . . . respect you if you wearing stuff like that how they gonna respect you?! |

## Self-Control and Choice

In the context of a discussion about Beyoncé's new video where she is provocatively dressed, I asked Abigail if Beyoncé's outfit bothered her in any way:

| | |
|---|---|
| Abigail: | Not with her because I think she knows how to control herself, but like J-Lo [Jennifer Lopez, female pop star], I don't think [J-Lo] knows how to control herself or Britney Spears [female pop star]. |
| K: | What do you mean by control themselves? |
| Abigail: | Like the way they dress, they need to control the way they dress and like the way they act. |

For Abigail, and for the girls generally, Beyoncé could wear provocative clothing because she knew how to control her actions and how to respect herself; it seemed she had ownership of her body and career.

Self-control, generally, meant not acting 'out of control' and not being too 'outgoing', which for some girls meant not being 'innocent' or acting out of the confines of traditional models of femininity. Being out of control also meant being unfaithful in a marriage, having multiple marriages, and/or, for instance, taking someone else's partner. Talking about pop icon Britney Spears, Abigail describes how she used to like Spears but no longer does because of Spears's choices:

Abigail: I don't like her choices anymore
K:          What kind of choices does she make?
Abigail: Like the choice that she wanted to marry her husband, and she only knew
            him for like a month, and she married him. So I don't like that choice, I
            think you need to know someone for longer.

The value of choice was central to the girls' negotiation of femininity and had two connected aspects: making poor choices, choices which jeopardised one's self-respect, or choices outside the conventions of traditional femininity that privileged institutions such as marriage; and free will or self-determination. Based on the growing choices for girls and on other contemporary discourses, it seemed the girls assumed women, including the dancers, artists, and actors they drew on, had the power to make the 'right' choices. That is, the dominant gender order circulated the value of choice for girls and mediated the girls' understanding of the actions and behaviours of embodied VMC. For example, Shanti, Latoya, and Valentina spoke about the girls in the rap videos:

Shanti:     I feel sorry for [them]—
Valentina: They messed up inside—
Shanti:     At first I feel sorry, and then I think oh well that's their choice.

Shanti assumes that the girls in the videos have a choice – that women have choice – that they can decide for themselves whether they will respect or disrespect themselves. Similar to respecting your body, the data suggest the value of choice was also reworked in resonance with the girls' local experiences, in particular as black and Latina girls positioned in a particular way, often with meagre material resources in comparison to their white counterparts from middle-class families in the suburbs.[9] Within particular material and social constraints, I would suggest that choice for the girls was confined to the themes of controlling their actions and respecting their bodies: with/in their particular histories and circumstances, choice was not necessarily about choosing to be 'whoever you wanted to be' but was located in their lived experience, in what they realistically had choice over: here, their actions and their bodies (see also Aapola et al., 2005, p. 37).

---

[9] Examining various discourses of femininity, Walkerdine, Lucey, and Melody (2001) note the material constraints on working-class girls in Britain, which limit their access to forms of self-determination (see also in Aapola et al., 2005, p. 37).

## Heterosexuality

Being heterosexual rather than lesbian or bisexual was an important part of being a girl as well as a valued quality of femininity championed through various institutions. Aapola et al. (2005, p. 147) write that '[d]iscourses of compulsory heterosexuality are part of a network of power relations governing women's lives, and they have traditionally been crucial for girls and young women in positioning themselves as "properly" female and mature'. As heterosexuality was shot through all aspects of feminine identities, I focus here only on aspects which most profoundly intersected with VMC.

For the girls, heterosexuality was about being interested in, talking about, and/ or being romantically involved with boys. Hours were spent poring over and deciphering love letters and recounting what had happened in school with the particular crush of the week. Throughout interviews, girls would talk about boys in school often in the same breath as their thoughts about embodied male VMC. For example, Abigail compared the boys she did not like to teen hip-hop artist Chris Brown, whom she said was 'full of himself'. Girls used interviews to talk about actors and artists they liked, hated, and found attractive; they spoke about who was 'sexy' and who was not.

Yet, the girls used VMC to assert a unique kind of heterosexuality, one that went against traditional models of heterosexuality that emphasise the desires and asser- tiveness of men and position women as objects. Instead, the girls took control of their sexuality, using embodied male VMC to at once assert their interest in boys as well as to, in a sense, objectify the opposite sex. Using VMC, the girls would often act as the aggressors, telling me what they would 'do to' a particular male rap artist. They would objectify male VMC, subjecting them to severe scrutiny. Talking about rapper 50 Cent and male hip-hop artist Bow-Wow, Latrice told me:

Latrice: 50 Cent, he has all muscles and he's cute and he has a, he's got, well everybody thinks it's a dimple, but it's not, it's a bullet [scar] and when he smiles [pretends to be visibly overheated]... Bow Wow ... he's so cute and he has musk-cles cause he doesn't have muscles yet, so he has musk-cles.

VMC offered girls a 'safe place' to negotiate the mixed messages and dicho- tomies of the gender order with respect to heterosexuality (Lemish, 1998). The girls used VMC, including plots and characters from shows such as Degrassi,[10] to think about what was right/wrong, good/bad and what they found romantically acceptable – always (for the most part) within the existing gender constraints. Gender constraints were based on a central dichotomy with respect to girls' heterosexuality: being good or bad, innocent or sexual.[11]

---

[10] *Degrassi* is a television drama series set in a Canadian high school. The show deals with a wide range of social issues from dating and having sex to racial issues and self-harm. This was one of the most popular shows amongst all of the girls. As Tonya told me, 'I love that it's so real, and I love the drama, and I love how hot they are on that show'.

[11] In between, as Cowie and Lees (1981) might write, being a 'slag' and a 'drag'.

## Individuality

Individuality in discourses of neoliberalism is about pushing against traditional ideals of femininity and taking action in the creation of new selves (Aapola et al., 2005, p. 36). While the individuality the girls constructed was certainly drawn from these widely circulating themes, the girls worked with/in their own circumstances, where the intersections of class and race constrained the girls' individuality and where the girls could not simply 'be anything they wanted'. Individuality for girls was about not being afraid to go against traditional representations of femininity or against the constraints of peer culture. The girls spoke of individuality as being 'your own self' with friends, about finding your own qualities and articulating them, and not following others. The girls used female characters from *Degrassi*, pop stars, and actresses who possessed individuality, who were not scared to be 'themselves', to invest meaning in this ideal.

At the same time, there was considerable confusion and contradiction surrounding this ideal, as the girls were always constrained by the traditional norms of femininity where you could, in fact, be 'too much of an individual'. The girls continuously used VMC to negotiate the boundaries of conformity and to locate selves, others, and VMC as moving too far outside norms of femininity. For example, actress Cassie Steel, who played the character Manny[12] on *Degrassi,* was often debated by the girls: on the one hand, Manny embodied individuality. As Latrice told me, 'Manny, she's not afraid to be her own person'. On the other hand, Latoya spoke about how Manny was more 'innocent' when she was younger but that her actions now lacked self-respect:

Latoya: Manny's too dirty now—
K:       What do you mean dirty?
Latoya: Shows her body. She didn't respect it, and that guy got her drunk.

What made someone 'too much of an individual' depended on the individual young person. Though the girls had collective histories, they also had individual histories, values, emotions, and experiences, and as such, the boundaries of individuality were continuously reworked both collectively and individually. For example, though heterosexuality was a traditional norm and ideal of femininity for the girls, for Tonya, individuality was about crossing norms and constraints, in this case about crossing this enduring norm. Talking about role models, she told me:

Tonya: I really don't care how my role models dress that's not what I'm looking at them for. I'm looking at them for what's inside, what they do, their actions. And I like Madonna. A lot of people don't like her because she kissed Christina Aguilera and Britney Spears, I like her for that. I like that she stood out and she did what she wanted to do and she didn't care. She's an individual.

---

[12] In *Degrassi*, Manny is an outgoing, attractive, Filipina/Canadian student who attends Degrassi High School.

Though there was a collective value system among the girls that stressed self-respect, this was made of numerous voices, with countless lived experiences and particular histories and families.

### Strength

Strength for the girls was associated with the discourse of 'girl power'. Though a widespread discursive formation, the meaning of girl power was localised and understood through the girls' lived individual and collective experiences as black and Latina youth in an urban context. Based on these discourses of strength and tenacity drawn from female black and Latina rap artists and VMC, for girls at the Hope, girl power was about independence, assertiveness – standing up for yourself, or what the girls referred to as having an 'attitude' – and overcoming obstacles.

For example, independence included having strength and power to make it on your own, not having to rely on men, not having to be degraded to get ahead, and being able to do what you want for yourself, by yourself. As Latrice told the camera in her video, 'Stay beautiful, stay fly, and don't let nobody tell you, you can't get by on your own'. Strength and girl power were about being assertive, about standing up for yourself. Standing up for yourself meant respecting yourself. The girls made sense of this quality through forms of VMC and through the expression of attitude. Shanti referred to Halle Berry as the 'ultimate female actress' because of her attitude in the movie Catwoman:

Shanti: Like at first she was one of those girls who let people walk over her but then when she died—
K:      In the movie?
Shanti: Yeah, but then when she died and then she came back to life, she had this new attitude. She was like, I don't care what nobody think or whatever. And like she wouldn't let people push her around anymore. It was so good.

Fierce independence, making it on your own, and standing up for yourself were further tied to the girls' respect for embodied female VMC who had overcome various obstacles. The girls held in high esteem those actresses and artists who struggled and survived and never forgot where they came from. Tonya summarises by telling me why she respects actress Drew Barrymore:

Tonya: Cause she grew up tough and you know she's in a industry and she's still living her life she's doing what she wants to do and she grew up tough and I admire that about her.

Drawing together respecting your body, self-control and choice, heterosexuality, individuality, and strength, the girls' navigation between the good and the 'bad' and the continuous reworking of ideals of femininity was a constant project (Connell, 2002, p. 82). Constrained by traditional norms and models of femininity, as well as by their own positional identities as raced and classed youth, the girls used VMC in conjunction with these ideals to negotiate a unique identity which began to elide binaries. Using a quote from female pop star Beyoncé, Shanti would often tell me, 'well, you know, "good girls gotta get down with the gangstas"'. In other words, being a girl did not mean being all good or all bad but something in between. As Shanti said, 'I'm not a goody girl cause goody girls they're innocent cause they don't do nothing and not a bad girl, I'm normal in the middle'. The girls used VMC, their own experiences and desires, and models and discourses from the prevailing gender order to negotiate a local femininity, indeed a new gender narrative, between complex and contradictory messages.

In fact, it could be argued that for both boys and girls, these reworked ideals of masculinity and femininity were the aggregates of new local narratives: of gendered selves which young people, drawing on VMC, not only negotiated but simultaneously asserted and performed through various expressive practices. Before concluding, I expand briefly on this idea.

## *Performing Gendered Selves*

Gender performance could be conceived through the Butler's (1990) concept of 'performativity' as well as through sociocultural theories where, as in racial identity production, performances are *gendered behaviours* (e.g. feminine behaviours such as particular ways of walking or talking) or cultural artefacts at once produced, employed, and internalised by youth in the construction of their own gender identities (see Holland et al., 1998).[13] Though youth continuously performed and constructed their gender identities, through participation in this study (i.e. through interviews and projects using photography and video making), the performance and articulation of gender identities were made more visible.

For example, employing the expressive medium of film, the boys, including Louis, Freddie, Malcolm, and Juan, asserted and performed a local masculinity including reworked ideals of toughness, survival, community, friends and family, and talent. For their video titled *New York Boys Gone Mad*, the boys decided to patch together scenes of them, for instance, breakdancing, doing the 'Harlem Shake' (a dance), and mock fist fighting – scenes representing ideals of talent and toughness. Performing the ideal of talent in the realm of expressive media and technology, the boys integrated into the final film a clip of the video as it was being edited on the computer. Taking breaks from dancing, the boys watched artists such as Chris Brown on my laptop; concentrating on the steps, they would then try them out for themselves.

---

[13] The idea that gender is not fixed or 'given', that gender identities need to be 'achieved', effectively 'performed' (Frosh et al., 2002; Paechter, 2001), is most often drawn from the theories of 'performativity' (Butler, 1990; Schechner, 2002), where performances themselves (actions, behaviours, gestures, and the like) instantiate that which they name. As Butler (1990, p. 25) famously writes, 'identity is performatively constituted by the very "expressions" that are said to be its results'.

Throughout the video, the boys drew on motifs from gangsta rap and hip-hop aesthetics including autobiography. At the end of the video, Louis wanted photos of each of the boys in 'tough gangsta' poses with 'R.I.P.' (rest in peace) and their birth and death dates over the tops of the images using nicknames they gave themselves. At one point parodying the 'flash' of gangstas, Louis told the other boys, 'Get your phones out! Pretend like we rich'. The boys' video was a pastiche of the qualities of masculinity they valued as well as a reminder of what they respected, who they were, who they were not, and what their material circumstances were. Performing talent and toughness, imitating flash, drawing on autobiography, referencing artists, and using narrative and aesthetics from hip-hop, in this video, VMC was not only part of the subject matter, it was a means of performance, a tool of representation and identity.

Overall, as the boys danced and as the girls, for example, had attitude, youth negotiated, performed, and produced unique gendered selves.

## Gender Sites, Gender Selves

Of the almost infinite ways youth used VMC in their everyday lives, to understand and construct gender was a significant theme in data. Though gender could be approached from multiple positions, staying close to the data, I took a narrow focus in this chapter and limited my discussion to gender identities – in particular to the ways youth used VMC to understand and negotiate gender identities. To make sense of data, I drew on the concept of narratives conceived as both identities and artefacts constituted of the norms and ideologies that are part of the gender order or patterns in places and instantiated in embodied forms of VMC. I described how youth used embodied VMC to understand and produce broad overarching gender narratives including gangsta, girlie girls, and tomboys which were locally produced: dependent on young people's lived experiences, VMC, and sociocultural place. Using the work of Connell (2002), I suggested that girlie girls, tomboys, and gangstas were connected to and comprised of the powerful cultural artefacts derived from the more traditional (and compelling) gender order in place which propagates those dominant ideologies with respect to what means to be, for example, a boy, girl, man, or woman. As such, I proposed that youth could not fully reject narratives as they held powerful sway nor fully invest in them as the use of artefacts is always constrained and enabled by sociocultural and material contexts. Therefore, I illustrated how young people used VMC to rework and negotiate ideals and valued qualities of masculinities and femininities and to produce unique gendered selves: selves created at the crossroads of their own lives and desires, of VMC, and of confusing and often conflicting discourses, values, and ideals constituting the dominant gender order in place. In this discussion, I take some time to examine the intersection where youth lives, VMC, and the local gender order in place meet in the continuous negotiation and production of gender identities.

Gender, as Jackson and Scott (2002, p. 1) underline, is an identity marker and embodied form 'produced, negotiated and sustained' through lived experiences *as well as* a structural form 'embedded in both social institutions and social practices'. The more enduring structures of gender that make up the gender order, including, for example, traditional gender roles, rules, and norms of a community, are part of sociocultural and material aspects of local places – they are woven into and constitute local places.

The gender order, like place, is not static, but rather it is made up of shifting flows of gender discourses, roles, ideals, and the like. The gender order might be conceived as a layer of place that is continuously undergoing change and transformation as global flows of, for example, gender discourses are localised and where, similarly, the local gender norms of, say, communities interact with wider gender values of institutions and nation states. In this conception, again like places, the gender order is neither essential nor closed but open to continuous change.

In this research, this dual nature of gender – as identities which are lived and as gender structures – does not mean that the gender order was impressed upon young people or that youth could produce gender identities without external constraints. Instead, identities and gender contexts could not be separated: working with/in and through the local gender order, at a particular historical moment, youth used available cultural artefacts from the dominant order itself to negotiate their gender identities (Frosh et al., 2002, pp. 3–5; Connell, 2002).

In this chapter, I have argued that the two central artefacts used by youth in the negotiation and production of gender identities were gender narratives and VMC. Gender narratives were not only stories of gender such as the tomboys and the girlie girls, they were key resources in the construction of gendered selves. As artefacts, narratives, and, in particular, the constituents of narratives including, again, ideals, discourses, and so forth, connected identities and place (Bruner, 1990), narratives and their constituents might be thought of as the link between individuals and places, as the substance between young people and the local gender order in place which constrained and enabled them. Like all mediating artefacts, narratives in this study were produced in place, were products of history and human agency, and were constantly reworked in use.

At the same time, artefacts were layered (Cole, 1996), and it was not only narratives and the constituent ideals that mediated and connected youth and local gender order: I suggest that VMC had a central role in the negotiation of gender identities. As described throughout this chapter, gender narratives were often instantiated in VMC (e.g. Paris Hilton instantiated the girlie girl narrative for the girls). Moreover, embodied VMC, male and female, not only conveyed and represented artefacts, they *were* artefacts, another layer of artefacts which mediated youth negotiation and production of gender identities: the lives, actions, and physicality of these forms were material artefacts mediating the negotiation of gendered identities. This mediation through layers of artefacts was by no means straightforward; instead, there seemed to be a continuous flow of mediation and remediation. Mediation often doubled back on itself, where, for instance, as VMC mediated youth understanding of narratives and constituents (e.g. 50 Cent mediated an understanding of gangsta and toughness), narratives from the gender order were simultaneously brought to bear on VMC (e.g. choice and self-control were used to critique embodied VMC).

Like all artefacts, the meanings of VMC were not essential or *a priori* but rather were produced in practice, produced through situated mediated action (see Bruner, 1990). Generally, we make things meaningful by the way we talk about, employ, perform, and represent them (Hall, 1997). Artefacts are, as I have touched on throughout this book, polysemic spaces, spaces in which some voices – some meanings – will be more dominant, more powerful than others. Bringing in the lives of youth at the Hope, young people came to artefacts, including narratives and VMC, with individual and collective experiences. Their engagement with these forms – the meanings they invested and the artefacts they invested in – was limited and enabled by the meanings of the artefacts themselves, by their personal experiences as youth living in and through aspects of place including the gender order in place, and by contexts that positioned them depending on colour, creed, disability/ability, sexual orientation, and other axes of difference.

Drawing together youth, artefacts (including VMC and narratives), and place, most saliently the gender order in place, I suggest the meeting point of these aspects, the crossroads, might be thought of a 'site', as multidimensional space, not of place nor of gender order nor of person nor of VMC or narratives, but a space with a 'process ontology' (e.g. Sawyer, 2002): a relational space made of the continuous negotiation between elements – where gender identities and gender worlds (including the dominant rules, roles, and norm which make up those worlds) are endlessly negotiated, reworked, and remade. The crossroads might be considered 'construction sites' (Weis & Fine, 2000) where, in this study, there was a continuous transformation of youth, place, and artefacts.

More broadly, sites produced at the crossroads of youth lives, VMC, and the gender order in place (or place more generally) are discursive and nondiscursive junctures which at once produce and are constituted of gender stories, stories produced by specific youth, in certain places, using particular forms of VMC. It is possible that with/in and through these sites of gender, the meanings of artefacts, including the meanings of identities and gender norms, are reworked to produce new stories – new narratives – indeed new mediums of self- and world-making.

In the following and final analysis chapter, I pick up on several of the themes described from the Hope including racial and gender identities, place, and authenticity and, tracing my own path through fieldwork, focus on youth identity production in Barlow, Canada.

# References

Aapola, S., Gonick, M., & Harris, A. (2005). *Young femininity: Girlhood, power and social change*. New York: Palgrave Macmillan.

Archer, L. (2003). *Race, masculinity and schooling: Muslim boys and education*. Maidenhead, UK: Open University Press.

Boyd, T. (2002). *The new H.N.I.C.: The death of civil rights and the reign of Hip Hop*. New York: NYU Press.

Bruner, J. S. (1990). *Acts of meaning*. Cambridge, MA: Harvard University Press.

Budgeon, S. (1998). 'I'll tell you what I really, really want': Girl power and self-identity in Britain. In S. Inness (Ed.), *Millennium girls: Today's girls around the world* (pp. 115–144). Oxford, UK: Rowman & Littlefield Publishers.

Butler, J. P. (1990). *Gender trouble: Feminism and the subversion of identity*. New York: Routledge.

Cole, M. (1996). *Cultural psychology: A once and future discipline*. Cambridge, MA: Harvard University Press.

Connell, R. W. (2002). *Gender*. Cambridge, UK: Polity Press.

Connell, R. W., & Messerschmidt, J. W. (2005). Hegemonic masculinity: Rethinking the concept. *Gender & Society, 19*(6), 829–859.

Cowie, C., & Lees, S. (1981). Slags or drags. *Feminist Review, 9*, 17–31.

Dimitriadis, G. (2001). *Performing identity/performing culture: Hip hop as text, pedagogy, and lived practice*. New York: Peter Lang Publishing.

Eckert, P. (1989). *Jocks and burnouts: Social categories and identity in high school*. New York: Teachers College Columbia University.

Eglinton, K. (2010). 'I got a lotta respect for him …': Boys use of visual material culture to negotiate local masculinities. *Journal of Cultural Research in Art Education, 28*, 10–24.

Frosh, S., Phoenix, A., & Pattman, R. (2002). *Young masculinities: Understanding boys in contemporary society*. London: Palgrave.

Gottlieb, A. (2002). Interpreting gender and sexuality: Approaches from cultural anthropology. In J. MacClancy (Ed.), *Exotic no more: Anthropology on the front lines* (pp. 167–189). Chicago: University of Chicago Press.

Hall, S. (1996). Introduction: Who needs identity? In P. Du Gay & S. Hall (Eds.), *Questions of cultural identity* (pp. 1–11). London: Sage.

Hall, S. (1997). *Representation: Cultural representations and signifying practices*. London: Sage.

Hannerz, U. (1983). Tools of identity and imagination. In A. Jacobson-Widding (Ed.), *Identity: Personal and socio-cultural – A symposium* (pp. 347–360). Atlantic Highlands, NJ: Distributed by Almquist & Wiksell International; Humanities Press (distributor).

Harris, A. (2004). *All about the girl: Culture, power, and identity* (pp. xvi–xxv). New York: Routledge.

Hess, M. (2006). From bricks to billboards: Hip-hop autobiography. *Mosaic, 39*(1), 61–78.

Holland, D., Lachicotte, W., Skinner, D., & Cain, C. (1998). *Identity and agency in cultural worlds*. Cambridge, MA: Harvard University Press.

hooks, b. (2004). *We real cool: Black men and masculinity*. London: Routledge.

Jackson, S., & Scott, S. (2002). Introduction: The gendering of sociology. In S. Jackson & S. Scott (Eds.), *Gender: A sociological reader*. London: Routledge.

Lemish, D. (1998). 'Spice Girls' talk: A case study in the development of gendered identity. In S. Inness (Ed.), *Millennium girls: Today's girls around the world* (pp. 145–167). Oxford, UK: Rowman & Littlefield Publishers.

Luttrell, W. (2003). *Pregnant bodies, fertile minds*. London: Routledge.

Mac an Ghaill, M. (1994). *The making of men: Masculinities, sexualities and schooling*. Buckingham, UK: Open University Press.

Majors, R. (1990). Cool pose: Black masculinity and sports. In M. A. Messner & D. F. Sabo (Eds.), *Sport, men, and the gender order: Critical feminist perspectives* (pp. 109–114). Champaign, IL: Human Kinetics Books.

Majors, R., Tyler, R., Peden, B., & Hall, R. (1994). Cool pose: A symbolic mechanism for masculine role enactment and coping by Black males. In R. Majors & J. U. Gordon (Eds.), *The American Black male: His present status and his future* (pp. 245–259). Chicago: Nelson-Hall Publishers.

Nayak, A. (2003a). *Race, place and globalization: Youth cultures in a changing world*. Oxford, UK: Berg.

Nayak, A. (2003b). 'Ivory lives': Economic restructuring and the making of whiteness in a post-industrial youth community. *Cultural Studies, 6*(3), 305–325.

O'Donnell, M., & Sharpe, S. (2000). *Uncertain masculinities: Youth, ethnicity and class in contemporary Britain.* London: Routledge.

Paechter, C. (2001). Using poststructuralist ideas in gender theory and research. In B. Francis & C. Skelton (Eds.), *Investigating gender: Contemporary perspectives in education* (pp. 41–51). Buckingham, UK: Open University Press.

Quinn, E. (2005). *Nuthin' but a 'G' thang: The culture and commerce of gangsta rap.* New York: Columbia University Press.

Reay, D. (2001). 'Spice girls', 'nice girls', 'girlies' and tomboys: Gender discourses, girls' cultures and femininities in the primary classroom. *Gender and Education, 13,* 153–166.

Renold, E. (2000). 'Coming out': Gender, (hetero)sexuality and the primary school. *Gender and Education, 12*(3), 309–326.

Renold, E. (2007, January 25–26). Between spaces: Young girls, ambivalent femininities and contemporary tomboy/ism. ESRC-funded seminar series. *New femininities: Postfeminism and sexual citizenship,* LSE.

Renold, E. (2008). Beyond masculinity?: Re-theorising contemporary tomboyism in the schizoid space of innocent/heterosexualized femininities. *International Journal of Girlhood Studies, 1*(2), 129–151.

Sawyer, K. (2002). Unresolved tensions in sociocultural theory. *Culture & Psychology Online.* http://www.artsci.wustl.edu/~ksawyer/articles.htm. Accessed 29 July 2004.

Schechner, R. (2002). *Performance studies: An introduction.* London: Routledge.

Thorne, B. (1993). *Gender play: Girls and boys in school.* New Brunswick, NJ: Rutgers University Press.

Tobin, J. (2000). *'Good guys don't wear hats': Children's talk about the media.* New York: Teachers College Press.

Walkerdine, V., Lucey, H., & Melody, J. (2001). *Growing up girl: Psycho-social explorations of gender and class.* Basingstoke, UK: Palgrave.

Weekes, D. (2004). Where my girls at? Black girls and the construction of the sexual. In A. Harris (Ed.), *All about the girl: Culture, power, and identity* (pp. 141–154). New York: Routledge.

Weis, L., & Fine, M. (2000). *Construction sites: Excavating race, class, and gender among urban youth.* New York: Teachers College Press.

West, C., & Zimmerman, D. H. (1987). Doing gender. *Gender and Society, 1*(2), 125–151.

# Chapter 7
# Northern Landscapes: Place- and Identity-Making in Sub-Arctic Canada

## Introduction

In this chapter, I take off from the North: a space in the world where nature matters; where you can feel time; where histories, people, place, land, fire, mud, myth, tribe, Northern Lights, dreams, snow, gold, sun, ice, colonialism, artists, families, salmon, and river congeal, grow, and change – form and reform the landscape – and where landscape, I argue, is a space of meanings, a context that constrains and enables, and a powerful 'tool of identity' (Hannerz, 1983).

Picking up on some of the themes discussed at the Hope and focusing on place-making and identities (racial and gender identities specifically), I begin by providing an ethnographic description of my early days in Barlow. As noted in Chap. 1, this book is heavily weighted towards the Hope where I spent the most time, as such I spend more time in this chapter describing the context – this 'thick description' (Geertz, 1973) serving as a means of supporting some of the claims that follow. After this description, I start to underline the ways in which landscape – for now, physical geography and 'narratives of land' – and youth everyday experiences intersected youth place-making. Throughout, visual material culture (VMC) is considered part and parcel of the human-made landscape shaping youth under-standings of place: it includes everything from the local architecture to media representations of Northern Canada often propagated by the territorial and federal governments. In fact, in Barlow, as everywhere, VMC was part of the landscape: it was the gold rush architecture, Interpretive Centre, beadwork, Aboriginal dance, smoke huts, caps and fleeces of the Elders, and broken-down cars, as well as so-called popular or global forms such as practices from hip-hop and, for example, skateboard fashion worn by some of the youth.

In the second half of this chapter, I return to the themes of racial identities and authenticity described in Chap. 5 and to aspects of gender identities described in Chap. 6. Using the example of the 'Original Gangstas' or 'OGs' (a group of Indigenous boys who identified as black and drew heavily on the lexicon and performances of hip-hop artists), I push into relief the negotiations youth needed

K.A. Eglinton, *Youth Identities, Localities, and Visual Material Culture: Making Selves, Making Worlds*, Explorations of Educational Purpose 25, DOI 10.1007/978-94-007-4857-6_7, © Springer Science+Business Media Dordrecht 2013

to make when drawing on urban hip-hop, often raced as black, in the construction of their racial and gendered identities as First Nations boys. I begin to argue that landscape – more specifically, the narrative of marginality it cradled – was not only a social and physical context constraining and enabling particular identities, it was also a tool that youth in Barlow reworked and strategically deployed in an effort to forge credible identities. In particular, I conclude by extending Appadurai's (1990, 1991) 'scapes' (e.g. mediascapes, ethnoscapes) to include 'landscapes', which, I argue, at once releases the concept landscape from discourses constructing it as immobile and supports the idea of landscapes (like mediascapes) as cultural artefacts youth used in the production of their identities. More generally, I argue the OG identity is neither local nor global but a hybrid form produced at the intersection of the social-political-material landscape, the inequitable conditions of globalisation, and the global cultural flows (including VMC).

## Early Days in the North

If early days at the Hope can be described through a series of interactions with the youth, my time in Barlow might be characterised through understandings: by a constant coming to know between me and the community – Elders, parents, teachers, and youth; between me and the landscape – the physical, social, and temporal space; and between the researcher and person I was in New York City and the one I was becoming in Barlow.

I arrived in the closest city to Barlow about 1:00 a.m. on July 1. Neil, a historian and catalyst for my working there, picked me up in his truck. Although just a few hours before I had seen the sun setting in Vancouver (one of my three layovers en route), the sun was now out again, not a bright sun, more like dusk. I had just come off fieldwork in New York City, and I was grieving leaving the youth there. This new 'city' seemed small to me. Like really small. But I would never say that to Neil. My gracious host took me home and had a bed waiting for me. Closing my eyes tight, trying to block out the light, I shook in my bed, my heart pounded, and I heard blood rushing in my ears. I thought of a story my mother told me about people going crazy because of the midnight sun.

The next day, early evening, I went for a walk in the bush, on my own, scared of bears, but somehow I melted into the experience. I looked out over the oxbow of a river painfully blue – it looked fake. Earlier I had gone with Neil and his wife on the same walk; they knew a lot about the bush. They are both white and in their mid-50s; they also knew about traditional medicine and First Nations people, about the purpose of the land and the layers of complex meanings, about community, and about how everything is connected. In the evening, salmon was cooked on cedar blocks; raw eggs were eaten in the salad; I was far from home. I showed Neil some of the videos from the Hope. New York appeared uninteresting 4,500 miles away; the images almost meaningless, a form of visual culture for my host to make his own meaning from. Everyone was relaxed; the fire crackled; I felt I came off coarse, loud, and crude.

The next morning, Neil and I took the long ride up to Barlow. I still felt out of place. I longed to connect with the landscape or people, but as I wrote in my fieldnotes, 'for me, it is just too foreign'. We passed small First Nations communities nestled in bends on the river; Neil talked with passion about camping trips, history, and fish. Coming into Barlow, we went straight to the local bar; the bartender also worked in the local arts centre. She said I should come in, help out with the summer camp, and get to know some of the youth in the community. School did not start up again for 6 weeks, and it was up to me to find youth to start working with.

Neil continued to introduce me to people over the course of 48 h. We went to the Band Hall or First Nations' administrative building. Someone immediately asked me to volunteer for a community function; desperate to be liked, I said yes. I quickly learned that everyone pitches in for events. Some of the people in the office were talking about a swallow's nest they had found. A short First Nations girl with dark shaggy hair and small chubby hands took it gently off the shelf. She said she 'saved it in a box'; she thought she would 'make something out of it'. As she fingered the delicate form, Neil and several others (both white and First Nations) talked about inspiration and about how they 'are swimming in it in the North' – how they 'have too much of it' and simply 'can't stop thinking' – Neil said, 'Give me some bread to lap up this gravy'.

Walking over to the First Nations' Interpretive Centre, Neil introduced me to Nina, an Elder who worked in the centre. A short, sturdy First Nations woman with dark hair and a devilish twinkle in her eye, she was strong, funny, sensitive, and intuitive. Looking me up and down, when I asked her a question, she laughed loudly and called me a 'pushy American'. Neil also laughed and said, 'She is from New York' and 'so she is very pushy'. 'That's fine because I am rock', Nina retorted. She had a beaded brooch pinned to her fleece vest; I told her I liked it, and she said she would teach me how to make one. I liked her instantly – I think the feeling was mutual. After this initial meeting, I would go visit her at the Interpretive Centre; she taught me to bead, spoke to me about the practices of the First Nations people, about their history, and about life in general.

Before Neil left to go back to his family, he took me to the top of one of the hills surrounding Barlow. Alaska was close by. He welled up as he looked out beyond the hills. I longed to feel the inspiration too. Quietly panicking, I shut my eyes as he spoke; my mind raced: what if I can't find young people to work with? What if I never fit in? Neil left. I moved into a large draughty wooden house on my own.

## Going Upriver

Early on I started drinking my morning coffee on a bench looking out over the river. A few of the Elders would often sit there with me, making small talk, telling jokes, or just sitting in silence (though not often). I felt like we (many of the Elders and I) shared a sense of humour. One morning soon after I arrived, one of my neighbours, well-known Elder G – , and I sat together. As we took in the river, he spoke slowly about an important First Nations site. I told him I wanted to go; he told me he would take me there – like, that minute. Gathering our mugs, Elder P – pulled up to the shore in a rickety wooden speedboat he and his brother built. We both got in, and off we went. Passing fishing nets and islands, it was beautiful; the air smelled of sage. Arriving, we pulled up at the dock; both men were wearing windbreakers and baseball caps and had wispy moustaches growing from deeply tanned skin. They both showed me around. G – talked about how he was 'taken away and sent to a school for English far away'. At 16, he left the residential school because 'he could'. I told him about the degree I was studying for, and he said, 'The earth is my university'. He talked about 'clean living' in the North and about the lifestyle. He told me how all the meat is fresh, how the fish is fresh, and how a moose will last him from autumn to autumn (when he can hunt again).

I gave P – ten dollars for taking me upriver on the boat. 'I throw it in the river; that is tradition, then tomorrow I come and get the ten dollars with this fishing net', he said, smiling. I took some photos, and he laughed as he steered the boat sharply from side to side, jokingly miming an attempt to throw me overboard. We all giggled as we motored back to Barlow. The river, the hills, and the tiny islands where massive trees huddled – I was overwhelmed by the space, the people, the light, the history of my guides and neighbours, and the cold river rushing beneath us. They asked if I was going to First Fish camp where young people (both First Nations and white) learn about traditional modes of catching, preparing, and smoking salmon; I decided I would go to everything. As we pulled into Barlow, youth were getting into boats to go to First Fish. Barlow suddenly felt like a bustling port city. My own sense of space and time was being altered.

## Locating Youth

Meetings with the education coordinator for the First Nations (an earthy, sporty white woman) led to a list of names of youth who might be interested. I had also sent out an email before I arrived to some of the parents. But nobody took too much notice, and I was a bit of an anomaly at first in Barlow: constantly walking around town, a somewhat goofy, loud New Yorker, being extra friendly and taking lots of photos. I took the bartender up on her offer and hung out at the summer camp for a few hours during the day. I put posters up asking youth and/or parents to call me if the young people wanted to participate in a 'photography and film project'. I approached youth wherever I saw them. Armed with my list, I would ask if their name was on it – if it was, I would act excited and shamelessly – for better or for worse – use a kind of New York 'capital' to get them interested in the project by telling them I worked with youth in New York and would like to do the same in Barlow. Many of them were polite – though I found out after getting to know them they did not have a clue what I was talking about.

I also pedalled through town on the bike I bought. This bike later became a joke between the youth and me: they would hop on it and make me chase them for it, hide it from me and watch my reaction, and see it parked somewhere and come and find me. One day as I rode up to a shop, I found Will hanging around outside. Eleven, small, and thin, with longish dark hair and green eyes, he was wearing a fitted cap and black T-shirt. He watched as I clumsily tried to park my bike against a fence, and then he followed me in. His mom was there, and she and I got into a conversation. I told her I was doing a research project trying to find out about the lives of young people in the community and how they are using VMC. I told her Will would have the opportunity to take photos and make videos with me. Will said he was 'kind of interested', and his mom, a short, white woman with dark hair and Will's green eyes, simply said, 'It up to him'.

Sitting by the river an hour later, I saw Will again. I watched as he and two other boys did jumps along the dike on skateboards and bikes – I thought they looked like some of the boys at the Hope. Will's thin frame, athleticism, and tough attitude reminded me of Freddie. As the summer wore on, Will and I worked together, and he introduced me to his friends. I continued to meet young people on the streets, through a designated youth centre and by volunteering for several of the festivals and First Nations celebrations, gatherings, and cultural events. Throughout the summer, a few parents did start to call me, word started to get out, and before school started I had a handful of young people working with me and others following me around, knocking on my door wanting to 'work', waiting on the roads to chat with me at night after the bars closed, and constantly asking to make videos.

Once school started, I worked with youth during and after school. The art teacher let me hang out in her room during her classes and work with the young people (see Appendix 1 for phases of the research in Barlow). By the end of the first week of school, I felt I had been in Barlow for years: youth and adults, including many of the teachers, in the community already knew me. The young people had a good feeling I was on their side, the adults and the Elders knew I had fallen for the place, and overall I had a sizable number of young people wanting to join the project or, more simply, spend time talking with me.

## Place-Making in Northern Canada

One of the first days of working with youth was with Will over the summer. We met outside the art centre; he walked up with his skateboard wearing his knit hat (his 'toque'). We decided we would take a walk around town, and he could tell me about some of the places he likes to go to and things he likes to do. I offered him my camera, and he thought for a while about what he would like to photograph and show me. On the way, we stopped to see his mother at work. She was friendly as usual but, since our first meeting, seemed slightly suspicious of me. She asked again where I was from, and I told her again I was from New York. She pounced as if she had been waiting a while to speak and asked if I meant 'New York as in New York

City'. I told her yes. 'Well, what will you do here without the opera?' she asked. Though she was half joking, I felt ashamed and lamely apologised, for what I cannot say. I told her that I never go to the opera, and she said, 'In small towns you have to make your own fun'. We talked about some of the young people in town going camping during First Fish, and I told her I would go to First Fish but that 'I am not a great camper'. 'You don't camp? And you are here?!' she exclaimed. 'I bet the kids in New York don't even know how to skin a fish', she chided. 'I'm sorry, I'm just teasing, I bet I would be a weirdo in New York, I never even been there'. I said that most people are weird in New York and that she would not stand out; she protested, 'Oh, but me, especially so'.

As we spoke, a middle-aged man walked into the building. He heard us talking about making your own fun in small towns and told Will, 'See, life is boring here, even as an adult'. 'But you seem happy', Will said to him. 'That's because I just got paid', the man replied. Will and I left and started to take photographs around town. He wanted to take me to all the places where the young people hung out. In one shop he and his friends liked to look at the knives; in another they would laugh at the tourist gifts including the bottles of hot sauces and spices that have 'dirty words' and, as Will said, 'ladies' tits' (which they did) across the labels. He spoke about sports (snowboarding, skateboarding, biking) as we walked along the river. He told me to come back in the winter so I could photograph him riding through the snow on a Ski-Doo or snowmobile. He also mentioned the skateboard park in town but said it was 'broken'. He talked about how the town does not have any stores that he can buy clothes in but only 'tourist T-shirts'; he also told me how he has to buy his clothes in the closest large town, which is over 8 h away by car; during festivals when vendors come to Barlow; or through a catalogue. In the local trading post, he spoke excitedly about more of the local VMC – about the furs, traps, and fishing rods; about the animals that were stuffed and standing at attention on shelves; about the hides; and about the beading.

## 'In a strange land north of sixty': Constructing Barlow

Barlow, it seemed, was more than place: it was a multilayered, multidimensional space of shifting histories, meanings, and practices (Ingold, 1993, p. 152) – a changing, messy knot in the landscape often referred to simply as 'the North'. The Northern landscape is constituted of what Shields (1991) refers to as 'place-images', 'myths', or what I refer to interchangeably, and more broadly, as narratives of place or land. Narratives include the real and imagined understandings, meanings, and conceptions 'associated with real places or regions regardless of their character in reality' (Shields, 1991, p. 60): narratives are collections of images or discourses which tell a story or constitute a perspective of place or region for particular groups of people at particular points in history. Place-images and, more broadly, narratives are often circulated and propagated through VMC including postcards, websites, and other media (ibid., p. 47). Moreover, narratives have real consequences in the social production and physical development of places and regions – Shields argues they are 'key in the transformation of purely discursive ... notions of space and of "imaginary geographies" into empirically-specifiable everyday actions gestures of the living persons' (ibid., p. 7). These narratives mediate our understanding of places including the ways in which we might be, do, and interact with/in and through places.

My walking tour with Will seems to embed some of the central narratives and organising concepts that intersected youth place-making in Barlow including most primarily a narrative of marginality. In his historical overview of what he calls the 'social spatialisation' of Canada's Arctic and sub-Arctic region (i.e. the cultural production and circulation of discourses or narratives of this region), Shields describes the social production of the North as 'marginal' or 'peripheral' and highlights how place-images and narratives at once are underpinned by and support powerful geographic binaries and dichotomies.

For youth in Barlow, marginality – in conjunction with their own experiences – was at once a primary narrative they produced and drew on in their construction of Barlow and part of the dominant binary which included centre/periphery (or centre/margin) and connected dichotomies of urban/rural and city/country, which organised and mediated their place-making. Shields (1991) reference to marginal places as those which might be geographically 'out of the way', spaces of 'low' cultural practices, and/or places positioned or represented as 'other' to, for instance, cosmopolitan and/or urban counterparts (pp. 3–4), provides a useful starting point for mapping youth production of Barlow. That is, using a mix of 'half-real, half-imaginary' narratives of land that held the North as isolated, untamed wilderness, a place of recreation, a frozen tundra, and an 'extra-ordinary region out of the patterns of ... working like in the cities' (ibid., p. 190), youth at once constructed marginality and Barlow as marginal.

### 'Barlow's so welfare': 'True North' and 'Real North'

Youth cited place-images propagated by adults in the community and based on scale and relationships to urban centres as they described Barlow in opposition to 'the city', as a 'small town', and, for instance, 'the country'. During fieldwork, it seemed my own background as New Yorker pushed this opposition into relief. At First Fish, for example, youth and Elders teased me about not having anyone to talk to in the city – 'nobody cares about you there', one of the Elders said to me. As she skinned a fish, the youth looked on, and she followed with, 'I would never want to live in a city, nobody talk to you; here we have the land, everything we need is right here'. These sentiments were echoed by many of the young people. Twelve-year-old Sammy, who identified as white, was into ice hockey and hunting with her dad, and lived 'in the bush' outside Barlow, told me with respect to city and country living:

Sammy: Country's way better. I'm sorry, no offence.
K:        Why?
Sammy: Because there's a lot more to do. Like in the city it's more crowded, I don't
        really like cities.
        ...
Sammy: They're too crowded and stinky. Here it's so open.

Youth commented on the country being a space of recreation and thus superior to the city. Images or 'postcards' (see Appendix 1 for this method) produced by youth in Barlow during this study included the horns of a moose killed in a hunt, photos of Ski-Doos, bikes, hunting guns, and hang-gliders. Fourteen-year-old Becker, tall with light hair and eyes, who identified as First Nations and was known for his athleticism, spoke about differences between the city and Barlow: 'Like if you moved to the city you can't really do much', he said. '[In a city] you have more stuff to do like games, buildings and stuff like that, arcades, but in a city you can't like go Ski-Dooing or anything like that... Or going hunting or something'.

While many youth would comment on how much they liked living in the country, echoing those place-images of the North as space of leisure circulated through Canadian national discourses of the North as a destination for holiday-makers and adventurists, they would soon draw on their own experiences in Barlow, often denigrating the conditions of place. Becker spoke for many of the youth with respect to the ice rink:

Becker: [H]ockey, like all the kids like playin' it but like we have shitty ice—
         ...
Becker: You only get to play hockey for like two and a half months a year.
K:       What is wrong with the rest of it?
Becker: Well like the ice doesn't last long cause it's real ice and like most places
         have artificial ice so they get it pretty much like 8 or 9 months of the year.

Shields (1991) describes the narrative or myth of the 'True North' as 'reality mediated by imagination' (p. 195) and a '*Southern image* of the North' (p. 194, emphasis in original), discursively propagating the North (p. 197) as wilderness, purity, truth, power, and freedom, and the 'Real North', or 'the reality of the Canadian North' which includes underdevelopment, poverty, and 'deep heartland-hinterland inequalities' (p. 193). For youth in Barlow, narratives of the True North were tempered by their own first-hand experiences. Though most of the youth, regardless of racial or gender identity, were very attached to their community, they would 'place-effacingly' (as if describing a younger sibling) describe Barlow as geographically, socially, and economically marginal. For example, drawing on images of rural isolation, best friends Lizzy and Jamie remarked how they are living 'in the middle of nowhere'. Using discourses of rural poverty, 12-year-old Agatha laughingly told me, 'Yeah, this town is a welfare town'. When I asked 13-year-old Chloe to describe Barlow, she told me, 'Really small... Like welfare, not really great. We always say Barlow's so welfare.' In addition to narratives of the True North, the material and geographical aspects impacted and mediated the imagined community of Barlow youth could create.

Though youth took great pride in the fact that they could Ski-Doo to school in the winter and stay out all night on safe streets in the summer, the out-of-the-way locale contributed to their sense of geographic marginalisation and to a kind of cultural marginalisation from VMC young people saw as coming from the 'centre'. Youth described exclusions and lack of access to services and goods in Barlow; all described how they would have to travel far to the town of J—to buy their clothes.

Asking about style, Becker spoke about particular shops: 'Yup all those places are in J—you can't get nothing here for clothes'. Will and others commented on the VMC around them in relation to accessing the styles and clothing they wanted:

Will: Well I would like to live in the city.
K:     Why?
Will: Well because you can't really buy anything here. Like if you want new clothes you have to order it from a book or go to J—or whatever. And I wish we had like Wal-Mart and stuff... here.
K:     It would be easier?
Will: Yeah it would be easier to buy your clothes. I mean stores, we have all these buildings we don't even use.
K:     Well maybe there's just not enough people to open up a shop like that?
Will: Like at least I would be happy if they had like not as big as those but still have clothes and stuff.

In an effort to bolster tourism and the town's economy, the territorial and federal government deliberately discursively and physically (re)constructed Barlow into a historical site featuring, for example, architecture and other VMC from the late 1800s – the time of the Yukon gold rush. Fourteen-year-old Marcus, who identified as First Nations, spoke about this in relation to going to the nearest city to buy his clothes, 'Cause Barlow's like a historical place and they just have, they just have sweaters and clothes with Barlow [written on them]'. This physical construction of Barlow as historical seemed to add to young people's feelings of marginality.

In fact, for many of the youth the reality of geography – in this case living in a place located geographically far from a city – excluded them from easily participating in some of the youth cultural practices and uses of VMC that young people in New York City had easy access to, at least geographically, though often not financially. Their location meant exclusion not only from particular flows of youth commodities but also from participating in particular youth culture movements. Twelve-year-old French Canadian Claire was one of the few youth that I worked with in Barlow who dressed in what might be considered an 'Emo' style. She and I spoke about this style:

K:      So as you get older do you think you'll become more Emo?
Claire: Maybe. It depends on how many times I visit Wal-Mart.
K:      Why what goes on there?
Claire: A lot of things. I spent three hours there last time.
K:      Do you wish you lived in J—[where there is a Wal-Mart] or do you like living in Barlow?
Claire: Sometimes I wish I was in J—. I'd be able to be with my sister and be with my friends, be able to buy clothes a lot of times.

For youth in Barlow, the inequities and imbalances of globalisation were a geographic reality. As superstores moved closer though just out of reach and as the styles and commodities of so-called global youth cultural forms and practices operated in their minds and were delivered and reinforced through media-scapes (Appadurai, 1990, 1991), their geographic (and economic) access to these forms was restricted.

## North as 'Other', Selves as 'Other'

Young people's production of Barlow was further mediated by common geographic and temporal place-images of the North as extraordinary, mythical, and uncivilised. In one of the first videos made in the community, Will and his friends, 10-year-old Devin and 12-year-old Lyle, both French Canadian, began the video with a scroll that read, 'In a strange land north of sixty...' (see Appendix 2). In this video, the youth articulated the physical boundaries of the North where 'sixty' refers to the 60th line of latitude, north of which lies the area around the North Pole. As they opened the video, they at once drew upon and created place-images of Barlow as 'other': as unknown, unexplored, mythical, and a 'strange land' not part of the daily grind of fast urban life. Place-images and the construction of Barlow as marginal simultaneously came from within and outside of Barlow. Agatha, who identified as white and whose family had a long history in the region, told me how other people in Canada understand Barlow:

Agatha: Like in Nova Scotia, Nova Scotia is in Canada, right, it's in Canada and they thought we like lived in igloos and that we go everywhere by dog sled and they couldn't believe that I went to school and it was minus 50 [Celsius]. The school never shuts down because it's always like minus 47, 48 and if it shuts down and the kid goes to school what's going to happen or something like that. Everyone would freeze to death.

Thirteen-year-old Ada, who identified as First Nations, spoke to me about how Barlow was constructed by a friend outside of the community:

Ada: Like I asked one of my friends from O—on MSN, well on Hotmail, if he ever been to Barlow and he's like, 'Yeah what's the legal drinking age? 13?' I said, 'No it's like 19, same as Canada'. He's like, oh and I was like, 'Why did you think it was 13?' He's like, 'Cause there's so many damn bars there'. I was like, 'Don't judge us by how we look!'

Irrespective of the multiplicity of comments from youth about the North being a place where they can hunt, fish, Ski-Doo, and partake in other outdoor activities – comments reinforced through common discourses about the North as a space of sports and leisure – youth still deemed their own cultural practices as 'low' in comparison to 'high' practices thought to exist for youth residing in the 'centre' (Shields, 1991, pp. 4–5). When I asked youth how they spent their time, they usually replied, as 12-year-old Rylee said, 'Doing nothing, just walking around'. In fact, there was an almost natural connection between narratives of the North as marginal, their everyday practices in place, and place itself. As 11-year-old Benji told me, 'There's nothing to do in Barlow, it's Barlow'.

Touching on the production of identities through everyday practices, youth called the walk around Barlow they would go on each night 'the loser lap'. As Becker and 14-year-old Penn, Becker's cousin, told me:

Becker: We just walk around.
Penn:   Sometimes we just like laugh at stuff or [go to the] video store.
Becker: Yeah laugh at people.

K:      Just walk, everyone keeps telling me this in interviews that they just walk
        around?
Becker: Just walk around—
Penn:   That's all you can do in Barlow there's nothing—
Becker: The loser lap, you go up this street, down that street, down S—street.
Penn:   It's one big square—
Becker: Yeah that's all it is a square.
K:      The loser lap?
Penn:   The loser lap.
Becker: We walk that probably like ten times a day.
K:      Everybody walks the loser lap?
Both:   Yeah.

Citing the loser lap, Penn and Becker start to underline a connection between the
practices of place and a kind of 'spatial identity' as 'other' produced with respect to
place – identities also organised around a centre/periphery and corresponding
dichotomies such as urban/rural. Pushing this idea slightly further, 12-year-old
Madison, who racially identified as white, and Rylee, who identified as part First
Nations, spoke to me about being 'small-town girls':

Rylee:   I like the Toyota something and it's like … electric and so when you're
         sitting there it's not idling.
K:       I don't even know what that [idling] means.
Rylee:   When your car's—
Madison: Idling when you're not moving, only small town, only small town girls
         would know that.
         …
K:       Why do small town girls know about cars? … Like what kinds of things
         do small town girls know about?
Rylee:   We know how to live in the bush.
K:       Do you really?
Rylee:   Longer than some city people—
Madison: Like if you got, if you got in the bush, if someone dropped you off in the
         bush with like a thirty-aught-six [.30-06] [a gun].
         …
Madison: Thirty-aught-six, matches, and something else we would know how to
         survive.

In this excerpt, 'small-town girls' is a spatial identity mediated, afforded, and
limited by geography. Here the overarching narrative of marginality which positions
particular rural localities as 'other' in relation to more urban spaces and which
connects to a series of dichotomies including urban/rural is implicated in the girls'
understanding of self and place. Positioning themselves in opposition to city dwellers,
the girls' own experiences and practices in Barlow intersect with these tacit geographic mediating artefacts.

What is more, in addition to a narrative of marginality and on-the-ground material
circumstances, youth themselves – in the form of heavy policing with respect to the
use of VMC – were also implicated in place- and, ultimately, self-making in Barlow.

For example, girls in Barlow told me about their difficulty in wearing tight clothes akin to the dress of some of the girls at the Hope in New York – clothes which were not in keeping with the relaxed, sporty style adopted by many of the youth. Girls wearing certain clothes or make-up or doing their hair would be asked (in a negative way) why they were 'dressing city'. Box 7.1, which contains part of an interview transcript with Madison and Rylee, expands on this idea.

---

**Box 7.1 Madison and Rylee Describe 'Dressing City'**

Madison: Some people refer to some people as dressing 'city' [quotes with fingers].
. . .
Madison: It's just what everybody says.
. . .
Madison: Like 'you're so city today'.
K:       No they never! What does that mean?
Rylee:   Like skirt and high heels and -
Madison: 'Your dressing so city' like [imitating someone]—
Rylee:   And like you don't dress city at all—
Madison: I've been told I dress city, I been told—
Rylee:   But it's not a bad thing to dress city, it's just weird wearing it in Barlow.
K:       Like what would you be wearing if someone said that to you?
. . .
Madison: Okay, you know there's this girl, and she used to be my neighbour, and last year in grade seven I started wearing make-up and she always said 'you're so city I can't believe you're wearing make-up', and like straightened my hair—
K:       They say 'so city', what city are they referring to?
Madison: I don't know any city.
Rylee:   Well you know like all the fashion, like haven't you ever been to Vancouver, and you sit there and it's like a fashion show you just sit there and it's like everybody—
. . .
Rylee:   Like hats like not baseball caps.
Madison: Hair.
. . .
K:       And what else, your hair? Why does your hair look very city?
Madison: If you do like—
Rylee:   Do it every day—
Madison: That's what that friend said that also called me city, cause like I straightened my hair sometimes, I curled it sometimes—
K:       So if like you take care of yourself sometimes—
Rylee:   Yeah.
K:       They'll call you like city?
Madison: Yeah.

This expression (i.e. 'dressing city') connects the use of VMC, youth cultural practices and identities, and geography and points to the power of the centre/ periphery binary which underpinned youth place-making in Barlow. Further, this expression – dressing city – begins to highlight tensions involved when youth drew on VMC often considered part of 'the centre' or urban, that is, when youth employed VMC that was thought to belong to place-images and narratives of land that sat in opposition to their own – such as urban landscapes.

In the second half of this chapter, I continue a focus on geography with respect to marginality and explore some of these tensions using a salient example: a group of First Nations boys who drew on hip-hop, a distinctly urban form of VMC, in the construction of their own racial and gender identities as First Nations or, as youth put it, 'Native' boys.

## Identity-Making in Northern Canada

Early on in Barlow, I visited the youth centre – as I walked down the dirt road towards the centre, I could hear the young people outside shouting. I didn't go into the centre, but as I had already made initial contact with many of the youth in town, I walked to the back of the centre where the young people were hanging out. 50 Cent was playing; I knew that much from my time at the Hope, but I couldn't recall the title of the song. Nobody heard me say hi, and I stood there watching them all dance for a while, not breakdancing, but just kind of moving their bodies, jumping across some outdoor tables that had benches attached. There were about seven or eight boys there and two girls, all of whom I later found out indentified as First Nations, aside from Will, who was also there. A few of the boys wore fitted hats like I had seen in New York, but their general style was different – pants were not too low on the waist, and generally they dressed in a more sporty or outdoor style with fleeces or down vests. As Penn seemed to dress like this, I asked him about this distinct Barlow style one day. He told me it was between 'hip-hop and skate style', where 'skate style' meant skateboarding style. 'The pants are low, but not that low', he told me. 'And the labels are mixed between like G-Unit (rap artist 50 Cent's clothing line), and skate labels like Quicksilver', he added. As they danced, Otis, a 13-year-old boy, said, 'I'm gangsta' two or three times.

An adult came out. A white man between 30 and 50, he started laughing, telling me, 'They all think they are gangsters'. I got out my video camera and started filming; all of the youth hammed it up for a while, dancing for the camera and yelling out the words to the song. The music soon changed, and Slipknot (a white heavy metal band) came on; I never listened to them until I went to Barlow, and I quickly grew used to (and quite liked) the sound of it. Soon the music slipped back into something familiar to me: Chamillionaire's 'Riding Dirty'. Several of the youth said how much they liked the song, and I asked them if they knew what it meant. Some said yes, and a few said no; I asked if they wanted me to tell them, and they all said yes. At that moment, I was elated that I had gone to the Hope first. I told them what the girls had told me back at the Hope, and the boys grew excited.

They started making jokes about stealing a beat-up 'rat-bag' truck in Barlow and how the Mounties (Royal Canadian Mounted Police) would only need to walk to catch them because the truck's tyres would be 'all flat and shit'. One of the boys again said he was gangsta and shouted something explicit from the earlier 50 Cent song; the remaining boys started play fighting – though, as I wrote in my fieldnotes that night, 'for better or for worse, with more force and freedom than youth at the Hope'.

After this early visit, I soon learned a lot about gangstas in Barlow – or, more specifically, about the Original Gangstas. I learned the Original Gangstas were the only youth cultural formation that had a distinct name, a name that all young people knew about and the only group that youth mentioned in interviews and brought into casual conversations with me. It was also one of the only identifiable – through style, the deployment of other forms of VMC, and performance – youth group identities in the community. In fact, I soon learned Original Gangstas (or the OGs) was synonymous with a group of First Nations boys, was a unique raced and gendered identity in Barlow, and was similar in its production to the blackarican identity at the Hope: it was contingent on geography, produced through the deployment of VMC, and intersected with youth lived experiences and issues of authenticity.

## The Original Gangstas

Just as youth at Hope deployed racialised VMC to produce aspects of racial identities, a group of boys in Barlow drew on forms of urban hip-hop to produce a local understanding of black and/or what the youth referred to interchangeably as 'Native' (First Nations) identities. To clarify, many of the First Nations boys I worked with self-identified as 'black' – often remarking that they 'acted black', or citing their style as 'black style'. Young people in Barlow often conflated Native and black identities. In a discussion about 'acting black', a common phrase also used by youth in Barlow, Agatha, who identified as white, described how black in Barlow 'meant Native':

Agatha: [H]ere when you say you're black you're like Native.
K:      Cause a lot of kids keep saying that they're black.
Agatha: They mean Native, they all mean Native.
K:      So when you say 'acting black', you mean what?
Agatha: Native.
K:      Okay so what way do you act when you act black?
Agatha: Like when, like the Native [boys] they talk with kind of an accent, kind of, and they imitate that and they speak like 'whoa that's so black' and they'll be like, they'll say ghetto and stuff. They'll talk about the ghetto. It's different.
K:      Yeah, because in New York people talk about the ghetto also.
Agatha: But in New York when you guys talk about it like, cause I've never been there so I don't know what it's like, it's talking about African-American people... Here it's not like that, it is Native people cause there's no African-Americans here.

K:        And how do they act? Do they wear like certain clothing?

Agatha: They wear like name brand stuff... Like baggy clothes, jeans that like hang down around your butt and everything.

Agatha's insistence that black means Native instantiates a masculine First Nations identity produced using what might be considered global VMC, here, in part, hip-hop style. Agatha notes, the identity that the boys produce is not, in fact, African-American but Native. Fourteen-year-old Marcus, who identified as Native (and often as black), spoke at length about acting black and the construction of black/ Native identities in Barlow: describing black identities as something that could be managed, he told me, 'I only act black because my friend started doing it'. When I asked him why, he mentioned, 'I don't know, just cause black people are just so cool and they know what they're doing and I guess we just like their style'. Marcus's thoughts on 'black cool' mirror the racialised masculinities discussed by O'Donnell and Sharpe (2000, p. 3) (see also Chap. 5) which touch on both attitude and expressive practices of archetypal black identities including 'being "laid back" – in effortless control' (p. 3). It also speaks to the notion of blackness as 'an elastic sign' (Nayak, 2005, p. 145) and as signifier of 'urban cool' black identities propagated through hip-hop's spatial practices and connections.

The First Nations boys in Barlow, however, did not simply occupy a bounded racial form already in circulation – for example, the black identities that youth constructed at the Hope with their links to the spatial idiom of ghetto, to urban living, and to an African-American experience. Instead, though First Nations boys in Barlow drew on, reworked, and negotiated the values and ideals of the same embodied form of VMC and overarching gender narrative, the gangsta, drawn from gangsta rap (i.e. many of the First Nations boys called themselves the Original Gangstas after the original gangsta rappers in Los Angeles and New York City),[1] and though youth in Barlow might have constructed racial and gender identities using similar VMC as youth at Hope (see Chaps. 5 and 6), they did not (and could not) construct exactly the same identities as youth at the Hope.

The OGs in Barlow referred to themselves interchangeably as black and Native, and there were implicit links between gangsta, black, and Native identities. Young people spoke to me about how 'acting black' was synonymous with 'acting gangsta' and 'gangsta meant Native'. This gangsta identity was produced and articulated through an interplay of style and performance drawn from the gangsta narrative, as it is circulated through VMC and reworked by youth in resonance with their own lives and locality. Jamie told me how all the 'Native boys only wear G-Unit clothes and all that'. Marlow, a 13-year-old First Nations boy, told me that to be gangsta you have to wear 'G-Unit shoes' and 'baggy clothes'; you also had to 'be into rap' and use 'a lot of slang'. In fact, language coupled with performance was key: Marcus mentioned how acting black is 'gangsta'. 'It's like how you talked and how you dressed and what you did.' It included a way of using slang he got from TV, in particular from 'Dave Chappelle, [on] that black channel, BET [Black Entertainment Television] or something'.

---

[1] *Original Gangsta* was also the title of rap artist Ice-T's first album.

The OGs' identity performances were described by all of the young people. For example, Lizzy, who identified as 'a Native', described how the boys in town called themselves the "'Barlow youngsters," but they don't rap, they think that they're a gang'. Using aspects from the gangsta narrative championed through hip-hop that includes loyalty to friends and family, a small group of First Nations boys in Barlow performed their gang alliance in their video for this research titled 'The BK' (The Barlow Krew). Other youth touched on O'Donnell and Sharpe's (2000, p. 3) 'black macho' or 'hardness' when describing Barlow's OGs. For example, many spoke about the boys' resistance and performance in school. Chloe who identified as white spoke to me on a number of occasions about the OGs' rebellious behaviour:

K:      But the kids all get along?
Chloe:  Yeah, pretty much, except for the gangsters usually start trouble cause they're so rude.
        . . .
K:      So they're identifiable, the gangstas?
Chloe:  Yeah.
K:      How are they identifiable?
Chloe:  Because they always swear and they try and act like each other and they're all rude to teachers, and they always listen to really hard core rap and have like Slipknot and stuff in their lockers.

Many of the OGs felt connected to and identified with various embodied forms of VMC, mainly rap artists. For example, Marcus's nickname was Tupac (or 2Pac) after the deceased rapper. Marcus inscribed his nickname on everything from class lists to desks, to his knuckles. Tall and athletic, with dark, short, shiny hair, dark eyes, and caramel-coloured skin, Marcus was, as many boys and girls told me, one of the most popular boys in the school. A central OG, he spoke a lot about the Original Gangstas in Barlow. In this excerpt, he had just finished telling me how you have to be Native to be an OG as well as dress a certain way. I asked him about getting in trouble as part of the OG performance:

K:      Okay you have to be Native; you have to dress a certain way—
Marcus: Yup.
K:      You have to get in trouble?
Marcus: Yup, cause my friends when we're in a group it's like the biggest group in the school.
        . . .
K:      What do you get in trouble for?
Marcus: Talking back to the teachers and not doing your work.
K:      Do you have to do these things to be part of it?
Marcus: You don't have to it, but it's just what we always do.
        . . .
Marcus: You have to like get into a fight to be in it, and kind of be how we act.
        . . .
K:      Who do you have to fight with?
Marcus: Just whoever, just pick a fight with someone.

This toughness as part of the OG performance points to the undoubtedly gendered (i.e. masculine) nature of this identity. First Nations girl Ada often dressed in a style I would have considered to be gangsta and had brothers and cousins who were self-proclaimed OGs. When I asked her if she was an OG, she exclaimed through her laughter and disbelief, 'Only boys are OGs, girls can't be OGs!' Citing and reworking many of the same ideals of masculinity that boys cited at the Hope (see Chap. 6), Marcus described how you have to 'be tough' to be an OG and what this meant:

Marcus: If someone like calls you down, you can't just like stand and take it. You
          have to stand up for yourself. It doesn't matter how big they are or
          anything, you still have to stand up. Cause if you stand up then you'll be
          the good person not him.
K:       And standing up means what?
Marcus: Like calling them back down and fighting back.

While the OG identity was unquestionably a masculine First Nations identity, mediated and produced using forms of VMC, what was questionable was the authenticity of this identity. In fact, comparable to the Hope, though under a different set of sociocultural and geographical circumstances, youth in Barlow needed to work hard to produce credible identities. In Barlow, as in the Hope, authenticity intersected the OGs' identity production and maintenance and operated on two interconnected and continuously in dialogue fronts: in the first instance, a kind of racial authenticity was constructed and invoked by the OGs themselves to give them entitlement to black-identified forms of VMC, as well as to police the borders of this identity. In the second, a more local or, even, place-based authenticity, in some cases based on cultural marginalisation, was invoked by non-OG peers, as a means of both supporting and critiquing the credibility of the OGs' identity and use of black and, more importantly, urban VMC.

Focusing on the first intersection, the OGs constructed a local racial authenticity based on biology, access to particular services, and belonging to, and taking part in, First Nations traditions, which they invoked to claim a 'real' First Nations or non-white identity; in Barlow, only First Nations youth were entitled to use VMC commonly raced as black, and therefore, only First Nations youth (in particular boys) could potentially be OGs. Marcus, for example, spoke about skin colour as a marker of a First Nations identity and, therefore, entitlement to racialised performances drawn from VMC (and ultimately to being an OG):

Marcus: That's about it, oh, dark skin because there's kids here who are white-skinned
          and they talk black and people just call them wangsters [white gangstas].

Luke, who identified as white, told me, 'Their skin's darker than mine cause they're Natives and so they're closer to being black and gangsta than everyone else'. First Nations boys also cited connections to the tribal community through matriarchal lineage and verified their identity by referring to their access to particular programmes and benefits received as First Nations peoples, including national and regional government initiatives (e.g. entitlement to particular work schemes and participation in certain activities such as sporting events and/or trips out of town).

Significantly, as means of claiming (and constructing) an authentic First Nations identity, youth would refer to the traditions they took part in such as First Fish and hunting with Elders. When asked what set them apart from their non-First Nations friends, many cited particular values including taking care of family and friends; Ada remarked on how the OGs took care of each other and how they performed the important value of, as she put it: 'thinking about your other family and friends and [not] ... just always think[ing] about yourself'. The boys also described how they knew about various forms of Indigenous VMC including knowledge of traditional dance. They would often perform belonging to and pride in their First Nations identity by wearing rubber bracelets and baseball caps with the words 'Native Pride' stitched across the back. When I asked Marcus about being Native, he showed me the rubber bracelet that made him part of the 'redskin' club and spoke excitedly about working at the First Nations' festival when he got the bracelet – how he served food to the Elders and worked with his extended family members in preparing various feasts. Fourteen-year-old Lizzy summarised setting themselves apart and performing belonging and pride in their identity – indeed, performing authenticity:

Lizzy: Native people here they just like they, you know how some people try to hide their religion, they try to act like their something else? Everybody here they say that they're Native and stuff and their like proud of it and stuff.
K:       Are you proud that you're Native?
Lizzy: Oh hell yeah! [laughs]. And, like we got these redskins bracelets it's like Native Indian and stuff like that.

Simultaneously instantiating their identity as First Nations (and, therefore, entitlement to the use of particular VMC), as well as maintaining the borders of this specific identity, many of the First Nations boys engaged in police work with respect to who could and could not use these racialised forms of VMC often derived from hip-hop. For example, with respect to the 'n-word', as Marlow told me, 'You have to be gangsta' (i.e. First Nations) to use the n-word; Agatha agreed that 'white people can't say it, but they [OGs or First Nations] can say it'. In Barlow, only First Nations youth (which, for boys, the gangsta identity was almost synonymous) could, as many youth told me, 'drop the n-bomb'. Thirteen-year-old Allen, who identified as half First Nations, spoke to me about the n-bomb:

Allen: Okay, you're like you walk up to someone and you're like, 'What's up *nigga*' then somebody like T—or somebody like that will come punch you. That's done with.
K:       Okay why does that happen?
Allen: Why? Because they [think] they [First Nations youth] were the only ones who could say it.

As Barlow was a place where there weren't any African-American or, for instance, Afro-Caribbean youth to challenge them, youth who could claim a credible First Nations identity were able to use black racialised VMC with relative ease (see also, e.g. in Archer, 2003). However, while most youth (both First Nations and white) accepted the OGs' use of racialised forms of VMC – indeed, even their identification as 'black' – it was Barlow's rural environment, its construction through a centre/periphery binary, and the ever-present narrative of geographic marginality that posed the biggest threat to their authenticity. That is, non-OG peers questioned the boys' use of VMC associated with urban environments. As described in Chap. 5, hip-hop credibility comes not only from being black but also from living through the difficulties of the urban landscape. In Barlow, the urban discourses of rap could not be easily mapped onto the rural landscape.

It was here that authenticity intersected the OGs' identity production and maintenance a second time: again, in this second case, it was produced and invoked by non-OG peers as a means of both critiquing and supporting the credibility of the OGs' identity and simultaneously their use of black and, more importantly, urban VMC typically associated with the 'centre'. Thirteen-year-old Luke, who spent much of his time out in the bush where he lived with his mom, spoke to me about the OG identity. In the following excerpt, he is talking about how he is different from his friends.

K:     Why are you different?
Luke:  I don't know. They're more into gangsta stuff and I don't really believe in
       gangsta and I know they're not from the 'hood. And yeah they live in town
       and I live out in the bush, so mainly that. We have some similarities I guess.
       . . .
K:     You don't think Barlow can be the 'hood?
Luke:  Well it could be, but it wouldn't be like the South Side, living in trashy
       houses and drive by [shootings]. It's not like that here. It's just jeans and hats
       and pushin' people and gettin' in fights.
       . . .
Luke:  Yeah so that's not anything compared to like Tupac [rap artist], how he lived.

Luke's mention of the physical landscape was common among youth where Barlow's rural landscape, it seemed, sat in tension with the identities the First Nations boys sought to produce. Lizzy and Jamie were quite close to many of the OGs, and Lizzy's cousins were central OGs in the school. As the girls talked about the OGs, they kept saying that they are not 'real' gangstas. I asked the girls why the OGs in Barlow could not be 'real' OGs:

Lizzy: Because—
Jamie: Because they're from here—
Lizzy: There's no ghetto here really.

Yet, they immediately went on to say:

Jamie: Well—
Lizzy: Actually Barlow's just like one big ghetto.
K:     Do you feel that?
Jamie: Well yeah people they just like hang out by the bar and drink that is pretty
       much like the 'hood, just 'cept no one's gettin' shot.

Almost authenticating the OG identity, Lizzy and Jamie start to rework a construction of ghetto as a distinctly urban form (as it commonly produced through hip-hop) and of Barlow itself as *only* rural by calling upon particular images and larger narratives of place. In this excerpt, the girls push into relief that powerful narrative of cultural marginality that youth often used in their constructions of Barlow broadly (as illustrated in the first half of this chapter). Here the girls deploy this narrative by citing the so-called 'low' practices associated with marginal places including hanging out and drinking (Shields, 1991). In another example, rather than referring to popular place-images of Barlow as gold rush town, historical, and even a space of outdoor recreation (images circulated both locally and nationally), when I asked Chloe about the spatial concept of the ghetto, she drew on the realities of the Real North – of youth experiences in place:

K:       Do you ever use the word ghetto? Is something ghetto?
Chloe: Gangstas do that.
         . . .
Chloe: But like we'll say the ghetto is like [names an area of Barlow] cause usually
         people get hurt over there.
K:       So that's like the ghetto there and people get hurt there?
Chloe: Yeah. It's more like most drugs and alcohol is always there.

Significantly, landscape – and its constitutive narrative of marginality – was at once a physical context which constrained youth identities, and, arguably, an arte-fact or tool youth in Barlow altered and tactically deployed in an effort to construct a credible OG identity.

What is more, in this authentication, youth went beyond simply citing particular place-images over others; rather, I would suggest they began to push past a domi-nant centre/periphery binary that, as I described in the first part of this chapter, seemed to underpin their constructions of Barlow. That is, as they instantiated the OGs' credibility, youth appeared to, in a sense, push through what seemed to be static notions of periphery and marginality with respect to geography and place-making by emphasising the social, cultural, and political referents of marginality. Illustrating some of these ideas, Jamie and Lizzie spoke to me about some of the First Nations boys in the community:

Jamie: I mean some of the kids here don't have it that great, like [they] live in the
         H—part of town and like they're like—
Lizzy: Yeah, they been through some rough shit like their parents divorced and
         crap and then like they're broke and stuff.
Jamie: Like their parents don't really pay attention to them and let them do
         whatever.

In their negotiations and authentication of this identity, youth continuously produced Barlow as 'Native territory' where, it could be argued, Barlow as a 'Native space' rather than a rural place (which would work in opposition to an urban place) moved youth discourses from the geographic (i.e. rural/urban) to the more sociocultural discourses of marginalisation which underlined the social inequalities that were an everyday reality of many First Nations youth and their families. Agatha's comment that '[Barlow] is Native territory, everything that is here is owned by Natives or something' was echoed in various forms by many of the young people. Though not necessarily a statistical reality, youth would often say, as Penn did, 'That's just the way Barlow is. Pretty much every kid here is Native'. Positing Barlow as a Native space, youth cited some of the difficult conditions for First Nations people in the Yukon and elsewhere. For example, Jamie and Lizzy spoke about a small First Nations village near Barlow:

Jamie: T—is like the ghetto

. . .

Jamie: Like nobody's shootin' each other up, but I mean there has been like deaths there. It's like this small little town and there's this like broken-down shacks and stuff that people stay in and it's like a Native little village upriver.

In their authentication of the OG identity, youth called upon those aspects of the boys' lives that might, arguably, resonate with some of the struggles of 'real' urban and black gangstas. For instance, young people, both First Nations and white, described historical oppression and colonialism, poverty, school exclusion, and racism at once, it seemed, offering a portrayal of the lives of these First Nations boys and instantiating their credibility as OGs. For example, Agatha touched on histories of some of the boys: 'We took their land. . . It wasn't our fault, it was the gold rush'. Becker, too, spoke about some of the history:

Becker: It's just like who was here first was the Natives—

. . .

Becker: And then we got like a village down there [down river]

. . .

Becker: And we used to have one over there at K—and got kicked out.

Both white and First Nations youth cited racial profiling directed at the First Nations boys (and OGs); as Chloe mentioned, 'Everyone blames them [First Nations boys/OGs] right away for anything that happens'. Marcus told me, 'They just think I'm too disrespectful in class but I don't think I am. And I skipped French class once and another kid skipped with me and they didn't even mention that kid and they mentioned just me. And I kind of find that racist cause he's white and I'm Native'.

As hip-hop forms including style, music, and vernacular are the most imitated and prevalent form of popular culture in the world today (see Warikoo, 2007), it is not surprising that First Nations youth used aspects of hip-hop in the construction of their identities. Archer (2003) describes the gangsta identities produced by the Muslim boys she worked with in England. She comments on the popularity of black-identified culture with non-white youth as a space of difference and belonging, 'as a shared site of solidarity against racism, as a resistance to whiteness' (p. 64, citing Archer, 2001, p. 98). What is interesting is that the boys were producing a new racial and gender identity: in addition to border crossing (where Native youth were drawing on black-identified VMC), the OGs were arguably using VMC to blur and even rework racial and powerful geographic borders (here, demarcating black and First Nations identities and an urban and rural dichotomy) and, in the process, producing a unique identity.

That is, similar to the blackarican identity described in Chap. 5, wearing certain styles and using certain vernacular, the OGs constructed and asserted a particular racial and gendered identity tied to place and to their experiences in place. Where boys at the Hope produced a video with rap and R&B music, breakdancing, and engagement in what are arguably place-based and gendered performances drawn from urban-identified hip-hop (see Chap. 6), some of the OGs made a video where heavy metal played in the background rather than rap, where they wrestled in the outdoors rather than danced inside, but where their nicknames and hand gestures were drawn from black and urban hip-hop. Speaking about the OG style, many youth said, as Agatha did, 'Well it's like a gangsta skate mix'. The OGs' baggy pants were worn differently than they were at the Hope. The boys in Barlow spoke to me about wearing pants that were made for skateboarding and sports. These pants were described as baggy but not 'so baggy'. The OGs did not wear do-rags but hats with skateboard logos and mixed the clothing labels of black rap artists with outdoor and skate brands to create a style that reflected their daily experiences of playing outside, engaging in sports, and living, as they often said, 'in the bush'.

## Relational Landscapes, Relational Identities

This chapter focused on the North – on Barlow, Yukon, specifically. Through ethnographic description and interview material, I drew primarily on Shields (1991) to underline the geographic binaries, place-images, and narratives – in particular the narrative of marginality, centre/periphery binary, and other dichotomies such as urban/rural – underpinning and structuring youth production of Barlow. Moving from a production of Barlow based on the natural physical landscape and widely circulated place-images of the North as space of leisure and recreation, youth's production of Barlow was further mediated by the built environment, the town's history, and their own experiences growing up in Canada's North where the lived realities – including lack of access to certain forms of VMC, particular styles, and the everyday cultural practices of place – were deemed, from both within and outside Barlow, marginal. I further touched on how geographic concepts not only organised youth understanding and production of Barlow but structured spatial identities including 'small-town girls'. Turning more fully to identities, I focused on a specific racial and gender identity in Barlow: Original Gangstas or OGs. Using the example of the Original Gangstas, I described the negotiations youth needed to make when drawing on urban hip-hop as a tool in the construction of self, and I touched on the notion of landscape – in this case the place-images and narratives of land – as an artefact or tool of self-making which youth in Barlow reworked, negotiated, and deployed in their identity construction. That is, I started to demonstrate how landscape, in this case the narrative of marginality youth used in the production of place, was a tool in the authentication of the OG identity.

Taking off from this point, I support a driving argument of this book that holds young people's use of VMC in the construction of their identities is a process involving youth lives and experiences, localities, and VMC. I argue that the OG identity, which was, in part, a product of this postcolonial space, the physical landscape, Indigenous values, VMC, and the like, was not a local *or* global identity but a relational form continuously produced in the space where the warp of communities or places, the weft of scapes, the conditions of the global postmodern, and the (constrained) agency of youth intersect.

Appadurai (1990, 1991), as I have cited throughout this book, writes of scapes: flows or spaces carrying meanings, objects, capital, and people across constructed borders – wefts rocking seemingly stable warps. Scapes that may stealthily infiltrate, creep in, or sometimes violently grind against, through, or into so-called 'stable' communities. Communities that, for instance, the 'centre' may deem the 'periphery', the urban, the rural, the cosmopolitan, the provincial, the big, the small, and, in Canada more simply, the communities constituting 'the North' – real and imagined.

Yet, while the metaphor of weaving fosters a particular understanding of the character of (seemingly) global flows, it does not help unravel the space where the warp and the weft meet – where the local and the global, if we pretend there is a separation, touch, negotiate, and sometimes blend. It is in this space that youth in Barlow made sense, negotiated, and constructed aspects of their selves and the world around them. What is more, in this metaphor, 'stability' with respect to community is a relic, discursively produced through history. Instead, communities – like places – are, by their nature, dynamic, continuously produced through human (inter)actions throughout time (Massey, 1993).

Building on these ideas, communities, as well as localities or places, are part of landscapes. Landscape, Ingold (1993) tells us, is more than place. '[T]he landscape', Ingold (1993) writes, 'is constituted as an enduring record of – and testimony to – the lives and works of past generations who have dwelt within it' (p. 152). Through the 'taskscape' (i.e. the '*inter*activity' (p. 163, emphasis in original) of people as they live out their lives), there is a mutual constitution of land and cultural practices – where landscape is '*the taskscape in its embodied form*' – as well as a 'temporality' of landscape: the landscape is 'neither "built" nor "unbuilt", but perpetually under construction' (p. 162, emphasis in original). In Barlow and the surrounding region, for instance, for centuries, First Nations peoples set up seasonal fish camps; later the rich natural resources brought prospectors and government rule to the area; the activity of the miners altered the history and subsistence practices of the First Nations people and forever altered the landscape – the physical and social space, including the narratives the landscape now incorporates and inspires.

Landscapes, as I have pointed to in this chapter, are made up of the multiple narratives, place-images, and ideologies of place (see Shields, 1991). These images and narratives are cultural artefacts we draw on to shape and understand ourselves and our worlds: youth in Barlow drew on various place-images and larger narratives that were part of overarching binaries and dichotomies in their efforts to understand and produce their localities and identities. Coming back to this space where the warp and the weft meet and holding this particular conceptualisation of landscape in mind, I suggest landscapes are similar to Appadurai's scapes – to, for example, mediascapes and ideoscapes (1990, 1991). That is, landscapes, and the narratives they fold and flower, are transient, malleable, and processual (Ingold, 1993); landscapes are not fixed or essential forms but rather carry meanings across human-made borders and infiltrate, mediate, and shape our understanding and, hence, production of place and self. Imagined like this, landscape for youth in Barlow was a context limiting and affording youth action as well as a tool or artefact used to construct place, and that was tactically deployed in their production of authentic identities.

Landscapes, therefore, are at once local/global, continuously reworked from within and outside. Like culture – and cultural artefacts – landscape too is both rooted and routed: narratives of place are circulated, they mediate thinking, and they are continuously reworked in and through cultural work – through a kind of physical and social (re)tilling over time. Describing place-myths (collections of place-images), Shields (1991) argues that place-myths – what I would refer to as narratives – are both consistent and shifting – the narrative begins to change as 'core images change slowly over time' (p. 61). Place-images, and the narratives they constitute, are deployed by people in different ways for different reasons at different times – this deployment and the ensuing practices slowly shifting the landscape throughout history. Youth employed particular place-images and practices to produce Barlow as, for example, a First Nations space and emphasised a narrative of cultural marginality – a narrative which, arguably, not only lent credibility to their identity by connecting them to some of the struggles of gangstas in urban surrounds but shifted the image and ultimately narrative of place – of Barlow – itself.

Thinking again about the space where the warp and the weft meet – and bringing in the work of Bhabha (1990) (see Chap. 5) – I suggest that landscapes as scapes themselves – as non-essential temporal forms – woven with other non-essential dynamic flows including popular VMC, people, and capital – produce a space of hybridity, which, as I described in Chap. 5, is a 'third space', a space which fosters new narratives, landscapes, and selves. The OG identity – produced where the warp meets the weft – was not a global identity youth occupied, nor an isolated local identity without links to wider youth movements; rather, it was a relational form youth worked hard to produce as the postcolonial context brought history and power to bear on the identities youth were able to construct and where, for example, physical geography excluded youth from access to forms of VMC and impacted the ways in which youth could use popular VMC.

Finally, I would add: the spaces where the warp and weft meet are fully participatory spaces: they are spaces of embodiment, relationality, and engagement. Youth in Barlow (and the Hope) were active participants in the (re)construction of their identities and borders and ultimately the racial and gendered landscapes of their figured worlds. 'Human agency', Holland, Lachicotte, Skinner, and Cain

(1998, p. 5) state, 'may be frail, especially among those with little power, but it happens daily and mundanely and it deserves our attention'. Drawing on participatory perspectives, Reason and Bradbury (2001, p. 2) posit: 'Human persons are agents who act in the world on the basis of their own sensemaking'. Though youth worked within the constraints of place and their circumstances, they still actively made sense of identities, produced and reworked borders, and started to produce, in this case, a new OG identity that was adaptable to and reflective of their lived experiences.

# References

Appadurai, A. (1990). Disjuncture and difference in the global cultural economy. *Theory, Culture & Society, 7*, 295–310.

Appadurai, A. (1991). Global ethnoscapes: Notes and queries for a transnational anthropology. In R. G. Fox (Ed.), *Recapturing anthropology: Working in the present* (pp. 191–210). Santa Fe, NM: School of American Research Press.

Archer, L. (2001). Muslim brothers, black lads, traditional Asians: British Muslim young men's constructions of race, religion and masculinity. *Feminism & Psychology, 11*(1), 79–105.

Archer, L. (2003). *Race, masculinity and schooling: Muslim boys and education.* Maidenhead, UK: Open University Press.

Bhabha, H. K. (1990). The third space: An interview with Homi K. Bhabha. In J. Rutherford (Ed.), *Identity: Community, culture, and difference* (pp. 207–221). London: Lawrence & Wishart.

Geertz, C. (1973). *The interpretation of cultures: Selected essays.* New York: Basic Books.

Hannerz, U. (1983). Tools of identity and imagination. In A. Jacobson-Widding (Ed.), *Identity: Personal and socio-cultural: A symposium* (pp. 347–360). Stockholm, Sweden: Almquist & Wiksell.

Holland, D., Lachicotte, W., Skinner, D., & Cain, C. (1998). *Identity and agency in cultural worlds.* Cambridge, MA: Harvard University Press.

Ingold, T. (1993). The temporality of the landscape. *World Archaeology, 25*(2), 152–174.

Massey, D. (1993). Power-geometry and a progressive sense of place. In J. Bird, B. Curtis, T. Putnam, G. Robertson, & L. Tickner (Eds.), *Mapping the futures: Local cultures, global change* (pp. 59–69). London: Routledge.

Nayak, A. (2005). White lives. In K. Murji & J. Solomos (Eds.), *Racialization: Studies in theory and practice* (pp. 141–162). Oxford, UK: Oxford University Press.

O'Donnell, M., & Sharpe, S. (2000). *Uncertain masculinities: Youth, ethnicity and class in contemporary Britain.* London: Routledge.

Reason, P., & Bradbury, H. (Eds.). (2001). Introduction: Inquiry and participation in search of a world worthy of human aspiration. In *Handbook of action research: Participative inquiry and practice* (pp. 1–14). London: Sage.

Shields, R. (1991). *Places on the margin: Alternative geographies of modernity.* London: Routledge.

Warikoo, N. (2007). Racial authenticity among second generation youth in multiethnic New York and London. *Poetics, 35*, 388–408.

# Chapter 8
# Theoretical, Methodological, and Pedagogical Possibilities

## Introduction

Cultural productions, including this book, serve to mediate and incite further action; moreover, mediating artefacts are always unfinished, their edges and centres open – made to mean in infinite ways, in infinite contexts, through infinite (inter)actions. In this chapter, I exemplify the unfinished, mediating, and dynamic nature of artefacts, and rather than sealing this book, wrapping it tightly within itself, I use it to provoke further possibilities and future processes. As such, I summarise the main findings and couch them within the current literature in youth studies in education and educational research broadly. I then toy with theoretical, methodo-logical, and pedagogical ideas inspired by inquiry. In particular, I consider the local/global binary, explore ideas around transformation and play, and reconsider the potential of multi-sited ethnography. In the second part of this chapter, I introduce a pedagogical possibility and focus on what I call an 'ethnographic pedagogy'. I imagine this mode of pedagogy as a possible starting point for releasing some of the tensions and disconnections between youth lived experiences and theoretical and pedagogical approaches in an education focusing on all forms of visual material culture (VMC).

## Youth, (Global) VMC, and Place

The findings and relationships I have illustrated are not an objective reality – a '"real" picture of youth' (Pilkington, 1994, p. 198) – but rather a unique perspective and interpretation: one of infinite outcomes created using particular methods and theories at the intersection of time, place, my assumptions as a researcher, and the lives of the youth described in these chapters. Despite this singular perspective, with Pilkington, my hope is the insights I have provided inform 'alternative starting points for further study' (p. 198), set in motion new ways of thinking about youth

K.A. Eglinton, *Youth Identities, Localities, and Visual Material Culture: Making Selves, Making Worlds*, Explorations of Educational Purpose 25, DOI 10.1007/978-94-007-4857-6_8, © Springer Science+Business Media Dordrecht 2013

engagement with VMC and, ultimately, new ways of supporting this engagement in and out of formal school contexts. Throughout this book, I have postulated a central thesis suggesting young people's use of VMC is a relational process involving youth lives, localities, and VMC. Using a multi-sited approach not to compare sites, but to generate empirical data pushing into relief local understandings, physical contexts, and the lives of particular youth, I have offered an analysis illustrating the ways in which youth people might be negotiating and authoring new selves using VMC – often the same VMC – in two corners of the world. Across two sites with a more primary focus on the Hope in New York City, I have described two main relationships and a central finding identified and illustrated through three major themes.

To summarise, first, using data generated at both the Hope after-school club in New York City and in Barlow, Yukon, Canada, I have demonstrated a tie or relationship between youth lives, VMC, and place. In this relationship, aspects of local place simultaneously impinged upon and afforded the identities, meanings, and practices youth could construct and/or engage. While I entered the study using the literature, gaps in the literature, and personal experiences as my guides, it was only through empirical study that I could understand, describe, and more deeply theorise this relationship.

Second, most saliently, I found that of all the ways young people across both communities used VMC in their everyday lives, constructing, negotiating, and/or making sense of aspects of selves and worlds were the most significant. Articulating the role of local place in this process, I argued aspects of localities including, for example, the gender order in New York and narratives of place in Barlow, in addition to the material conditions of both sites at once limited and provided the resources for youth identity-making using VMC. Youth in both communities, I suggested, continually worked in relation to the constraints and affordances of local places – constraints and affordances wholly tied up with their individual, collective, and historical circumstances.

Third, as data suggest, youth identity construction and world-making were interrelated: as youth used VMC to make sense of and construct aspects of their identities (e.g. racial identities), they simultaneously produced aspects of their worlds (e.g. at the Hope the borders of race). Willis (2000, p. xiv) writes, 'in making our cultural worlds we make ourselves'. This mutual constitution was located in the space where youth lives, VMC, and aspects of local places intersected – a space I will come back to in a moment.

Four ethnographic chapters spanning three significant themes including place, race, and gender brought together, supported, and illustrated the central relationships and findings noted above. In Chap. 4, I argued that youth at the Hope used VMC to produce aspects of place and place-based identities. I demonstrated how youth used cultural practices from VMC to simultaneously create the imagined communities constituting their worlds and construct, represent, and perform their own place-based identities. Similarly, in Chap. 5, I underlined how youth at the Hope used VMC to participate in the active (re)construction of race including racialised identities and the borders of race. These borders were not fixed, but malleable, constantly reworked by youth in light of their own circumstances in place, using various forms of VMC. To maintain borders, I argued youth invoked a form of racial authenticity and that authenticity was also socially produced and flexible, where, for example, themes from hip-hop informed some of its constituent aspects. In seeking to maintain racial borders, the theme of struggle opened up rather than closed down possibilities for the blurring and reworking of racial borders. I speculated that struggle might have been a 'way in' for all youth to make claims to particular forms of VMC and that in authentically drawing these forms of VMC, youth began to rework racial borders and construct new racial identities.

In Chap. 6, I brought in the theme of gender at the Hope. I demonstrated how young people used VMC, in particular embodied VMC, to make sense of, construct, negotiate, and perform aspects of gender including gender identities and what I have called gender narratives. Identifying three central gender narratives – 'gangstas', 'girlie girls', and 'tomboys' – I suggested employing these narratives in the production of gender identities was not straightforward, but rather involved what appeared to be a continuous negotiation among youth lived experiences, aspects of the traditional gender order, and VMC itself – where youth circumstances in local places impacted the construction and use of narratives. Further, I noted how youth used VMC and the constituents of narratives (e.g. values, behaviours) as artefacts, reworking them in light of their own circumstances and in concert with the gender order of places. In the process of this reworking and negotiation, youth performed and produced local gender identities.

Following the path of fieldwork across two sites, in Chap. 7, I moved from the Hope in New York to Barlow, Yukon, Canada, where place, race, and inevitably gender were central themes. Here, I argued a narrative of marginality, the centre/periphery binary, and other geographic dichotomies such as urban/rural, structured youth understanding Barlow, and what might be considered spatial identities including 'small town girls'. I underlined how the production of Barlow and subsequent identities were not only based on the physical landscape and place-images of the North as a space of recreation but were mediated by the town's history, buildings, and location as well as by the young people's lived experiences growing up in the far North.

Concentrating on the intersection of youth lives, VMC, and locality, I focused on the raced and gendered Original Gangsta or OG identity in Barlow. Here, I described the negotiations youth needed to make when drawing on certain forms of VMC as a tool in the construction of self. I extended Appadurai's (1990, 1991) 'scapes' to include 'landscapes' – as a global flow in constant flux produced and reworked from both inside and outside place; as such, I began to work with the idea that landscape (in this example, a narrative of marginality) was a tool youth deployed to produce an authentic OG identity. The OG identity, I concluded, was not a local and/or global identity, but a relational identity which bore the imprints of locality, history, (sometimes global) VMC, and individual and collective experiences.

## Theoretical and Methodological Possibilities

Discussions throughout the ethnographic chapters align with and support strands of education scholarship including youth studies in education and educational research broadly. A significant aspect linking the research presented in this book with strands of youth studies in education is a methodological and theoretical emphasis on what the conditions of the 'global postmodern' (Hall, 1997) might mean with respect to understanding youth engagement with VMC – an understanding crucial to the development of relevant pedagogical practices in the broad area of visual material culture (see Chap. 1).

Various youth researchers across education have started to consider mobilities, movements, and flows as key concepts in understanding youth identities and lives (e.g. Dillabough & Kennelly, 2010; Dolby & Rizvi, 2008a, 2008b; Kelly, 2006, 2008). Empirical projects, including the work presented in this book, challenge commonly held understandings in education of culture, identities, and localities as bounded or static. For instance, McCarthy, Giardina, Harewood and Park (2003) describe culture as 'significantly undertheori[s]ed' in education, 'treated', for example, 'as a pre-existent, unchanging deposit' (p. 452). Arguably then, what this study and others like it point to is the need to reconceptualise culture, places, and identities including identity markers such as race and gender as fluid, relational, and dynamic. In reconceptualising culture, place, and identities, a more nuanced picture of youth engagement emerges, and practices in education can start to align themselves with youth experiences, with their engagement with VMC, and with contemporary cultural dynamics broadly (Buckingham, 2003).

What is more, in light of the global postmodern, in education and educational research, it seems local places have been lost in the theoretical agenda as educators and, for example, researchers commonly assume the global bears down on the local (Pilkington & Johnson, 2003). Consequently, throughout this book, I have attempted to open up thinking and analyses through a truly relational, non-dualistic perspective, which considers youth, VMC, and place in the same frame. Through various theories including the sociocultural theory of artefact mediation (e.g. Cole, 1996) and the concept of place as a nexus of social relations (e.g. Jess & Massey, 1995; Massey, 1993), I was able to explore and emphasise a more relational understanding and offer a new narrative of how places might impact youth action, meanings, and experiences.

At last, what this study and projects like it demonstrate is the need for deeper speculation on the link between local and global practices; it is here that I want to draw attention to a local/global binary often implicit in youth studies and educational research. This binary is significant: it is part of the global postmodern and continues to organise scholarly thinking about place, VMC, and identities in education. Moreover, it carries with it a host of issues with respect to, for example, the exclusions of globalisation and harbours various geographic dichotomies including centre/periphery and urban/rural (see Chap. 7). McLeod (2009, p. 290) writes 'that a pressing challenge for youth researchers today is how not to render the local as a miniature or reflection of the global and, further, how to keep in analytic play the shifting intersections between these various levels of place and affiliation'.

Thinking about McLeod's challenge, my discussion in Chap. 7 theorising the meeting point where the warp of localities and the weft of global flows intersect, and my appropriation and extension of Appadurai's (1990, 1991) scapes to include landscapes – as at once local and global as well as malleable tools in the production of self – arguably helps hold in analytic focus these local and global scales as we attempt to understand youth engagement with visual material culture. With Pilkington (2004, p. 119), I also suggest this binary might more appropriately be considered a nexus: it *is* the space where the warp and weft meet and is always implicated in the site where youth lives, VMC, and localities intersect. In fact, this nexus might again be theorised using Bhabha's (1990) third space (see Chap. 5). Here, I would argue that at the intersection of VMC, youth lives, and localities, the identities youth produced – the masculinities and femininities at the Hope, and, as described in Chap. 7, the OG identity in Barlow – were not specifically local identities, as they included aspects of what might be considered global VMC, nor were they simply reproductions of global identities, but relational forms continuously produced in the discursive and nondiscursive space where youth lives, the warp of place, and the weft of scapes (including, again, landscape as narratives of place and VMC) cross, blur, and merge.

Appadurai (1991) suggests media and images, which include forms of VMC and place-images circulated locally and (inter)nationally, offer possibilities for making self and world (p. 197). This conceiving of possibility is not a unique gift, but inevitably, where, in globalisation, global flows of, for example, hip-hop, people, and place-images offer individuals and groups all over the world possibilities for living. However, as was intensely obvious in Barlow, the enactment of these possibilities is almost dictated by the physical and sociocultural aspects place itself: life is not just in 'the givenness of things' but in the 'ironic compromise between what they could imagine and what social life will permit' (Appadurai, p. 198). Again, youth in Barlow and at the Hope did not simply reproduce local places or even global identities, but (re)constructed places and selves in the space between the sociocultural and physical conditions of place, their lived experiences and histories, and possibilities found and lived through VMC.

Going further with some theoretical possibilities, it could be argued that the site where the local/global, youth, VMC, and place entangle is laced with aspects of 'play'. Thorne (1993) describes play as an active doing, performing, inventing (p. 5). Consequently, it is possible that imagination and elements of play not only fuel these sites but are a means of inciting change and transformation in youth identities and figured worlds. Holland, Lachicotte, Skinner, and Cain (1998) write:

> It is the opening out of thought within the activity of play, what we might call the cultural production of virtualities, that allows for the emergence of new figured worlds, of refigured worlds that come eventually to reshape selves and lives in all seriousness (p. 236).

It is possible that youth engagement with VMC offers young people opportunities for play that, as Luttrell (2003, p. 180) writes,[1] is a 'source of human agency'. It is

---

[1] Luttrell is drawing on the writing of Holland et al. (1998).

also possible that the continuous engagement of the imagination through the use of VMC and through play is a possible means of moving beyond present selves.[2] Holland et al. (1998, p. 236) suggest that 'through play imagination becomes embodied ... experienced in activity ... Through play our fancied selves become material'.

It could be that through expressive practice in the negotiation of identities, through engaging with VMC in particular places at particular times, youth are effectively pressing on a fault – a potential crack that allows them to move beyond – beyond anything just local or just global, beyond these spaces, beyond constraints, beyond selves which, as a consequence of power and enduring structures, can sometimes get fixed or simply reproduced.

Knotting together imagination, play, and identities, Hannerz (1983) writes of portraiture and other representations of self as 'identikit[s], ... inventor[ies] of elements that one might use in putting together an identity of one's own' (p. 355). 'Such externalities', he writes, 'seem to be tools of both identity and imagination. They serve an expansive sense of what an individual may be or can become'. Both with/in and through this study, where youth used expressive media to participate in the recording and constructing of their own stories of self, as well as in their everyday lives, as they used VMC to think about and engage in expressive practices, telling stories, investing in narratives, recording, indeed constructing, their lives, desires, and pleasure through raps, handshakes, style, behaviours, and expressive media including photographs and videos – 'new genres [were] created and recorded in the durable media, old ones [were] refigured, and new worlds and new identities ... created' (Holland et al., 1998, pp. 238–239).

In fact, it is possible that through imagination and play, through embodied and expressive cultural practices, the young people in this research – in fact all young people – in particular places, with individual and collective lives and desires, continuously draw on their world to create their world. And, as they do, they not only move beyond any kind of local or global identity – beyond place-based, raced, and gendered selves – they endlessly construct new possible selves and new possible worlds. Turning to methodological possibilities, multi-sited ethnography permeates this space where identities are constantly being remade in and through local places often using global forms of VMC. Aligning itself to those approaches that hold culture as rooted and routed, identities as material and ideal, and place as in process and anchored, local and global, multi-sited approaches begin to unravel the proliferation of difference which characterises the global postmodern – pushing into relief 'the marginal and the local' (Hall, 1997, p. 183), where the 'margins come into representation' (p. 183), in particular the voices of those often silenced young people such as black and Latina/Latino youth in New York City and Indigenous youth in Canada.

---

[2] 'To tap into imagination,' Maxine Greene writes, 'is to become able to break with what is supposedly fixed and finished... It is to see beyond what the imaginer has called normal' (1995, p. 19).

Indeed, in the global postmodern, there is a 'proliferation of difference' (Hall, 1997, p. 181) including new sexualities and nationalities; it is a time when, as Hall writes, 'marginality has become a powerful space. It is a space of weak power, but it is a space of power, nonetheless' (p. 183). Though the Original Gangstas, for example, worked within the constraints of place, they still actively and creatively made sense of race, still produced and reworked borders, still produced a new racial and gender identity which gave them voice and representation, which was adaptable to and reflected their unique experiences. Multi-sited ethnography offers a 'window into [this] complexity' (Candea, 2009, p. 39) – into the complex geographies of youth cultures, meanings, and lived experiences not only inside and outside school but across national and international borders.

Multi-sited projects align themselves with the idea of places as 'articulated moments in networks of social relations and understandings' (Massey, 1993, p. 67), as constantly shifting, open to global forces, as well as *anchored* and *specific* (Massey, pp. 66–68). As places are at once dynamic, anchored, specific, global, and local, multi-sited projects can demonstrate how particular identities will be (im) possible at particular times and in certain places (Gupta & Ferguson, 1997). For instance, as I illustrated, the location of New York (i.e. a port city on the Atlantic Ocean) and historical events including heavy immigration produce a specific place where black and Latina/Latino youth, living an inner-city experience, use racialised VMC to construct and understand localised white, black, and Latina/Latino identities. Similarly in Barlow, youth in a remote town first inhabited by Indigenous or First Nations peoples displaced by an influx of (predominantly white) gold miners also used racialised VMC to construct particular white and First Nations identities. Though both used VMC to construct identities – in many case the same forms of VMC (usually derived from hip-hop) – the racialised identities youth constructed at the Hope, for instance, were not the racialised identities produced in Barlow.

A multi-sited approach can support a deeper examination of the link between spatiality and identities – the implication of local values, ideologies, and global media on the formation of youth identities and on the geographies of identity markers as they are (re)produced and negotiated with/in and through various local/national/global spaces (see also Dimitriadis & Weis, 2007, pp. 336–338). As I have tried to make clear, this approach is not meant to compare sites, but rather offers an analytic space to, for instance, think about youth lived experiences of the local/global, examine the aspects of power that weigh down on and/or silence particular identities while supporting others (Leonard, 2009, p. 169), and consider how the uneven processes of globalisation impinge on the lives of youth.

# Pedagogical Possibilities

This study persuasively illustrates Grossberg's (1989, p. 94) claim that popular VMC is 'precisely where our identities and experiences are produced'. Connected to this, it implicitly calls for deeper reflection and emphasis in education on the idea that all forms of VMC are pedagogical sites where young people make sense of themselves and their worlds. Moreover, what this study has started to demonstrate is that the experiences youth have with VMC, the meanings they make, the ways in which they engage with these forms are not passive, but rather fully engaged activities. For education, this means that the lives of youth themselves – their meanings, desires, and pleasures – should be central to pedagogical practice (Grossberg, 1989).

Yet while this study illustrates the rich insights gleaned when primacy is given to youth lives and experiences, as noted in Chaps. 1 and 2, many approaches in education that value all forms of VMC (including popular forms) do not necessarily begin with youth experiences, but are commonly underpinned with a concern for ideology embedded in texts. A pedagogical task is to reveal meanings rather than elicit them: it seems that youth lives, their voices, hopes, and desires, have been taken out of the pedagogical equation.[3] I would argue that a consequence of this practice is a continued gap between youth lived experiences with VMC and pedagogical and theoretical perspectives often used across educational areas concerned with bringing VMC into the classroom.

In Chaps. 1 and 2, I touched on the idea, and throughout the analytic chapters (see Chaps. 4, 5, 6 and 7) I have demonstrated how a more dynamic and relational understanding of young people's cultural practices, working in tandem with visual-based ethnography, provides insights into the lived discursive and nondiscursive space where youth, VMC, and aspects of local places intersect. Here, I add this kind of research cannot only potentially link the lives of youth with pedagogical, theoretical, and empirical practices in education – but can serve as a model for pedagogical practice. That is, I would like to argue that an ethnographic pedagogy which makes expressive use of the visual might offer educators a 'way in' to youth lives and support a more youth-centred education in and through VMC.

## *An Ethnographic Pedagogy?*

Staying with this idea of forging a link between youth experiences and pedagogical practices, using this study as a tool to mediate my thinking and this chapter as a space of exploration, I close this chapter with a possibility – in this case, I join the conversation on the potential of what I will refer to as an ethnographic pedagogy: more simply a mode of pedagogy which draws on the practices and principles of what I referred to in Chap. 1 as 'new ethnographies' (in, e.g. Lather, 2001) including

---

[3] While Grossberg (1989, p. 92) writes of pedagogy, 'Unless one begins where people live their lives, one will be unable to engage with the struggles over larger and more explicit ideological positions', and despite calls to start with youth, asking youth to, say, teach us their meanings, their experiences (e.g. Darts, 2004), in the contexts of popular VMC in visual art education and forms of media education, an emphasis is often on textual analysis (see Chap. 2).

accessing youth meanings, a focus on representational issues, questioning the authority of the researcher (or educator), and an emphasis on youth participation in the research and/or pedagogical process.

Ethnography (with anthropology) is often presented and debated as a model for visual culture, art, and design education where the research presented in this book finds its roots (e.g. Chalmers, 1978, 1981; Jagodzinski, 1982; Janesick, 1982; Stanley, 1986; see also Desai, 2002). Chalmers (1981, p. 6), for example, describes the possibility of 'art as cultural artifact' and of teachers and students as 'ethnographers'. Stanley examines the use of an anthropological model in the context of multicultural art education; Desai turns her attention to the increasingly common phenomenon of 'artist as ethnographer'.[4] My discussion here, nested within this dialogue and taking into consideration criticisms and debates (see Jagodzinski, 1982; Janesick, 1982; Stanley, 1986), begins to consider participatory ethnography that draws heavily on visual-based methods as an inclusive education and possible way of linking pedagogical practices with respect to VMC and youth experiences with these forms. While I am not advocating that educators necessarily become ethnographers, I am postulating that tools and ideas from new ethnographies can serve as fruitful resources for the diverse educational perspectives concerned with the role of visual material culture in youth lives.

Though I do not offer a description (or prescription) of exactly what an ethnographic pedagogy looks like or how it might be implemented (I do not pretend to know these answers, nor is this necessarily desired), in the following, I will first offer the trajectory of my imaginings: imaginings which I believe can be used as tools providing another starting point to enter into this conversation, as well as methods which might be taken up, further conceived, constructed, and used in pedagogical practice. Second, I will touch on some of the theories, perspectives, practices, and methods that might lend themselves to this pedagogical approach. And, third, using practical examples, I will point to the significance of ethics in an ethnographic pedagogy which uses visual-based methods and focuses on VMC by drawing on several ethical issues which arose during fieldwork at the Hope and in Barlow.

## Imagining an Ethnographic Pedagogy

It was the notion of ethnography as 'praxis' that inspired my thinking not only about the possibility of an ethnographic pedagogy but also about ethnography as a link between youth practices, pedagogy, and theory in education broadly. Specifically, throughout this study, I thought about ethnography (and research more generally) as a form of praxis at the most basic level, where theory and practice come seamlessly together, but also where praxis refers to 'self-creative activity through which we make the world' (Lather, 1991, p. 11).[5]

---

[4] For a discussion of art teachers and ethnography, see Denscombe (2008).

[5] Lather (1991, p. 11) is citing Bottomore's (1983) *A Dictionary of Marxist Thought.*

In fieldwork, drawing on Harvey (1991), I began to envision ethnography as 'intrinsically praxiological' (p. 23) – a space where theory and practice are brought together on multiple levels – a transformative practice that not only generates knowledge but transforms both researcher and participants in the 'research act' (Denzin, 1978). As we carry out research, we at once enact and are led empirically by the theoretical perspectives underpinning our understanding of social reality. Further, through ethnographic work, as new knowledge is produced, old knowledge is transformed, and there is a continuous integration of theoretical perspectives with raw, sensuous, cultural processes of life in practice (Willis, 2000). Drawing on participatory perspectives, I believe the recognition of this transformation, even transformation on the most basic epistemological level, is potentially empowering and, to an extent, emancipatory (see Kincheloe & Steinberg, 1998 for a discussion on the limits of emancipation).

In the study presented here, and in the context of possibilities for educational practice that starts with the lives and experiences of youth, it was this connection between praxis and transformation, (partial) emancipation, and empowerment that stretched my methodological and pedagogical imagination. While I would not label the research presented in this book as emancipatory research (Lather, 1991), I have remained cognisant of Maxine Greene's (1995) idea that giving young people tools, space, and time to produce their visual worlds supports a transformation of knowing and being – a *potentially* empowering act. What is more, based on some of the theoretical possibilities with respect to play, imagination, and the use of expressive media, since carrying out this study, I would argue more vehemently about possibilities of visual-based ethnography as transformative praxis.

Most importantly, however, it was ideas around empowerment and transformation through the research process itself, this coming together of theory and practice in ways that transform our worlds, and the emphasis on youth experiences and meanings, which planted the seeds for understanding ethnography – in particular participatory visual-based ethnography – as the possible link between youth experiences and practices in education concerned with VMC and, connectedly, possibly, as a model for pedagogy itself. That is, a model for an inclusive education which not only connects youth lives (including those struggling in formal education) and pedagogical perspectives, but which is truly relational and contextual, starts with the lives of young people, and emphasises identities, place, and VMC.

## Possible Perspectives, Theories, and Methods

An ethnographic education as imagined here is a reflexive, youth-centred, participatory practice. It is a mode of pedagogy that brings together the importance of place, youth meanings and experiences, and their engagement with VMC in shaping their worlds and selves. An ethnographic pedagogy will include various perspectives, theories, and methods. In particular, it would respond to some of the needs underlined through this study. Of significance, an ethnographic pedagogy would position youth as active agents taking part in the construction of their own lives. As described in Chaps. 1 and 2, in certain approaches in education, including, for example, in visual culture art education (VCAE) and social reconstructionist approaches, youth are enlightened to the structures of domination, and through the recognition of dominant ideologies, through recognising their own and others' oppression, there is transformation (both individual and social) and empowerment. Yet, in these approaches and others like them across educational fields (see, for instance, a discussion in Buckingham, 1998), pedagogy, theory, and research seem to be based on the implicit assumption that educators and/or researchers know the right answers, that 'the teacher understands the right techniques to enable emancipatory and transformative action' (Grossberg, 1989, p. 92).[6]

However, what this study has emphasised and provided examples for is the idea that youth already are active agents continuously constructing their worlds and further that youth already are engaging in so-called democratic action – action which is transformative. Therefore, I suggest an ethnographic pedagogy might be underpinned by a different kind of thinking about agency and transformation where youth are repositioned as active beings continuously engaged in democratic acts – acts which ultimately transform both themselves and society (see a thorough discussion in Dolby (2003) which I draw on here).

To reposition youth, agency might be better thought of, not from the humanist perspective of individualism, but rather from a more relational perspective, where people are considered fully situated and part of the world around them, a world which affords particular actions and disallows others. As Grossberg writes (1989, p. 93), an agency which imagines that 'people do make history even if they have to use what they have been given, within the constraints and tendential forces pushing them in certain directions and limiting their possibilities'.

Rethinking transformation and democracy, in an ethnographic pedagogy, transformation might simply be about the small changes to our world that youth are continuously making. That is, through mediated action, using artefacts including VMC, youth at once change both themselves and the world around them. Further, the concept of democracy might more powerfully shift from the historic understanding of democracy as action that transforms society and takes place in and through the exclusively public sector to a more 'radical democracy' which elides the public and private binary and, in so doing, articulates youth (private) engagement with VMC as a form of democratic action (Dolby, 2003, p. 269).

Writing about radical democracy, Dolby (2003, p. 269) argues that as youth use VMC to learn about, construct, and negotiate selves and worlds – through 'their creative production' or, as Willis (1990) might write, through 'symbolic creativity' (see Chap. 2):

> [youth] contribute to the multiple sites in society: their homes, families, schools, and communities. In this way, young people are not just refashioning private spheres and private identities, but are contributing to the transformation of public spheres, citizenship, and democracy. (Dolby, 2003, p. 269)

---

[6] Grossberg is describing three types of pedagogical practice impeding radical pedagogy including 'hierarchical, dialogic, and praxical'. In each of these practices, people are constructed as lacking agency, and educators are construed as knowing 'better than they [youth] do' (p. 92).

Repositioning youth as active agents and reflecting with youth on the ways in which they construct and make their worlds move us beyond traditional notions of transformation and democracy and into new and more radical ways of understanding youth engagement with VMC.

Bringing together theories and practice, I would argue that some critical pedagogical perspectives as well as place-based education offer possible support to an ethnographic pedagogical model. In particular, I would suggest a 'critical place-based pedagogy' (Gruenewald, 2003; see also Graham, 2007; Gruenewald & Smith, 2008) offers promise. Rather than focusing strictly on ecological issues, critical place-based pedagogy brings together critical pedagogical perspectives (e.g. see Giroux, 1992; see also in McLaren & Kincheloe, 2007), which sometimes begin with the terrain of popular VMC, where youth experiences with popular culture in particular are prioritised, and place-based approaches which support the examination of the ways in which inequalities, power, and the relations constituting places shape identities and places themselves. A critical place-based pedagogy features youth and educators interrogating the relationships, social structures, and institutions, as well as community and family beliefs and values, constituting local places (Gruenewald). A critical place-based pedagogy summons youth and educators alike to explore the multiple identities constituting places and the ways in which those identities are constructed and continuously transformed in concert with the dynamics of localities (Freire & Giroux, 1989).

An ethnographic pedagogy would postulate the importance of local places including the symbolic, material, and social aspects of place that at once limit and release us. It would be critical, recognising the ways in which aspects of places bear down on identities, youth actions, and meanings, and underpinned by relational and non-dualistic perspectives such as sociocultural theories that envision culture, youth, and the social and material world in mutual interaction.

Bringing in a focus on practice (part and parcel of the more theoretical discussion above), I would suggest that the growing and diverse literature on youth/students as researchers in education and/or youth action research in anthropology and, for example, in human geography are key literatures lending support to an ethnographic pedagogy (e.g. Akom, Cammarota, & Ginwright, 2008; Cahill, 2007; Cammarota & Fine, 2008; Guajardo, Guajardo, & Casaperalta, 2008; Steinberg & Kincheloe, 1998). I would also suggest drawing on ideas from the large body of work in youth voice, pupil consultation, and participatory inquiry (e.g. Flutter & Rudduck, 2004; Hertz, 1997).

Connected to some of these perspectives, an ethnographic visual-based pedagogy might put into practice forms of 'participatory aesthetics' (Gablik, 1991), where cultural production is directly tied to the transformation of self and the betterment of communities. Participatory aesthetics construes cultural production as a device to enact social change; here, artists – cultural producers – indeed, the youth we seek to work with, can potentially reconstruct and transform social conditions. The relevant assumption is that people are at once perceivers, shapers, and (re)constructors of their world.

Linked to this, a medium of an ethnographic pedagogy could arguably include the visual-based methods that constituted this study: methods which were not simply about recording, but were construed as an active means of producing, representing, and constructing identities (see Chap. 1 and Appendix 1). Visual methods in an ethnographic pedagogical practice would be used for cultural production (here art- or media-making): drawing on visual ethnography, an ethnographic educational practice would turn to postmodern ethnographies, where the expressive (and sometimes ambiguous) nature of visual material forms in the production of ethnographic knowledge is capitalised on. In visual anthropology, examples abound (e.g. Edwards, 1997; MacDougall, 1997; Pink, 2001) where there appears to be a cross-fertilisation between ethnography and the visual and media arts.[7]

Visual methods could be used that seek to understand visible cultural processes and practices, as well as the ways in which the physical landscape, social interaction, and discourses are part of these processes. Cultural expression would be viewed not only as producing culture and identities but as fodder for past, present, and future explorations of self and others (Hannerz, 1983). Visual and expressive tools could be used by youth to reflect on their meanings and identities, to unpick the local, and to explore for themselves the affective, the lived, the hybrid, and the space where their lives and experiences, the cultural artefacts which are the media of their lives, and aspects of local places intersect.

As visual methods are designed to spark dialogue, thought, and further production, their use in pedagogy begins to move us beyond some thinking in areas of media education where youth cultural production is a key facet. Focusing on the area of new media literacy, Livingstone (2004) describes the importance of media production – of understanding people as at once consumers and producers of media. In an ethnographic pedagogy, through the production of media using visual methods not only are the expressive aspects of media deeply engaged with, young people's everyday acts of production (including anything from managing online identities, to keeping a blog, to wearing particular styles) are pushed into relief, articulated, and critically explored (see also, e.g. literatures in participatory content creation (e.g. Burgess, 2006); see also the diverse literatures in media studies and production in education (e.g. Sefton-Green, 1999, 2007)).

A final possible practice of ethnographic pedagogy might be drawn from multi-sited approaches. Using a multi-sited approach – or mode of thinking and analysis – educators and youth can consider the uneven aspects of the global postmodern by examining connections between rural and urban sites and, say, exploring how youth in various places are experiencing the proliferation of a visual culture and are excluded and included in global media and how, as in the ethnographic illustration provided, they are incorporating media texts into their own lives, producing 'new subjects, new genders, new ethnicities, new regions, and new communities...' (Hall, 1997, p. 183).

---

[7] For example, visual artists have begun to draw on ethnography, working in communities and sites across the globe, and similarly ethnographers who are trained in visual media have widened their forms of representation and generation of data to include the expressive use of the visual (Pink, 2001; Desai, 2002; Sullivan, 2005). In anthropology, Edwards (1997) describes the production of visual forms that move past realism, documentation, and reporting, to examine the aesthetic possibilities of 'expressing culture visually' (p. 55).

**A Focus on Ethics**

A central aspect of new ethnographies and, ultimately, of an ethnographic pedagogy is ethics (the discussion on ethics provided in this chapter is published and adapted from Eglinton (2013)). Primary concerns in the study presented in this book and ones I argue are key in any pedagogy meant to support youth practices with (often popular) VMC and involve questions about roles, authority, responsibility, and the relationships educators and researchers forge with the young people themselves. An ethical stance taken in an ethnographic pedagogy could be similar to the one which underpinned the research in this book where I drew on feminist perspectives which postulate a link between ethics and power, as well as on feminist and new ethnographic views of researcher (and, I add here, educator) subjectivity and positioning where particular social positions afford researchers and educators certain authorities (e.g. Conrad, 2006, pp. 438–439; Kirsch, 1999; Murphy & Dingwald, 2001, pp. 343–344; Pilkington, 1994). This ethical stance requires researchers and educators to be fully self-reflexive with respect to inequalities, hierarchy, authority, and identities in the process of knowledge production (Ramazanoglu & Holland, 2002; see also Kelly & Ali, 2004).

As a way to articulate some of the various challenges which could crop up when visual-based ethnography is used as a means of working with youth in the area of VMC (in school and out) and as a means of providing a final self-reflexive context for the work presented in this book, in the final part of this section, I touch on some of my own experiences from this study with respect to ethical challenges (see Eglinton, 2009 for an extensive discussion of ethics in this study). In particular, the issues that expressed themselves most profoundly in this research could be grouped into several themes including youth self-representation, the nature of VMC, and roles and relationships. With respect to self-representation, using expressive media and visual-based methods to produce self-representational images speaks to a particular tension throughout my time in the field between the ways in which youth wanted to 'portray' themselves on camera and my discomfort with their choices. For example, though the boys at the Hope were actively against gun use, there were occasions where they playfully asked to be photographed pretending to be holding a gun. In other cases, some of the girls would bring in a particular skirt or shirt they wanted to be photographed in or wanted to pose in ways (often based on dance moves) which from my perspective sometimes seemed age inappropriate. Throughout the production of self-representational images, I had to continuously examine the space between what I considered an appropriate self-representational image for youth and affording youth room to explore, construct, perform – indeed, represent – their identities.

A second theme with respect to ethics included the nature of VMC. This theme was threaded throughout my interaction with the youth in this study and is highly significant to any pedagogical modes concerned with popular forms of VMC. The notion that popular VMC circulates racist, sexist, and/or homophobic ideology is not new; it is also known that bringing these forms into the classroom is a source of tension between teachers' (and institutional) values and youth knowledge (Buckingham, 1998). However, what is less understood are the rules of engagement in research and pedagogy when an aim is to let youth speak (see Grace & Tobin, 1998 for an excellent example). In the study presented here, as my primary aim was to access youth meanings, I decided at the start of the study to remain as neutral about VMC as possible – while I believed I could certainly question youth about ideology embedded in images, I decided I would work hard not to overtly judge the forms themselves or young people's likes and dislikes. This approach proved more difficult that I imagined, and I often found myself stuck somewhere between interested (and a (wanna-be) hip and open) researcher to being completely unable to temper my reaction to, for example, particularly misogynistic rap lyrics. The question that remains for all involved (youth, educators, researchers) is how a more critical stance might be rectified with research and pedagogy which seeks out youth meanings and perspectives.

The third and final theme with respect to ethics in this study and, potentially, in an ethnographic mode of pedagogy includes roles and relationships. Throughout this study, I struggled with finding a comfortable position between forming personal relationships with youth and being the (adult) researcher. Moreover, I found that as my relationships with youth deepened, so too did ethical concerns. For instance, any ethnographic project brings with it issues around trust and responsibility to participants; over time, in both communities, I worked hard to gain the trust of youth, and consequently as I gained this trust, I felt an intense responsibility to young people – to, for example, not only protecting them, but to letting them know if I thought something was, say, a bad idea. And, yet, I did this with immense trepidation as I was very much aware of the power I had. That is, even though I struggled for equality in our relationships, I knew I was always in a position of power (if for no other reason than because I was an adult and, therefore, to many youth, an authority). Reflecting on fieldwork and bringing in issues and possibilities for an ethnographic pedagogy, which prioritises ethics, I still often wonder if I got too close to youth in this study and if closeness in any ethnographic enterprise is inevitable. I question the depth and even the 'authenticity' of understanding and empathy in the context of projects both educational and empirical where we continuously and consciously reflect on our emotions. I also question whether or not ethically and morally researchers and educators working within the contexts of youth lives and VMC can ever really fully negotiate their roles and relationships, their authorities, and subjectivities. That is, I don't think there are any straightforward answers with respect to ethics as we all – pedagogues, researchers, young people themselves – engage in this knotty process of constructing and performing an education which is inclusive of all VMC and which holds at its heart the significance of young people's voices, meanings, and perspectives.

## Concluding Thoughts

I close the way I began: with a short narrative. This time, I tell about a moment at the Hope – a moment when insights struck me, when I felt I was looking at phenomena perhaps from the back, maybe from side, even from the centre, but never as I had before.

It was a dry, chilly, late afternoon in mid-March just after an interview with Abigail. She and I grabbed my book bag and materials from the Hope office and went outside where most of the youth were playing basketball. Walking past the sweaty bodies, it was still cold enough to see our hot breath meet the air. Malcolm flew by me and grabbed one of the two video cameras that were still in my hand from the interview. He ran, actually started skipping, over to Freddie and asked Freddie to start playing basketball, telling him he would film him. Freddie brushed him aside; walking over to one of the brick walls that enclosed us, he slid down it on his back into a squat; crossing his arms in front of himself, he told Malcolm to leave him alone. Malcolm did not give up. Holding up the camera, he started filming. 'Who's your favourite rapper?' he asked. Freddie told him he wasn't 'playin'. Malcolm of course persisted.

About the same time, Abigail, who was still with me, sat behind me and played with my hair. As she did, she talked incessantly about her own hair and, of course, about Mia's hair from *Rebelde*. Shanti soon found us and sat down next to me. She immediately started asking who I thought was cuter, pop star Chris Brown or rapper 50 Cent, and I told her I didn't know. She took this to mean that I thought they were both cute and therefore liked both of them, but more importantly that I had romantic feelings for 50 Cent specifically. Shanti started shouting that I liked 50 Cent. As she laughed and teased me, we started play fighting. I jokingly tried to cover her mouth, and as she dipped down to protect herself, she deftly pulled a book out of my bag. I tried to grab it from her, and as I did, she tossed it to Abigail. This game went on for about a minute – Abigail to Shanti and back again, me flailing about between them. Shanti started saying she knew what the book was about. 'No you don't', I answered back, laughing. 'I do', she repeated. She told me that it was about 'a bunch of rich white people in the suburbs' who 'have a lot of sex' (surprisingly she was almost correct!). She and Abigail burst into laughter and continued tossing the book back and forth. The insanity momentarily stopped when Tonya walked over. She was upset. It seemed that some of the girls were teasing Freddie, telling him that Tonya wanted his 'laffy taffy', a term used in a song by hip-hop group D4L and slang for backside, behind, or butt – putting it in context, D4L writes, 'shake dat laffy taffy'. Apparently, Freddie was upset about this, and so was Tonya.

As Tonya walked away, back into the space where youth were playing, singing, teasing, fighting, running around, it hit me: youth use culture, including most significantly VMC, to make culture. Culture is a tool that is everywhere: in our minds, guiding our steps, constituting our identities and the places we live, forming our desires and our passions, forging the chains that hold us and the keys that release us. What I realised was that youth, just like me and just like you, are always and everywhere – actively, imaginatively, creatively – making culture. That is, making selves and making worlds – selves and worlds wholly situated, fully engaged, positively unique, and totally dynamic.

Since that moment and since finishing fieldwork, it has been hard to look at the world the same way again. In a sense, I feel I have opened a door or, more accurately, that youth themselves have opened a door for me, where the connections found on the other side have not only reconfigured my thinking and opened up possibilities but have inspired, no – demanded – that I ask questions – including, most significantly, how is it possible to support youth in a process that is ubiquitous, fluid, embodied, relational, at once private and public?

What I learned is that it is certainly not about telling youth about their world, nor about unpacking their worlds for them. Rather, it goes deeper than that: it is about listening and watching, as well as engaging, and providing tools and time. It is about seeing youth as active agents and beckoning them to join in the conversation – to be the educators, reflectors, and fully participatory beings they *already* are. And for educators – and researchers and theorists – it is about using our theoretical, methodological, and pedagogical imaginations. It is about using the artefacts around us to participate in cracking open processes, exploring spaces, opening doors, and ethically and reflexively entering into the lives of young people. It is about rethinking our approaches and actively participating in unpicking, shedding light on, and, yes, capitalising on our own power to construct new worlds *with* young people themselves.

Finally, it is about taking seriously local places and the cultural lives of youth in order to create and support an education where all young people are considered unique contextual cultural agents who, through local cultural practices, are actively producing, navigating, and using their visual material world.

While the research I have presented in this book begins to make some progress, as a tool – as a cultural artefact itself – it inspires possibilities, remains open and unfinished, and as such, the process continues.

# References

Akom, A. A., Cammarota, J., & Ginwright, S. (2008). Youthtopias: towards a new paradigm of critical youth studies. *Youth Media Reporter, 2*(4), 1–30.

Appadurai, A. (1990). Disjuncture and difference in the global cultural economy. *Theory, Culture & Society, 7*, 295–310.

Appadurai, A. (1991). Global ethnoscapes: Notes and queries for a transnational anthropology. In R. G. Fox (Ed.), *Recapturing anthropology: Working in the present* (pp. 191–210). Santa Fe, NM: School of American Research Press.

Bhabha, H. K. (1990). The third space: An interview with Homi K. Bhabha. In J. Rutherford (Ed.), *Identity: Community, culture, and difference* (pp. 207–221). London: Lawrence & Wishart.

Bottomore, T. (1983). *A dictionary of Marxist thought*. Oxford, UK: Blackwell Reference.

Buckingham, D. (1998). Introduction: Fantasies of empowerment? Radical pedagogy and popular culture. In D. Buckingham (Ed.), *Teaching popular culture: Beyond radical pedagogy* (pp. 1–17). London: UCL Press.

Buckingham, D. (2003). Media education and the end of the critical consumer. *Harvard Educational Review, 73*(3), 309–327.

Burgess, J. (2006). Hearing ordinary voices: Cultural studies, vernacular creativity and digital storytelling. *Continuum: Journal of Media & Cultural Studies, 20*(2), 201–214.

Cahill, C. (2007). Doing research with young people: Participatory research and the rituals of collective work. *Children's Geographies, 5*(3), 297–312.

Cammarota, J., & Fine, M. (2008). *Revolutionizing education: Youth participatory action research in motion*. New York: Routledge.

Candea, M. (2009). Arbitrary locations: In defence of the bounded fieldsite. In M. A. Falzon (Ed.), *Multi-sited ethnography: Theory, praxis, and locality in contemporary research* (pp. 25–45). London: Ashgate.

Chalmers, F. G. (1978). Teaching and studying art history: Some anthropological and sociological considerations. *Studies in Art Education, 20*(1), 18–25.

Chalmers, F. G. (1981). Art education as ethnology. *Studies in Art Education, 22*(3), 6–14.

Cole, M. (1996). *Cultural psychology: A once and future discipline*. Cambridge, UK: Harvard University Press.

Conrad, D. (2006). Entangled in the sticks: Ethical conundrums of popular theatre as pedagogy and research. *Qualitative Inquiry, 12*(3), 437–458.

Darts, D. (2004). *Visual culture jam: Art pedagogy and creative resistance*. Unpublished doctoral dissertation, University of British Columbia, Vancouver, Canada.

Denscombe, M. (2008). The art of research: Art teachers' affinity with ethnography. In R. Hickman (Ed.), *Research in art and design education* (pp. 25–34). Bristol, UK: Intellect.

Denzin, N. K. (1978). *The research act: A theoretical introduction to sociological methods*. New York: McGraw-Hill.

Desai, D. (2002). The ethnographic move in contemporary *art*: What does it mean for *art education*? *Studies in Art Education, 43*(4), 307–323.

Dillabough, J., & Kennelly, J. (2010). *Lost youth in the global city*. London: Routledge.

Dimitriadis, G., & Weis, L. (2007). Globalization and multisited ethnographic approaches. In C. McCarthy, A. Durham, L. Engel, A. Filmer, M. Giardina, & M. Malagreca (Eds.), *Globalizing cultural studies: Ethnographic interventions in theory, method, and policy*. New York: Peter Lang Publishing.

Dolby, N. (2003). Popular culture and democratic practice. *Harvard Educational Review, 73*(3), 258–284.

Dolby, N., & Rizvi, F. (2008a). Introduction: Youth, mobility, and identity. In N. Dolby & F. Rizvi (Eds.), *Youth moves: Identities and education in global perspective* (pp. 1–14). London: Routledge.

Dolby, N., & Rizvi, F. (Eds.). (2008b). *Youth moves: Identities and education in global perspective*. London: Routledge.

Edwards, E. (1997). Beyond the boundary: A consideration of the expressive in photography and anthropology. In M. Banks & H. Morphy (Eds.), *Rethinking visual anthropology* (pp. 53–80). New Haven, CT: Yale University Press.

Eglinton, K. (2009). *Making selves, making worlds: An ethnographic account of young people's use of visual material culture*. Unpublished doctoral dissertation, University of Cambridge, Cambridge, UK.

Eglinton, K. (2013). Between the Personal and the professional: Ethical challenges when using visual ethnography to understand young people's use of popular visual material culture. Special issue ethics and youth research. *Young: Nordic Journal of Youth Research*.

Flutter, J., & Rudduck, J. (2004). *Consulting pupils: What's in it for schools?* London: Routledge Falmer.

Freire, P., & Giroux, H. A. (1989). Pedagogy, popular culture, and public life: An introduction. In H. Giroux & R. Simon (Eds.), *Popular culture: Schooling and everyday life* (pp. vii–xii). New York: Bergin & Garvey.

Gablik, S. (1991). *The reenchantment of art*. New York: Thames and Hudson.

Giroux, H. (1992). *Border crossings: Cultural workers and the politics of education*. New York: Routledge.

Grace, D. J., & Tobin, J. (1998). Butt jokes and mean-teacher parodies: Video production in the elementary classroom. In D. Buckingham (Ed.), *Teaching popular culture* (pp. 42–62). London: Routledge.

Graham, M. (2007). Art, ecology, and art education: Locating art education in a critical place-based pedagogy. *Studies in Art Education, 48*(4), 375–391.

Greene, M. (1995). *Releasing the imagination: Essays on education, the arts, and social change.* San Francisco, CA: Jossey-Bass Publishers.

Grossberg, L. (1989). Pedagogy in the present: Politics, postmodernity, and the popular. In H. Giroux & R. Simon (Eds.), *Popular culture, schooling, and everyday life* (pp. 91–115). Granby, MA: Bergin and Garvey.

Gruenewald, D. A. (2003). The best of both worlds: A critical pedagogy of place. *Educational Researcher, 32*(4), 3–12.

Gruenewald, D. A., & Smith, G. A. (2008). Introduction: Making room for the local. In D. A. Gruenewald & G. A. Smith (Eds.), *Place-based education in the global age: Local diversity.* New York: Lawrence Erlbaum Associates.

Guajardo, M., Guajardo, F., & Casaperalta, E. D. C. (2008). Transformative education: Chronicling a pedagogy for social change. *Anthropology & Education Quarterly, 39*(1), 3–22.

Gupta, A., & Ferguson, J. (1997). Culture, power, place: Ethnography at the end of an era. In A. Gupta & J. Ferguson (Eds.), *Culture, power, place: Explorations in critical anthropology* (pp. 1–29). Durham, NC: Duke University Press.

Hall, S. (1997). The local and the global: Globalization and ethnicity. In A. McClintock, A. Mufti, & E. Shohat (Eds.), *Dangerous liaisons: Gender, nation, and post-colonial perspectives* (pp. 173–187). Minneapolis, MN: University of Minnesota Press.

Hannerz, U. (1983). Tools of identity and imagination. In A. Jacobson-Widding (Ed.), *Identity, personal and socio-cultural: A symposium* (pp. 347–360). Stockholm: Almquist & Wiksell.

Harvey, L. (1991). *Critical social research.* London: Unwin Hyman.

Hertz, R. (Ed.). (1997). *Reflexivity & voice.* Thousand Oaks, CA: Sage.

Holland, D., Lachicotte, W., Skinner, D., & Cain, C. (1998). *Identity and agency in cultural worlds.* Cambridge, MA: Harvard University Press.

Jagodzinski, J. J. (1982). Art education as ethnology: Deceptive democracy or a new panacea? *Studies in Art Education, 23*(3), 5–9.

Janesick, A. (1982). Art education as experience: A reply to art education as ethnology. *Studies in Art Education, 23*(3), 10–11.

Jess, P., & Massey, D. (1995). The conceptualization of place. In D. Massey & P. Jess (Eds.), *A place in the world? Places, cultures and globalization* (pp. 45–85). Oxford, UK: Oxford University Press/The Open University.

Kelly, J. (2006). Hip hop globalization and youth culture. In S. Steinberg, P. Parmar, & B. Richards (Eds.), *Contemporary youth culture: An international encyclopedia* (Vol. 1). Westport, CT: Greenwood Publishing Group.

Kelly, J. (2008). Diasporian moves: African Canadian youth and identity formation. In N. Dolby & F. Rizvi (Eds.), *Youth moves: Identities and education in global perspective* (pp. 85–100). London: Routledge.

Kelly, M., & Ali, S. (2004). Ethics and social research. In C. Seale (Ed.), *Researching society and culture* (2nd ed., pp. 115–128). London: Sage.

Kincheloe, J., & Steinberg, S. (1998). Students-as-researchers: Critical visions, emancipatory insights. In S. Steinberg & J. Kincheloe (Eds.), *Students-as-researchers: Creating classrooms that matter* (pp. 2–19). London: Falmer Press.

Kirsch, G. (1999). *Ethical dilemmas in feminist research: The politics of location, interpretation, and publication.* New York: State University of New York Press.

Lather, P. A. (1991). *Getting smart: Feminist research and pedagogy with/in the postmodern.* New York: Routledge.

Lather, P. A. (2001). Postmodernism, post-structuralism and post (critical) ethnography: Of ruins, aporias and angels. In P. Atkinson, A. Coffey, S. Delamont, J. Lofland, & L. Lofland (Eds.), *Handbook of ethnography* (pp. 477–492). London: Sage.

Leonard, K. (2009). Changing places: The advantages of multi-sited ethnography. In M. A. Falzon (Ed.), *Multi-sited ethnography: Theory, praxis, and locality in contemporary research* (pp. 165–179). London: Ashgate.

Livingstone, S. (2004). Media literacy and the challenge of new information and communication technologies. *The Communication Review, 7*, 3–14.

Luttrell, W. (2003). *Pregnant bodies, fertile minds*. London: Routledge.

MacDougall, D. (1997). The visual in anthropology. In M. Banks & H. Morphy (Eds.), *Rethinking visual anthropology* (pp. 276–295). New Haven, CT: Yale University Press.

Massey, D. (1993). Power-geometry and a progressive sense of place. In J. Bird, B. Curtis, T. Putnam, G. Robertson, & L. Tickner (Eds.), *Mapping the futures: Local cultures, global change* (pp. 59–69). London: Routledge.

McCarthy, C., Giardina, M., Harewood, S., & Park, J.-K. (2003). Contesting culture: Identity and curriculum dilemmas in the age of globalization, postcolonialism, and multiplicity. *Harvard Educational Review, 73*(3), 449–465.

McLaren, P., & Kincheloe, J. (Eds.). (2007). *Critical pedagogy: Where are we now?* New York: Peter Lang.

McLeod, J. (2009). Youth studies, comparative inquiry, and the local/global problematic. *Review of Education, Pedagogy, and Cultural Studies, 31*(4), 270–292.

Murphy, E., & Dingwald, R. (2001). The ethics of ethnography. In P. Atkinson, A. Coffey, S. Delamont, J. Lofland, & L. Lofland (Eds.), *Handbook of ethnography* (pp. 339–351). London: Sage.

Pilkington, H. (1994). *Russia's youth and its culture: A nation's constructors and constructed*. London: Routledge.

Pilkington, H. (2004). Youth strategies for glocal living: Space, power and communication in everyday cultural practice. In A. Bennett & K. Kahn-Harris (Eds.), *After subculture: Critical studies in contemporary youth culture* (pp. 119–134). New York: Palgrave Macmillan.

Pilkington, H., & Johnson, R. (2003). Peripheral youth: Relations of identity and power in global/local context. *European Journal of Cultural Studies, 6*(3), 259–283.

Pink, S. (2001). *Doing visual ethnography: Images, media and representation in research*. London: Sage.

Ramazanoglu, C., & Holland, J. (2002). *Feminist methodology: Challenges and choices*. London: Sage.

Sefton-Green, J. (Ed.). (1999). *Young people, creativity and new technologies: The challenge of digital arts*. London: Routledge.

Sefton-Green, J. (2007). Youth, technology, and media culture. *Review of Research in Education, 30*, 279–306.

Stanley, N. (1986). On not liking what one sees: Anthropology and the visual arts. *Journal of Art & Design Education, 5*(1–2), 173–186.

Steinberg, S., & Kincheloe, J. (Eds.). (1998). *Students as researchers*. London: Falmer.

Sullivan, G. (2005). *Art practice as research*. Thousand Oaks, CA: Sage.

Thorne, B. (1993). *Gender play: Girls and boys in school*. New Brunswick, NJ: Rutgers University Press.

Willis, P. (1990). *Common culture: Symbolic work at play in the everyday cultures of the young*. Boulder, CO: Westview Press.

Willis, P. (2000). *The ethnographic imagination*. Cambridge, UK: Polity Press.

# Appendices

## Appendix 1: Methodological Points

### Methods Used

Interviews, participant observation, and visual-based tools were used throughout the study.

### Participant Observation

Participant observation and subsequent fieldnotes formed the core of this ethnography: as an embodied practice, it lent itself to understanding the nondiscursive, affective, and emotional (see Emerson, Fretz, & Shaw, 2001, p. 354) and allowed for the continuous informal interviewing and conversations central to this study (Fontana & Frey, 2000, p. 652). Sitting with young people, for instance, at the Hope, making films, watching DVDs, reading magazines, playing basketball, and walking home with them through the streets of New York offered me a chance to understand and be part of their everyday lives. Through this method, I forged a deeper understanding of how youth used, were constrained by, and constituted the world around them (Emerson, Fretz, & Shaw, 1995).

Participant observation and fieldnotes started with my first meeting at the Hope in 2005 and did not end until I returned to England in late 2006. I drew on Emerson et al. (1995) to think about my use of fieldnotes and throughout the fieldwork carried around a small notebook, often jotting down quotes, seminal incidents, and emerging ideas. Because this was a visual-based study, cameras were often rolling, and at the end of each day, I had a significant amount of footage of youth talk, action, and antics. Most days whether at the Hope or in Barlow, I would walk to a

K.A. Eglinton, *Youth Identities, Localities, and Visual Material Culture: Making Selves, Making Worlds*, Explorations of Educational Purpose 25, DOI 10.1007/978-94-007-4857-6, © Springer Science+Business Media Dordrecht 2013 coffee shop or cafe and sit down, and, after transcribing any useful jottings from the notebook, I would begin writing fieldnotes directly into my laptop. Each fieldnote had the same heading for easy accessibility, analysis, and future referencing.

I reflexively approached fieldnotes, constantly examining my 'own participation' (Tedlock, 2005, p. 467), and used narrative format mixing emerging concepts, theoretical musings, emotions, anecdotes, quotes, and reflections. This corpus of writing has been central to analysis and provides the history of inquiry, including the trajectory of my thinking, mistakes made, and directions taken (Silverman, 2000, p. 236). Approximately 181,332 words in fieldnotes which came to 323 single-spaced standard letter paper pages from the New York City site and 101,474 words which came to 179 single-spaced standard letter pages from the Yukon site were amassed.

## *Interviews*

Interviews were akin to Kvale's (1996) 'interviewer as traveller' where the interviewer engages participants in conversation or 'wandering together with' (p. 4). Rather than assuming that interviews accessed an external reality, I understood interview data as generated between youth and myself, providing accounts which were '"situated"... locally produced', and productive (Silverman, 2000, p. 123). Questions grouped under broad themes or prompts remained open and flexible and were largely guided by previous conversations and/or by themes presenting themselves in the data, as well as targeted to specific youth (see below for sample interview questions). Three rounds of interviews were conducted in both communities in addition to peer-to-peer interviewing which familiarised youth with the cameras and with interviewing more generally (see Packard, Ellison, & Sequenzia, 2004). Interviews were both individual and group (of no more than three youth). Youth decided whether they wanted to be interviewed in groups of two or three friends or alone. Many youth in both communities participated in the initial interviews that were based on collages they made. As the research progressed and themes started to present themselves, I conducted a second and third round of interviews with central participants; these interviews focused on aspects of the life histories, experiences, and narratives of these youth (Atkinson, 1998; Heyl, 2001; Plummer, 2001), as well as on developing themes, and questions which were individually tailored for particular young people.

During the final days of the study in both communities, after the exhibition or screening of youth work, many youth spoke on camera and shared reflections on the project. Further, several adults in both sites were interviewed (the director of the Hope and community officials and members in Barlow). Youth interviews were rarely conducted in a quiet classroom or community centre but rather took place in hallways, in alcoves, in small resource rooms, on the streets, and in abandoned storage rooms. Regardless of where the interview took place, all sessions were videotaped; young people often spent time setting up the camera, and interviewing was often a time of games and performances. Overall, 56 h of open-ended interviews (over 70 individual and 14 group interviews (with 2–3 youth)) and 18 peer-to-peer interviews (approximately 10 min each) were generated across both sites.

## *Visual Methods*

As described in Chap. 1, visual methods used in both communities included: (1) image-making by the researcher, (2) using pre-existing materials to generate ethnographic data, and (3) participatory image-making (see Chap. 1 for a discussion of theory underpinning these methods). Exploring each of these categories, I produced images (still and moving) throughout the study as a means of, for example, examining cultural processes, understanding context, rethinking and reconstructing ideas, and documenting the research process. For instance, hoping to capture some of the contexts of youth cultural production, I would often run a camera during participatory image-making documenting how youth arrived at a final product. In another example, images were essential to gaining a deeper understanding of young people's talk and action. Young people would often talk about 'acting black' or 'being a girlie girl' – and invariably these statements were accompanied by physical actions and performances more aptly captured through visual means.

Second, I used pre-existing materials to generate ethnographic data: sometimes called photo- or film-elicitation, images, music videos, and magazines were used throughout both formally in interviews and informally over the course of daily conversations. Youth too produced digital- and non-digital-based images such as digital self-portraits and collages that sparked discussion and were used in photo- or film-elicitation interviews.

More informally, young people and I would often bring in VMC to discuss. For example, I frequently brought in magazines young people asked me to purchase. Hours were spent sitting with youth flipping through the pages of these magazines discussing, among other things, the images and articles. Young people also brought in VMC to show me. In particular, youth would regularly bring in family albums, and we would talk about the content of image as well as mull over the 'materiality' (Banks, 2001) of the objects. As video cameras were often running, many of these conversations were recorded or otherwise documented for later reflection and analysis.

Using the digital still and video cameras I always had with me, images were constantly generated (by me and the young people) and discussed on the spot. Young people would often take my laptop and with friends sift through and discuss the images taken over the course of the research. At the Hope, many of youth had phones with cameras: photos were taken, instantly critiqued, erased, and reshot.

In a kind of film-elicitation, video was a major resource in this study. Many of the young people would use my laptop to watch DVDs, listen to music, and view the videos they produced through the study. Youth and I would often set up impromptu screenings of their work where young people would crowd around a table or bench and watch the videos made by their peers. These sessions were often caught by a second video camera held by one of the young people. Additionally, much time was spent listening to music together: perhaps in a kind of 'music-elicitation', we would discuss, for example, the artist and/or VMC surrounding the music. I also had an MP3 player; youth used it regularly to record raps and download these recordings into my laptop, then would play them back, discussing them with me and/or their peers.

Participatory image-making was the third and final visual method used: young people created a variety of self-representational and place-based videos, collages, and still images. As described in Chap. 1, both alone and in groups, youth produced (wrote, filmed, acted in, and edited) 3–12-min videos. Film-making started in phase one. We watched various DVDs to get an idea of genres, storyboarded ideas, and, rarely sticking to these initial ideas, started filming. In participatory film-making, how much training participants receive varies. While some researchers teach participants the skills needed to make their own videos after they vacate the site, others simply offer their expertise but do not necessarily train participants (Badger, 1995; Banks, 2001, p. 126). Believing young people should have the skills to continue producing videos, I trained those who were interested in filming and editing, using basic digital cameras and equipment, which was not time-consuming. Various participants and I worked almost every day on their videos. Some days, for instance, were spent editing, selecting music, and doing the credits, and other days were spent filming. Videos were screened for the community at the end of my time in each site.

Young people also used still cameras, both digital and disposable, to engage in various projects. There were several planned projects around still photography and inevitable spontaneous uses of photography throughout the project. One planned project included the creation of digital self-portraits which were produced collaboratively: young people would pick the place and pose, and either I or another youth would take the photo. Photos were then downloaded onto my laptop, and young people could, if they chose to, integrate text into the image or create a different setting.

Another photographic project included a series of still images, some of which we called 'postcards' (inspired by Edwards, 1997). For the postcards, youth used disposable cameras to capture their communities, friends, and favourite VMC. Using still photography, youth and I explored some of the places they inhabited and the spaces they created (Hastrup, 1992). Photography was used in spontaneous ways: young people would often take my cameras to shoot images of themselves, friends, or events, and/or document the other participatory projects they were engaging in.

Non-mechanical media including collage were also employed. The production of collage and other visual forms is common in art education research (e.g. Packard et al., 2004, Springgay, 2003a; Thompson, 2003). Engaging participants in cultural production as a method to understand identities and meanings has also been used sporadically in social science research (Pink, 2001). In sociology, Luttrell (2003) provides a significant example engaging a group of pregnant teenage girls in collage making. Interested in self-representation, Luttrell asks the girls to base their collages on the question 'Who am I?'. Drawing on Luttrell's (2003) work, one of the first projects that youth in both sites participated in was the production of collages. Focusing on the question 'Who am I?', youth were asked to look through magazines (which they requested and I brought in for them) and cut out images or text in order to produce collages that might portray areas of their identity as well as VMC they were interested in. These collages served as the basis for the first round of interviews.

Overall, over 8,000 images were shot, over half of which were produced by youth; there were over 50 h of miscellaneous video documenting youth actions, practices, and informal interviews and conversations during participant observation; 50 youth-produced collages; 180 youth-produced still photos from disposable cameras; 15 youth-produced videos (between 3 and 10 min each); and 20 youth-produced digital self-portraits.

## Sample Interview Questions and Probes (Hope Only)

Examples of general themes and questions for second and third interviews (questions were often designed for individual youth) (Hope interviews only):

Notions of home
Example questions:

- Where do you consider home?
- Are you proud of where you are from? Why?
- Why do you love Harlem? PR? Etc..
- What things represent home? Food? Music? Clothing?

Place and space
Example questions:

- What things do you think are important to people in your neighbourhood? What do people like to do there?
- What makes you sad or angry in the community? Outside the community?
- Is your family different to other families in the community? Why do you think? Can you give me an example?
- In your own home, can you describe your bedroom? Where do you hang out with friends? What do you do in your home?
- Where is your favourite place? Why? Can you describe it to me?
- Do you think the things you are into are very 'New York'? Why?

Personal experiences, meanings, and self-conceptions
Example questions:

- What do you think are three important events in your life so far?
- How would you describe your cultural background?

- What do you do for fun?
- What is a typical school day like for you? What about a summer day?
- Who are the most special people in your life? Why?
- What would you say is different about you to your friends?
- What nickname would you give yourself and why?
- Where do you see yourself in 10 years?
- What do you value? What is important and significant to you?
- Do you think teachers/parents understand you? Why? Why not?
- What is the role of religion in your life?
- What do you like to talk about?
- What is your favourite quote and where is it from?
- How would you most like to be known?

Role models
Example questions:

- How would you define a role model?
- Who are your role models?
- Why are they your role models?
- If you were talking to your friend about this role model, what would you say?
- How are these role models like you? How are you like them?

Language
Example questions:

- How would you describe something you liked? What words would you use?
- How would you describe something you didn't like? What words would you use?
- If you were talking to a friend, what would you say about your favourite movie, song, and person?

Genres and lifestyles
Example questions:

- What kind of music is there? Could you give me examples?
- What kinds of places in NYC? Could you give me examples?

Friendships and collective meanings
Example questions:

- What is different about you and your friends to other people?
- What are some fun experiences you have had with your friends?
- Can you tell me about each of your friends and what they are into? Are you into the same things? Why? Why not?
- Do you feel you and your friends are brought together around common likes? Can you give me an example of this?

Pop culture narratives
Example questions:

- What music artist or actor's story do you like the best and why?
- What are your thoughts on the lyrics of some of the rap songs?

- What do you look for first in a music/pop artist/actor/entertainer? Looks? Talent? Etc?
- What are some of the messages coming from your favourite music artists? Favourite movies? Favourite songs?

Examples of questions focusing on biographies (for key participants)

- Can you tell me a bit about your background?
- Where are you from? Where have you grown up?
- How many brothers and sisters? Where are you in the family?
- Where are your guardians from?
- When did you/they come to the United States/New York?
- How long have they/you been in New York?
- How do you think of yourself as (e.g. a New Yorker, a Dominican)?
- What traditions, rituals, and celebrations are important in your home-life?
- What beliefs do the adults in your home-life try to teach you?
- What is your neighbourhood like?

Example of several themes and questions for adult interviews (Hope only)
General questions about staff role at the Hope
Example questions:

- What is your role at [Hope]?
- How long have you been here?
- What changes have you seen?

General questions about the programme
Example questions:

- How many kids are in the programme?
- How is the programme funded?
- What kinds of programmes are offered (summer club, girls club)?

Programme ethos and philosophy
Example questions:

- What values/beliefs are you trying to instil and uphold?
- What three sentences would sum up the ethos/philosophy of this programme?
- What makes your programme unique?
- Where do the mission statement and the ethos we just talked about come from (i.e. funding body, education discourses, personal beliefs, etc.)?
- Do you believe the values you are trying to instil are the same as those of the parents?
- What do you think is the biggest encumbrance to attainment of your goals here (youth, parents)?
- What would you like people to take away with them who have visited [Hope]?

Questions about the GVHS for younger staff and volunteers
Example questions:

- How long did you go to this high school?
- Where did you grow up?
- What kind of changes have you seen in this high school?
- What kinds of messages do they want young people to come away with?
- What are the youth like?
- What three sentences might sum up the ethos of this high school?

## Phases of the Research in NYC and Yukon

Approximately 18 months were spent defining the research problem, conducting a pilot study, revising the overarching research question, and examining a wide range of literatures. During this time, I also selected and negotiated access into the Hope in New York City and made contact with Barlow. Based on the pilot study, literature, and research question throughout this initial 18 months, I developed flexible research methods, reflected on possible ethical issues, and fleshed out a tentative design. Rather than constructing a tight design before fieldwork commenced, I settled on methods and an overall approach and allowed the field design to develop in concert with each context, the needs of youth, and directions emerging from data (Hammersley & Atkinson, 1995; Silverman, 2000).

Fieldwork was carried out between November 2005 and October 2006. I was preparing in New York City from November 2005 and attended the Hope after-school as a researcher on a regular basis from December 2005 through the first week of June 2006 (just over 6 months). I travelled to Barlow on July 1, 2006, and stayed until the second week in October 2006 (just over 3 months). Initial data analysis started in the field as data came in: there was a continuous process of data collection, reviewing, and analysis which consistently guided and focused field-work (Silverman, 2000, 121). I returned to Cambridge in late October 2006 where I spent approximately 2 years transcribing, analysing, and writing the final text. In the following sections, I cover the phases of the project in each community in detail.

## Phases of the Project at the Hope, New York City

### *Phase One*

Phase one of the project took place over the first two and a half to 3 months. During this phase, in particular during the first few weeks, I followed the advice of Rock (2001) to simply 'look and see what can be seen' (p. 34); I also aimed to get to know young people and build relationships. Unless I had other appointments, throughout all three phases, I attended the Hope approximately 5 days a week, working with young people from 3pm to 6pm or soon thereafter. Throughout my time, for the most part, I simply 'hung out' with the young people as they themselves hung out in the classrooms or the cafeteria of the building housing the Hope.

As the Hope had multiple volunteers, and as I went in as a volunteer, young people were not surprised when I sat next to them and started a conversation. During phase one, I engaged in numerous informal discussions with young people. I also sought out participants, secured consent from youth and parents, and engaged youth in producing collages. During this phase, youth and I discussed video making and spent time watching genres of videos and working on storyboards for video making. While some of the young people started thinking about the kind of video they would make, others started filming. Throughout all three phases, I liberally lent out camera equipment both video and still, and much time was spent sitting around reading magazines, talking about VMC, and snapping photos of friends. I also gave out a short questionnaire looking at popular forms of visual material culture (likes, dislikes, getting a sense of what youth were interested in), worked with participants conducting peer-to-peer interviews, and conducted interviews with young people who completed collages. By the end of phase one, I had worked with numerous young people, and the key youth who ultimately formed the core of the study were slowly beginning to surface. Though it happened early on, by the time phase one ended, I had narrowed the central research question to focus on identity.

## Phase Two

In the second phase, I continued using participant observation, and while showing up to the Hope almost every day was affording me ample opportunity to understand youth cultural practices, I also volunteered to come in over school holidays. The Hope was open all day when schools were not in session, and this time offered me copious hours with youth – just talking, looking through magazines, using my laptop, watching DVDs, and generally spending time with them. During this phase, my relationship with youth deepened; some ideas or themes were beginning to present themselves more profoundly than others in fieldnotes, visual images, and interviews. Augmenting my understanding of developing themes, I conducted interviews probing the life histories of the small group of key participants. I also focused interviews on the developing theme of identity and the intersection of place and VMC in identity construction. During this time, interview questions were often targeted for particular youth where I followed up more formally on something they may have said informally earlier in the week or in a previous interview.

Youth and I continued working on the production of videos including filming and editing. Digital self-portraits were also produced and edited on my laptop; still cameras were given out, and young people produced a series of still photographs (some we called 'postcards') which documented their likes and dislikes and places and spaces they inhabited and created. Digital and video cameras were always available from me, and, as in the first phase, youth spent much time snapping photos of friends, dancing for the camera, talking to the camera, and simply documenting life. I too used visual methods to continuously document or more accurately grasp the local context (inside and outside the Hope) and to reflect on my position and perspective on place. By the end of this second phase, I felt I belonged at the Hope, and, though this is only my perspective, it seemed I was generally accepted by the end of this phase among youth.

## *Phase Three*

In the third phase, I worked with youth as they finished off their visual productions and prepared for the end of project show, exhibiting their work and the project more generally. Videos were edited, still photographs were titled, self-portraits were completed, and youth recorded comments about their pieces. Throughout this phase, participants continued informally videotaping and photographing themselves, their friends, and their activities (including this study itself, e.g., youth documented the final exhibition using video and still photography). Interviews continued to focus on youth cultural productions, on individual lives, and on augmenting, confirming, and/or reworking developing constructs (Charmaz, 2000). Incorporated into final interviews, or as a separate interview, youth reflected on the study. During this time, I also interviewed several of the staff including a coordinator, the director, and assistant director. All young people were given copies of their work and interviews, as well as any other material they generated and a personal letter thanking them. I also tried to confirm some of my developing understanding by speaking with participants about some of the themes presenting themselves more profoundly than others in the data, in particular identity. This phase ended with the exhibition and final reflections.

## Phases of the Project in Barlow, Yukon, Canada

### *Phase One*

Phase one of the project took place during the first 7 weeks (see Chap. 7 for my first few days in Barlow and locating youth there). By the end of the first month (when young people were out of school for the summer holidays), consent forms were signed for approximately nine youth whom I worked with almost every day (though not necessarily the same youth every day). Spreading the project across the physical space, youth and I made collages in a room offered by the arts centre; we took photographs outdoors and indoors, filmed sports and nights out on the streets, and had initial interviews based on collages again in a room in the arts centre. Also during this time, basic questionnaires (similar to those I gave out at the Hope with a focus on VMC) were given out to these nine youth, and there was an early focus on emerging themes which were then used to develop the interviews carried out in the second phase. While I entered Barlow with the more focused research questions of identity in mind, I was open to the multiple uses of VMC. However, similar to the Hope, in Barlow I found that the most salient use of VMC was to make sense of, negotiate, and construct aspects of self and world. This being the case, I continued to focus on this question. At the end of these initial 7 weeks, I had made close friends in the community, felt comfortable with many of the youth, spent copious time taking photographs in the community, and frequented the bars, coffee shops, and cultural centres, and, I believe, became a familiar face in the town.

## Phase Two

During this phase (approximately weeks 7 through 11), I continued intense parti-cipant observation, hanging out and volunteering throughout the community, and working with and spending time with young people in particular. During this phase, many of the summer visitors left (which included a group of friends I had made), and more intense relationships were formed between the year-round residents and myself. In week seven, I was granted access into the school by the principal. In addition to working with the group of youth outside of the school, I started volunteering and, as I was doing throughout the community, 'hanging out' in the art classroom with the seventh and eighth (and sometimes ninth) graders. Showing up to the school every day, I would bring cameras and other equipment to the art class. The art teacher seemed relaxed and happy to have me there. During art classes, young people and I worked on collages (in addition to other projects they were working on for the class) and also started doing still photography (with both disposable and digital cameras) and self-portraits, and groups of youth started making videos. During this time, all the participants I worked with in the school completed the basic questionnaire.

Overall, the school provided an excellent environment for the study. The time-table and rules in the school were flexible, and the art teacher allowed youth to leave the class with me to talk, to make videos, or just to take a walk. Also during art class, youth and I would play on my laptop, listen to music, download videos, and generally talk about their lives – the atmosphere in the class was conducive to getting to know youth in an informal and open manner.

During this phase, those youth who would become key participants were presenting themselves, and the first and second round of interviews were either initiated or continued with all youth (including those I worked with both in school and out of school). Initial interviews were based on collages; second interviews focused on emerging themes, contained questions for individual youth, and targeted the life histories and individual experiences of central participants. During this phase, I tried to deepen my understanding of emerging concepts through interviews and intense involvement in the lives of youth and in the community more broadly. Interviews were often carried out in a designated quiet room. The principal and educators were phenomenally accommodating; the principal offered me much needed support (for example, academic and emotional) throughout the study.

During this time, many of the youth seemed extremely comfortable with me. As I did at the Hope, I always had digital (and visual) equipment with me for youth to use, and I was relaxed about the young people taking video cameras home with them for a night or two. Youth would often stay after school ended to film or edit their videos with me, and they would often show up at my house on the weekends asking me to film or take photos with them. Many times young people wanted me to follow them around town filming them on their bikes or skateboards as they did stunts. Many youth would walk into my house without knocking, eat my food, and/or talk with me on my porch as they slurped down whatever I had left in my refrigerator. Overall, by the second phase, it seemed there was little barrier between my personal life in the community and my life as a researcher with youth in the community. For example, as Barlow was safe, many youth were out late at night, and it was not surprising to find them waiting for me outside of a pub on their bikes. As I walked home, they would ride next to me talking energetically about their lives. Parents would stop me in the streets and ask about my life, and people in the community would come by and take care of me.

## *Phase Three*

Generally, during phase three (approximately weeks eleven to thirteen and a half), I continued participant observation and volunteering throughout the community. I also continued working in the art room every day for a few hours. During this phase, interviewing was intense and focused on youth cultural productions, augmenting developing themes, clearing up confusion, and understanding youth meanings. Interview questions often targeted specific youth. During this time, I carried out final interviews with youth at once reflecting on the study and checking and refining my understanding of developing themes (feeding themes back to them). Two adults in the community were interviewed in order to construct a fuller picture of the local place including the social history. These adults, Caitlin and Elizabeth, grew up in the community. Caitlin identified as First Nations and white (though primarily First Nations), was in her mid-thirties, and worked in various institutions across the community. Elizabeth worked in the social sector, identified as white, was older than Caitlin, and had her own children now growing up in the community. These participants also helped confirm and dismiss developing themes with respect to local place.

More specifically, in the third phase, I worked with youth both inside and outside the school, finishing their visual productions, and preparing for the end of project show exhibiting their work. Videos were edited and put onto a loop to be projected on a large screen in the art room on a planned day after school. As it was expensive in Barlow to print the still photography including self-portraits, youth and I decided to put all of the digital work into a PowerPoint presentation which would also run on a loop and be projected on another large screen in the art room (at the same time as the videos were running). In Barlow, just as in the Hope, still photographs and self-portraits were titled, and comments about the work by individual youth were added, and all of these details were included in the PowerPoint. Signs were made inviting people to the screening and were put up throughout the community. All youth visual-based productions were put onto CDs, and letters were written to all youth who worked with me, as well as to certain adults in the community thanking them for their generosity. I left Barlow 3 days after the screening. Leaving was indescribably difficult, and in order to go I needed to promise myself that I would be back when I finished my degree.

## Framework for Analysis

Interviews, fieldnotes, images, and media generated through visual methods formed the corpus of data which I subject to a thematic analysis employing an overall 'grounded approach': specifically, I drew on tools from grounded theory (e.g. memo writing) to develop themes as they presented themselves in data (Charmaz, 2000; Clarke, 2003). In keeping with the interpretive perspective of this inquiry, the grounded approach I used enabled me to connect emerging themes, focus data collection, and study relations, processes, and complexities in the research (Charmaz & Mitchell, 2001). As young people's engagement with visual material forms is under-researched and connectedly under-theorised, I suggest a grounded approach lent itself to the development of a body of scholarship in this area. While early grounded theory developed by Glaser and Strauss (1967) has received a fair amount of criticism (e.g. forms of grounded theory have been labelled positivist, scientistic, mechanistic, even deterministic (Charmaz, 2000; Charmaz & Mitchell, 2001, p. 161)), I appropriated 'constructivist' (Charmaz, 2000) and 'postmodern' (Clarke, 2003) grounded approaches which assume a link between individual and sociocultural context, offer tools which extend the unit of analysis to include both the individual (or the micro) and the context (the macro), and help develop a reflexive contextual picture of social phenomena grounded in people's everyday experiences.

Theory was used throughout inquiry from conception to final text (Wolcott, 2001). Though some contend grounded approaches require researchers to 'suspend' beliefs, hunches, and/or theoretical knowledge before entering the field (Flick, 2002, p. 41), with Lather (1991) and postmodern and constructivist grounded theory, I see the importance of flexible *a priori* theory to help focus analysis, engage with new concepts, and shed light on practices. Throughout this process while some theories were used to understand the subject of study (in this case I used, for example, concepts from sociocultural theories), others referred to methods, procedures, and the construction of knowledge and reality more broadly (for instance, I drew on sociocultural constructivism (see Hickman & Eglinton, 2010)) (Flick, 2002). At the same time, my use of theory was flexible; data enabled the reworking or, in some cases, dismissal of particular concepts and required the introduction of new ideas.

With respect to producing theory, Daly (1997) argues postmodern ethnographers are against, wary, and/or unsure of how to engage in theorising in light of the postmodern critique where theory might be construed as a universally applicable 'truth'. However, I argue, theories – not grand theories or theories presented as 'objective truths', but 'local' theories born out a situated, reflexive, participatory, interpretive inquiry help us (researchers, practitioners, participants) build on, learn from, modify, and transform the social world (Daly, 1997). While I do not necessarily claim to be developing broad theories, I have been imaginative in my use of theory: using the data in concert with theoretical concepts from the literature, I have actively toyed with theory, augmented concepts, and reworked theoretical ideas based on local processes always with the hope that these musings can be used to think about youth lives and future practices in education.

## *Analysis Procedures*

As ethnographic research embraces context, complexity, and meanings, and as I started research with a broad brush or research question, I needed analysis procedures which supported the gradual focus of questions based on insights arising in the field (Hammersley & Atkinson, 1995; Wolcott, 1999). With this in mind, analysis began as data came in (Silverman, 2000, 2001). As described, every evening during fieldwork, I would write reflective fieldnotes and download images, video with informal conversations, youth performances, and, for instance, interviews into my laptop. Watching videos, for example, I would type notes directly into fieldnotes on the computer, and in another analysis book, I would list and flesh out possible 'codes' (i.e. 'tags or labels for assigning units of meaning to the descriptive or inferential information complied during a study') (Miles & Huberman, 1994, p. 56). Also in this book, I engaged in early memoing (i.e. exploration of codes and ideas through writing) (Charmaz, 2000, p. 517),[1] made notes about individual biographies, and drew on Clarke's (2003) postmodern grounded approach to create 'situational maps'. These maps organised ideas, forged connections, and grounded data in the sociocultural context. Strengthening research claims and supporting the reflexive stance taken in this study, fieldnotes, memos, and maps provide a history of this analytic process (Silverman, 2000, p. 236). During fieldwork, all data was examined in relation to concepts I brought with me to the field, and data was always reflected on before collecting more: listening to interviews, I would prepare further questions, prompts, and activities for the young people.

---

[1] Charmaz (2000, p. 517) describes memoing as the 'step between coding and the first draft of the completed analysis'; however, I used this tool throughout analysis.

All interviews were videotaped and fully transcribed; transcription began during fieldwork. While I transcribed 95 % of the interviews myself, 5 % were outsourced through a company in the United States.[2] I personally rechecked outsourced transcriptions for accuracy. As I transcribed (and rechecked) interviews, I continued to memo, note emerging codes, as well as develop the biographies of the young people who played key roles in the study. Returning to Cambridge in late October 2006, approximately 85 % of transcribing was complete. In Cambridge, I used the computer-assisted qualitative data analysis software ATLAS.ti to support analysis. This software systematised analysis through its organisational and retrieval capacity and supported making connections, theorising, and extensive memoing (Coffey & Atkinson, 1996; Seale, 2000).

Using ATLAS.ti, after leaving the field, data was then subject to a more formalised system of *open coding* (i.e. attaching meaning or categorising chunks of data, bringing together reoccurring words, ideas, practices, activities under a particular label) (Coffey & Atkinson, 1996, p. 27; Miles & Huberman, 1994, p. 56). Many codes were readily available as they developed in the field, and types of codes included descriptive, theoretical, and metaphorical (Miles & Huberman, 1994, p. 58).

Interviews were coded first in ATLAS.ti; reading transcriptions and simultaneously watching the video interviews, I applied open codes to lines or chunks of text. This process was supported by the memoing and reflecting I had done throughout fieldwork. All codes were kept open and active subject to revision in light of other data forms (Charmaz, 2000). Coding data and rereading interviews, codes that subsumed smaller codes and continued to reappear across data were given the label of themes or 'categories' (Charmaz, 2000, p. 519; Clarke, 2003).

Fieldnotes were printed and subject to the same process of coding as interviews. I coded fieldnotes by hand, using sticky notes for memoing and putting codes in the margins (Emerson et al., 1995). Though informed by the coding from interviews, fieldnotes were central to analysis affording an overall picture of inquiry. Reading and rereading fieldnotes, I examined the trajectory of the study and gauged the development of relationships (Emerson et al., 1995, pp. 144–45). As I was interested in individual lives, fieldnotes kept individual stories intact. Specifically, because coding breaks up the data, I first coded the fieldnotes and then examined them as a whole: rereading them, I plumbed them for youth stories as well as for narratives that constituted codes or larger themes (Coffey & Atkinson, 1996, p. 23).

---

[2] The outsourcing was through Elance.com where freelancers bid for the projects listed. This method of obtaining a freelance transcriber afforded me the opportunity to talk with a wide range of possible transcribers, read reviews about their work, and discuss the sensitive and confidential nature of the interviews before settling on a transcriber. In the end, I selected a transcriber with a great deal of experience transcribing from video and who had a perfect reviews from numerous of customers. She was located in Nevada far from the New York or Barlow sites. There was an agreement of confidentiality between the selected transcriber and myself, as well as a notation of confidentiality in my brief sent to her which was readily agreed.

Data, therefore, was analysed across youth, examining categories and codes and vertically looking at each young person I worked with.

Images, in particular the images produced by youth through participatory projects including the self-portrait, still photography, videos, and collages, were brought into analysis in the light of fieldnotes and interviews. Done by hand, codes at this point were further reworked and added. Based on art-based research, youth productions were not decontextualised rather they were understood in relation to the wider study, viewed holistically in comparison with other cultural productions they produced as well as with other forms of data (Darts, 2004; Pink, 2001; Rose, 2001; Springgay, 2003b; see also Weber & Mitchell's 1995 study). Images were subject to multiple examinations, and were not used to merely illustrate themes, but rather more primarily to focus on how young people saw, represented, constructed themselves and their worlds, and performed aspects of their identities.

Final codes and themes provided a fertile platform for thinking about connections and interpretations: using memos and graphic maps, I played purposefully with links and using ATLAS.ti creatively explored connections (Seale, 2004a). Data from Barlow and the Hope were coded separately beginning with the Hope.[3] Though initial coding yielded over 100 codes from the Hope, the final coding scheme which remained flexible consisted of 66 codes from the Hope, of which 9 were broad themes and several of which were sub-codes (or code within a code). From Barlow, there were 88 codes, again 9 themes and a selection of sub-codes. Tables A1.2 and A1.3 at the end of this Appendix 1 provide the final code lists for the Hope and Barlow. For code full definitions, see Eglinton (2009). While I provide these codes here, they remained flexible and open to change long after this process of open coding was completed (and these lists were created). Though the laborious process of open coding, defining codes and developing themes took approximately 1 year, data analysis did not end there. Rather, analysis continued through representation; the most interesting connections and interpretive possibilities happened while writing up this research.

Analysis of data stretched into representation as my attempts to organise and structure the final text deepened my understanding of the phenomena. As I started to pull the pieces together, I was not simply writing what I already knew, nor was it a passive activity, rather it was an active production (and construction) of knowledge and understanding. Indeed, playing with various ideas, attempts at writing and representation continuously provided a fresh perspective on the data. In Chap. 1, I touch on some of the representational issues and refer readers to Eglinton (2009) for further details.

---

[3] Because Barlow was considered in the same inquiry as the Hope and used the same tools and theoretical frameworks, the reader will find many of the same themes in both communities with variations in codes and code definitions depending on the unique context.

# Evaluating the Quality of the Research

Connected to issues of representation, in interpretive inquiry and new ethno-graphies, issues around legitimation abound. A central question is how to evaluate research which is mediated, co-created, and interpretive. Addressing this question and supporting the validation of research claims, I employed a framework articu-lated by Guba and Lincoln (1994) designed for the unique aims and objectives of interpretive inquiry. Guba and Lincoln (1994) criticise the use of a realist frame-work which, for example, seeks a single truth in interpretive forms of research based on the multiplicity of reality (Seale, 2004b). Instead the authors propose the overarching criteria of 'trustworthiness' and 'authenticity' as the basis for a more appropriate framework that resonates with the underlying epistemological and ontological assumptions of interpretive inquiry. In this model, 'trustworthiness' includes four nested criteria: 'credibility' (the honesty of the researcher's account), 'transferability' (how well the findings 'hold' in another context), 'dependability' (can research be repeated and obtain the same findings), and 'confirmability' (research is not 'overtly' biased) (Guba & Lincoln, 1994; Bryman, 2001, pp. 272–74) (see Table A1.1 for these criteria). 'Authenticity', on the other hand, is a more political criterion that examines whether the study benefits society in some way (Seale, 2004b). Though there are a number of criteria nested within authenticity (see Table A1.1), I thought most heavily about 'fairness' which reminds the researcher that all voices need to be represented in the research process and product (see Chap. 1; see in Eglinton, 2009).

I focus here on trustworthiness: in order to support the trustworthiness of the research claims, there are a number of techniques embedded within each criterion I employed (see Eglinton, 2009 for a full discussion of these techniques). For instance, the powerful tool of self-reflexivity and the use of participatory inquiry

**Table A1.1** Criteria used to judge the quality of the study

| Criteria | Aspects |
|---|---|
| Trustworthiness | Credibility: the honesty of the researcher's account. |
| | Transferability: how well the findings 'hold' in another context. |
| | Dependability: replicability of the research. |
| | Confirmability: the research is not 'overtly' bias |
| | (Guba and Lincoln, 1994) |
| Authenticity | Fairness: research represents multiple realities |
| | *Other criterion within authenticity:* |
| | Ontological authenticity: research supports participants' deepening understanding of 'phenomena' being examined |
| | Educative authenticity: educates participants to look to perspectives of others |
| | Catalytic authenticity: inspires social action |
| | Tactical authenticity: empowers people to action |
| | (Seale, 2004b, p. 81) |

support and increase the *credibility* (i.e. 'feasibility' or honesty) of research claims (see Chap. 1 where I touch on these tools and strategies). Several more tools I employed supported the credibility of claims, including spending extensive time in the field, 'triangulation', and 'member validation' or 'member checking' (Creswell & Miller, 2000).

In the first instance, through prolonged engagement in reflexive participant observation, I was able to build deeper relationships with youth and to use a grounded approach to analysis where I could continuously check my developing understanding and obtain a more holistic picture of phenomena. Connected to this, being in the field for an extended period enabled me to employ multiple methods and obtain various perspectives on phenomena. Though it could be argued I triangulated theories (i.e. analysis of data in light of several theories), as well as data (i.e. I used various data sources), here I note that I most profoundly triangulated methods (i.e. the use of multiple methods including interviews and participant observation) (Denzin, 1978; also in Patton, 2002, p. 247). In this study, triangulation or the use of more than one method to examine an issue was not necessarily about getting forms of data to agree with each other but rather I triangulated methods to intersect with various aspects of research questions, to access multiple accounts, and to ultimately provide the details for people to judge the transferability of this study to other settings (Denzin & Lincoln, 2000, p. 5; Patton, 2002; Seale, 2004b; Silverman, 2001).

Another technique I employed was a loose form of 'member checking' or member validation; this tool is considered one of the most significant means of ensuring credibility (Creswell & Miller, 2000, p. 127; Flick, 2006; Lincoln & Guba, 1985; Seale, 2004b, p. 78). I continuously checked and rechecked my understanding of youth meanings and practices throughout my time in both sites – often using interviews as an opportunity to clarify my understanding. At the end of my time in both communities, I discussed some of my initial thoughts with key participants. Youth used this time to reflect on the study overall as well as to correct and clarify my thoughts. All youth were given copies of their images and were asked to speak to me about images or quotations they did not want me to use. In both Barlow and New York City, I interviewed several key adults and asked two adults who had been living in these local places for a number of years, and who for various reasons had close links with these particular groups of young people, to recheck codes, themes, and definitions constructed from data. This kind of '"peer debriefing"' (Flick, 2006, p. 376) provoked further negotiations and clarifications and added to the credibility of the accounts I produced.

While interpretive forms of inquiry do not (nor do they aim to) generalise findings or accounts to other populations, what is important is whether I have provided enough detail to judge if insights are *transferable* to other settings (Seale, 2004b, p. 78). One means I used of supporting transferability is 'thick description' (Geertz, 1973) or detailed accounts of contexts, youth, and events (Seale, 2004b, p. 78). In this study, thick description, as Nayak (2003, p. 179) writes, 'enable[d] a more embodied account of young lives to emerge', and afforded me 'a contextual location from which to explore youth subjectivities'. Thick description supported the conveyance of 'action as well as speech' (ibid.). Drawing extensively on reflective fieldnotes which support highly detailed accounts, my descriptions in the final text include both the micro-context (for example, the field practices, aspects of the young person's life, immediate community) and the macro-context (for example, New York City itself, see Chap. 3); I would argue that these descriptions help the reader in judging the applicability of claims to other contexts. Thick description also supports the credibility of the study by providing enough details that the reader feels as though 'they have experienced, or could experience, the events being described in [the] study' (Creswell & Miller, 2000, p. 129).

As a final example, I also drew on the criteria of *dependability* and *confirmability*: where dependability assesses how consistent and reliable the procedures of analysis are, confirmability addresses issues of bias and honesty of the research account. These criteria are intertwined: the dependability of the study rests on the confirmability of the insights constructed, and the honesty of the insights reflects/results from a dependable analysis. I argue a grounded approach where I used established tools including memoing and maps, as well as the use of copious fieldnotes, which offer a full trajectory of the research and strengthen the dependability and confirmability of the research account I provide here (Flick, 2006; Silverman, 2000). Further, fully supporting and augmenting the confirmability of the account is self-reflexivity. As I noted in Chap. 1, self-reflexivity was threaded through the research process, not least through analysis and ethnographic representation, and was a central means of engaging with researcher subjectivity, bias, and beliefs which are always entangled in inquiry.

## Final Flexible Codes for the Hope and Barlow

Code definitions remained open. For a final list of all the code definitions, see Eglinton (2009). Bold indicates overarching theme, indent indicates sub-code (Tables A1.2 and A1.3).

**Table A1.2** Final flexible codes for the Hope

| Place and space | Identity | Making sense of self and world |
|---|---|---|
| Communities | Ethnoracial identities | Attribution of or reference to |
| National/political space | Gender identities |   physical attractiveness (self) |
| Constructing place |   Femininities | Attribution of or reference to |
| Places (other) not homeland |     Girl power |   physical attractiveness (other) |
| Public spaces |   Masculinities | Attribution of or reference to talent |
| Private spaces |   Expressions of |   and/or character (self) |
| Centre/periphery |     sexualities | Attribution of or reference to talent |
| Constructing homeland |   Group identities |   and/or character (other) |
| Other social spaces | **Representation** | Morality |
| Natural/Human-made landscape | Representing self | Myths |
| Using and creating spaces | Authenticity | Personal narratives |
| **Performance (general)** | **People and** | Role models |
| Performing ethnoracial, | **  relationships** | Social problems |
|   sexualities, gender | Parents/teachers/adults | Social justice, survival and struggle |
|   identities | Peers | Social/economic references |
| Performance from VMC | Family | Intertextuality |
| **Visual material culture** | **Language (general)** | Expressions of traditions and |
| Entertainers/VMC people female | Language and identity |   institutions |
| Entertainers/VMC people male | Language and VMC | Creative expression |
| Forms of entertainment | | Freedom |
|   Internet | | **Research related** |
| Genres of VMC | | Discussion of the research project |
| Indigenous VMC (all) | | Reference to camera |
| Clothing/fashion/styles | | Reflection or summary on research |
| Critiquing VMC (all) | | Researcher difficulty |
| Connecting to VMC | | Researcher story/connection |

**Table A1.3** Final flexible codes for Barlow

| Place and space | Visual material culture | Making sense of self and world |
|---|---|---|
| Community: Historical, | Entertainers/VMC people | Attribution of or reference to |
|   sociocultural, economic |   female |   physical attractiveness (self) |
|   Local places | Entertainers/VMC people | Attribution of or reference to |
|   Local issues |   female |   physical attractiveness (other) |
| National/political space/place | Forms of entertainment | Attribution of or reference to talent |
| Yukon place/space |   Internet |   and/or character (self) |
| Constructing place/space |   Sports | Attribution of or reference to talent |
| Places (other) not Barlow or | Genres of VMC |   and/or character (other) |
|   local places | Indigenous VMC | Discipline and authority |
| Public spaces/places | Style/clothing/fashion | Belonging and popularity |
| Private spaces/places |   Hats | Being tough and survival |
| Centre/periphery |   Brand names/labels | Being yourself |
|   Choice | Critiquing VMC (all) | Myths |
| Other social spaces | Connecting to VMC | Expression of traditional culture(s) |
|   Internet | Learning from VMC | Expression of social institutions |

(continued)

**Table A1.3**  (continued)

Natural/Human-made
  landscape
Using and creating spaces/
  places
**Identity**
Ethnoracial identities
  First Nations
Gender identities
  Femininities
    Girl power
  Masculinities
  Expression of sexualities
Place-based identity
Group identities: Local and/or
  global
Morality

**Performance (general)**
Performing ethnoracial,
  sexualities, gender identities
Performance and VMC

**Representation**
Representing self
Authenticity
Local youth culture
  Leisure time

**People and relationships**
Parents/teachers/adults/
  Elders
Peers
Family
  History: Family

**Language (general)**
Language and identity
Language and VMC

Environmental issues
Being yourself
Personal narratives
Respect
Role models
Social issues: Local, global, VMC
  Guns
Social/economic references
Intertextuality
Creative expression
Freedom
Local/regional activities and/or
  employment
Migration and travel

**Research related**
Discussion of the research project
Reference to camera
Reflection or summary on research
Researcher difficulty
Researcher story/connection

# Appendix 2: Samples of Participatory Media-Making

**Fig. A2.1** Selection of collages from the Hope (All artwork used with permission from youth in this study)

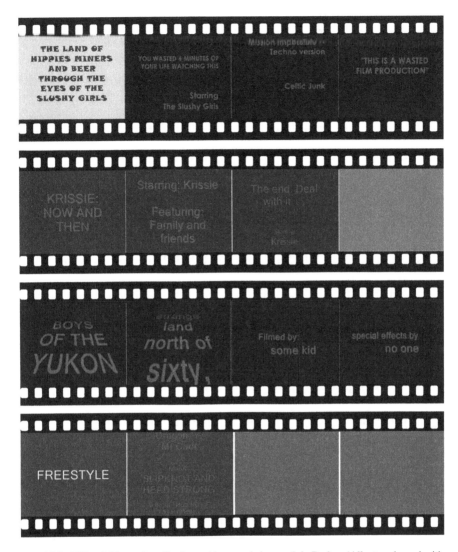

**Fig. A2.2** Stills of titles and credits from videos made by youth in Barlow (All artwork used with permission from youth in this study)

**Fig. A2.3** Stills of titles and credits from videos made by youth at the Hope (All artwork used with permission from youth in this study)

# References

Atkinson, R. (1998). *The life story interview*. Thousand Oaks, CA: Sage.

Badger, M. (1995). *Visual ethnography and representation: Two case studies in the Arctic*. Unpublished doctoral dissertation, University of Cambridge, Cambridge, UK.

Banks, M. (2001). *Visual methods in social research*. London: Sage.

Bryman, A. (2001). *Social research methods*. Oxford, UK: Oxford University Press.

Charmaz, K. (2000). Grounded theory: Objectivist and constructivist methods. In N. K. Denzin & Y. S. Lincoln (Eds.), *Handbook of qualitative research* (2nd ed., pp. 509–535). Thousand Oaks, CA: Sage.

Charmaz, K., & Mitchell, R. (2001). Grounded theory in ethnography. In P. Atkinson, A. Coffey, S. Delamont, J. Lofland, & L. Lofland (Eds.), *Handbook of ethnography* (pp. 160–174). London: Sage.

Clarke, A. (2003). Situational analyses: Grounded theory mapping after the postmodern turn. *Symbolic Interaction, 26*(4), 553–576.

Coffey, A., & Atkinson, P. (1996). *Making sense of qualitative data analysis: Complementary strategies*. Thousand Oaks, CA: Sage.

Creswell, J., & Miller, D. L. (2000). Determining validity in qualitative inquiry. *Theory into Practice, 39*(3), 124–130.

Daly, K. (1997). Re-placing theory in ethnography: A postmodern view. *Qualitative Inquiry, 3*(3), 343–365.

Darts, D. (2004). *Visual culture jam: Art pedagogy and creative resistance*. Unpublished doctoral dissertation, University of British Columbia, Vancouver, Canada.

Denzin, N. K. (1978). *The research act: A theoretical introduction to sociological methods*. New York: McGraw-Hill.

Denzin, N. K., & Lincoln, Y. S. (2000). Introduction: The discipline and practice of qualitative research. In N. K. Denzin & Y. S. Lincoln (Eds.), *Handbook of qualitative research* (2nd edn., pp. 1–29). Thousand Oaks, CA: Sage.

Edwards, E. (1997). Beyond the boundary: A consideration of the expressive in photography and anthropology. In M. Banks & H. Morphy (Eds.), *Rethinking visual anthropology* (pp. 53–80). New Haven, CT: Yale University Press.

Eglinton, K. (2008). Using participatory visual ethnography to explore young people's use of visual material culture in place and space. In R. Hickman (Ed.), *Research in art and design education: Issues and exemplars* (pp. 51–65). Bristol, UK: Intellect.

Eglinton, K. (2009). *Making selves, making worlds: An ethnographic account of young people's use of visual material culture*. Unpublished PhD Thesis, University of Cambridge, Cambridge, UK.

Emerson, R. M., Fretz, R. I., & Shaw, L. L. (1995). *Writing ethnographic fieldnotes*. Chicago: University of Chicago Press.

Emerson, R. M., Fretz, R. I., & Shaw, L. L. (2001). Participant observations and fieldnotes. In P. Atkinson, A. Coffey, S. Delamont, J. Lofland, & L. Lofland (Eds.), *Handbook of ethnography*. London: Sage.

Flick, U. (2002). *An introduction to qualitative research*. London: Sage.

Flick, U. (2006). *An Introduction to qualitative research* (2nd ed.). London: Sage.

Fontana, A., & Frey, J. H. (2000). The interview: From structured questions to negotiated text. In N. K. Denzin & Y. S. Lincoln (Eds.), *Handbook of qualitative research* (2nd ed., pp. 645–672). Thousand Oaks, CA: Sage.

Geertz, C. (1973). *The interpretation of cultures: Selected essays*. New York: Basic Books.

Glaser, B., & Strauss, A. (1967). *Discovering grounded theory*. Chicago: Aldine.

Guba, E., & Lincoln, Y. S. (1994). Competing paradigms in qualitative research. In N. K. Denzin & Y. S. Lincoln (Eds.), *Handbook of qualitative research* (pp. 105–117). Thousand Oaks, CA: Sage.

Hammersley, M., & Atkinson, P. (1995). *Ethnography: Principles in practice* (2nd ed.). London: Routledge.

Hastrup, K. (1992). Anthropological visions: Some notes on visual and textual authority. In P. I. Crawford & D. Turton (Eds.), *Film as ethnography* (pp. 9–22). Manchester, UK: Manchester University Press.

Heyl, B. (2001). Ethnographic interviewing. In P. Atkinson, A. Coffey, S. Delamont, J. Lofland, & L. Lofland (Eds.), *Handbook of ethnography* (pp. 369–383). London: Sage.

Hickman, R., & Eglinton, K. (2010). Exploring the ways in which youth engage with visual material culture in their everyday lives: a framework for inquiry. *Australian Art Education, 32*(2), 4–16.

Kvale, S. (1996). *Interviews: An introduction to qualitative research interviewing.* London: Sage.

Lather, P. A. (1991). *Getting smart: Feminist research and pedagogy with/in the postmodern.* New York: Routledge.

Lincoln, Y. S., & Guba, E. G. (1985). *Naturalistic inquiry.* Thousand Oaks, CA: Sage.

Luttrell, W. (2003). *Pregnant bodies, fertile minds.* London: Routledge.

Miles, M. B., & Huberman, A. M. (1994). *Qualitative data analysis: An expanded sourcebook* (2nd ed.). Thousand Oaks, CA: Sage.

Nayak, A. (2003). *Race, place and globalization: Youth cultures in a changing world.* Oxford, UK: Berg.

Packard, B. W.-L., Ellison, K. L., & Sequenzia, M. R. (2004). Show and tell: Photo-interviews with urban adolescent girls. *International Journal of Education & the Arts, 5*(3). http://www.ijea.org/v5n3/index.html. Accessed 20 April 2005.

Patton, M. Q. (2002). *Qualitative research and evaluation methods.* London: Sage.

Pink, S. (2001). *Doing visual ethnography: Images, media and representation in research.* London: Sage.

Plummer, K. (2001). The call of life stories in ethnographic research. In P. Atkinson, A. Coffey, S. Delamont, J. Lofland, & L. Lofland (Eds.), *Handbook of ethnography* (pp. 395–406). London: Sage.

Rock, P. (2001). Symbolic interactionism and ethnography. In P. Atkinson, A. Coffey, S. Delamont, J. Lofland, & L. Lofland (Eds.), *Handbook of ethnography* (pp. 26–38). London: Sage.

Rose, G. (2001). *Visual methodologies: An introduction to the interpretation of visual materials.* London: Sage.

Seale, C. (2000). Using computers to analyse qualitative data. In D. Silverman, *Doing qualitative research: A practical handbook* (pp. 154–174). London: Sage.

Seale, C. (2004a). Coding and data analysis. In C. Seale (Ed.), *Researching society and culture* (2nd ed., pp. 305–321). London: Sage.

Seale, C. (2004b). Validity, reliability and the quality of research. In C. Seale (Ed.), *Researching society and culture* (2nd ed., pp. 72–82). London: Sage.

Silverman, D. (2000). *Doing qualitative research: A practical handbook.* London: Sage.

Silverman, D. (2001). *Interpreting qualitative data: Methods for analysing talk, text and interaction* (2nd ed.). London: Sage.

Springgay, S. (2003a). *Communities seeing themselves seeing: Visual art as educational research.* Paper presented at American Education Research Association, Chicago, IL.

Springgay, S. (2003b). *Inside the visible: Youth understandings of body knowledge through touch.* Unpublished doctoral dissertation, University of British Columbia, Vancouver, Canada.

Tedlock, B. (2005). The observation of participation and the emergence of public ethnography. In N. K. Denzin & Y. S. Lincoln (Eds.), *Handbook of qualitative research* (3rd ed., pp. 467–481). Thousand Oaks, CA: Sage.

Thompson, C. M. (2003). Kinderculture in the art classroom: Early childhood art and the mediation of culture. *Studies in Art Education, 44*(2), 135–146.

Weber, S., & Mitchell, C. (1995). *That's funny, you don't look like a teacher: Interrogating images, identity and popular culture.* London: Falmer Press.

Wolcott, H. F. (1999). *Ethnography: A way of seeing.* Walnut Creek, CA: AltaMira Press.

Wolcott, H. (2001). *Writing up qualitative research* (2nd ed.). Thousand Oaks, CA: Sage.

# Glossary, Abbreviations, Notations

## Glossary

**Airhead(ed)**  Stupid, brain is filled with air

**Beef**  Fight or dispute both physical and/or verbal; complaint

**Bling**  Flashy jewellery

**Crunk**  Wild partying, drunk, crazy; genre of hip-hop

**Dis**  To disrespect

**Do-rag**  Tight fabric head scarf usually in a dark colour – 'do' is short for 'hairdo'

**Edgy**  Possessing something different, alternative, cool, daring

**Emo**  Youth movement where emphasis is placed on an emotional, expressive style of rock music and that is associated with fashion elements like slim-fit jeans and tight t-shirts

**Flash**  Having an impressive appearance; well-dressed

**Fly**  Cool, hip, well-dressed

**Freestyle**  Performance without prompts, improvisation

**Fresh**  Cool, hip, well-dressed, clean, new

**Gangsta**  Slang and/or short for gangster or gang member; a black-identified form of VMC derived from gangsta rap

**Hand sign/hand gesture**  Movement and/or symbols made using hands; can signify various localities or gangs

**Ho**  Whore or prostitute

**Homie**  Friend, term of endearment; for youth sometimes similar to 'home girl'; refers to males and females, though more generally to males

**Hoodie**  Sweatshirt or jumper with a hood

**Hot**  Cool, sexy, excellent, amazing, first-rate, best

**iPod**  Personal portable music player

**MP3 player**  Personal portable music player

**Playa/player**  Boy who goes out with many girls at once, 'plays' them; womaniser, sexy, flirt

**Preppy**  Style-based cultural form, often signifying upper socioeconomic status (derived from preparatory or private school); derogatory term for youth signifying, usually, white wealthy people

**Puffy-coat**  Thick down coat

**Shout-outs**  Practice derived from hip-hop, calling out the name of localities, friends, and others as a sign of respect and loyalty

**Smooth**  Describes someone as cool, sexy, laid-back; skilful; sometimes a womaniser

**Surfer dude**  Typified through a relaxed style, and a particular attitude. For youth this cultural form was based on movies featuring white California males who surf, wear colourful shorts or 'jams', and spend time hanging out on the beach. Use terms such as 'totally, man', and 'that's radical'.

**Swag**  From swagger; a way of walking, stride, performance

**Telenovela**  Short television serial drama

**Tims**  Work boots by Timberland

**Trucker hats**  Large baseball-style hat with mesh back

**Ups**  Basketball sneakers or trainers

**Walkie-talkie cell phones**  Mobile phones that are spoken into using a 'push-to-talk' style (like a 'walkie-talkie') rather than holding the phone to the ear and mouth; they make a beeping sound when used

**Yu-Gi-Oh cards**  Japanese Manga, collectable card game

## Abbreviations

**GVHS**  Greenwich Village High School
**OGs**  Original Gangstas (a youth identity formation in Barlow).
**VMC**  Visual material culture
**VCAE**  Visual culture art education

## Notations for quoted material

...  A series of ellipses indicates text has been removed
[ ]  Square brackets enclose added text
–  A long dash at the end of a segment of talk indicates an interruption or abrupt cut-off.

# Index

K.A. Eglinton, *Youth Identities, Localities, and Visual Material Culture: Making Selves, Making Worlds*, Explorations of Educational Purpose 25, DOI 10.1007/978-94-007-4857-6, © Springer Science+Business Media Dordrecht 2013